SUGAR

MY LIFE AS A SUGAR BABE

MONIQUE X

THISTLE
PUBLISHING

This is a true story. I have tried to recreate events, locales and conversations from my memories of them. But, in order to maintain their anonymity, I have changed the names of all individuals and sometimes also of places. Also for these purposes, I may have changed some identifying characteristics and details such as physical properties, occupations and places of residence.

There are a couple of people I would like to thank. I would like to thank my agent, Andrew Lownie, for believing in me. I would like to thank my friends, Amanda, Sarah, Barbara and Paul for standing by me. And Jamal the Pakistani and Aleksandar the Macedonian for sharing their wisdom with me.

And of course I would like to thank my Sugar Daddies – Mr. Viking, Mr. Iran, Mr. Singapore, Mr. Handsome, Mr. Yoga, Mr. Tantra, Mr. Japan, Mr. Happy Dick and The Professor. Thank you for the lovely trips and experiences. Thanks to you I could survive for almost two years.

Now Jamal the Pakistani has taught me that even the negative can be turned into the positive, so let me also thank Mr. America, Mr. Hideous, The Widower and – why not – Wilma for the lessons I have learned.

Yes, I was a Sugar Baby. For twenty-one months of my life. And though it started as a way to get fun dates, it ended as a way to survive. It was fun. It was interesting. And sometimes it broke my heart. But it was all, in my opinion, worth it. I could build up my life with my children thanks to Sugar and the proof are my girls. They are happy, balanced little girls. If I ever have to, I'd do it again.

So this is my story. Read on, and judge for yourself.

CHAPTER ONE:
SECRET LIFE

The kids wake me up at 6. They mostly do. Though they really do try, whispering is not an art they have mastered yet. Or it is at least one they forget when they get excited. I pull my pillow over my head and try to get some more sleep, but when Fuzzy the cat also starts meowing in my ear and scratching the pillow with his paw, I give up.

I stretch out in one nice long stretch before I get out from under my cosy warm duvet into the cold. Yes, it's getting cold again. Autumn has started early this year and the rain is not like normal British rain. It's more like a monsoon. It's hammering down on my roof like a tropical rainstorm. Without the warmth of the tropics that is. I'd rather be in the tropics with a rain like this...

Both girls jump on me, hugging the moment they see me and all I can do is smile while I kiss them on the top of their heads. *These are the moments that make it all worth it.*

Lisa is eight now. She's getting big. She's the serious one, her big blue eyes taking all in. Both her clothes and her long blonde hair are always neat. Since the divorce she feels like she is responsible for making sure her little sister behaves, no matter how many times I tell her she isn't.

Sophie is the tomboy of the two. Her ginger hair is always a mess. She doesn't care about her clothes, since she is mostly climbing trees anyway. She has a little heart-shaped face covered with freckles and usually a bump or bruise on at least one of her knees. She seems to be the least affected by the divorce.

Seems to be, I said. For Sophie *is* affected, in hidden ways. She keeps having 'accidents', wetting herself at school since the divorce. And many nights she ends up in my bed needing cuddles because of nightmares.

Like she is cuddling me right now. Holding me so tightly it seems she will never let go. But Fuzzy doesn't let us cuddle for very long. He is circling my legs with his tail in the air and strongly complaining now. For some reason he seems to think that six is way too late for him to receive breakfast. A cat's life is a hard life...

Feeding Fuzzy first, I make some extra strong coffee for myself – yawning abundantly – and start preparing breakfast and lunch boxes for the girls. In between I send a good-morning-message to The Viking. He is one of my Sugar Daddies, you'll hear all about him. We chat every day. Sometimes he comes to London and we have nice dinners – he always takes a nice present with him. But I shouldn't jump ahead.

I don't have time to dream about Sugar Daddies anyway. Upstairs the girls have picked up a fight. I sigh and climb back up. It turns out that Lisa thinks Sophie has stolen her socks and it takes my confession that I must have put the socks in the wrong drawers to stop the whining. I sigh some more.

With peace back in the house, the girls come down and have porridge. They used to have sandwiches, but I quit making those for now. Lisa takes ages deciding what she wants on her bread and Sophie will start moaning when she has to eat the bread crusts.

And *why* does she have to eat them? Because it is something you're supposed to do as a good mother? Who has written the handbook of perfect mothers anyway? It's us women who often make it hard for ourselves, by either judging ourselves, or judging others. In the end we're all having the same struggles. So why do we have to make it so hard for ourselves?

The porridge goes in well. And there are only some small fights. Lisa thinks Sophie is not eating decent enough and Sophie says Lisa is kicking her, but we're doing well this morning. I dress quickly as they brush their teeth, then pack their lunch and almost forget Sophie's gymnastic suit – luckily Lisa reminds me.

School is real close by, and there isn't a day since we've moved that I haven't truly enjoyed that. Before we lived a half an hour drive from school, now we walk to school in five minutes. And to the supermarket. The doctor. The dentist. All those necessary places you don't want to travel miles for. Now a bookstore close by would have been nice too, or a sex shop for that matter, but you can't have all in life.

At the school yard I stretch my neck to see whether I can get a glimpse of the cute Indian dad, but he is nowhere around. *Bummer. Seeing him always makes my day.* Lisa goes to class by herself now. Being seen with mothers is just not cool anymore. I can't hug her in public and need to keep a polite distance.

Sophie still wants me to kiss and cuddle before class starts. So I make sure to close my eyes and enjoy – I know it's not going to last long. When the kids are dropped off I hurry back home. It's preparation time. It's time for my secret life.

I love preparing myself for my dates. It has become some kind of ritual. Normally I have a facial mask the night before, sometimes also a hot bath – with lots of bubbles and candles of course. And if I really want to splurge, I'll also have a glass of wine. I love the feeling that splurging a little on myself gives me. Now if I'm in a naughty mood, I'll send some teasing picture to a SD. Sometimes to all of them.

Ah, what SD means? It's the abbreviation of Sugar Daddy. You're going to learn a lot of Sugar Terms. And though I have been living this life for almost two years now, even I don't know all of them and am still learning...

So I love a little splurging on myself. With a nice bath, a lovely mask. In my opinion there are so many mothers who don't spoil themselves enough. *And why not?* It feels good to spoil yourself. As my SD Mr. Tantra likes to say: 'only if you look well after yourself, you are able to look well after others.' Also it makes me feel totally and utterly woman. No, I don't think men and women are the same. We're totally different. And yes I LOVE being a woman. In every single way.

But I'm getting off track. It's not the night before anymore. It's date-day. First I meditate and do my yoga. Thanks to my SD Mr. Yoga that has become a part of my daily routine. Next I take a nice long hot shower and shave. Everywhere. Well, I do keep a Brazilian. I don't like a bald pussy, it makes me feel like a little girl.

I will only go bald if a SD especially requests it. Though to be honest, it annoys me when they do. *What gives them the right to tell me how to trim my pussy? I don't tell them whether or not to shave themselves...* But hey, life is too short to be annoyed for too long. I always manage to push those feelings aside. It's much better to focus on the fun, the trips. And the money of course...

See a Pakistani – you'll read all about him – has taught me that there are two ways you can see life. It all depends on your focus. You can either see it as something negative and complain, or you can see life as overall something nice and make sure you are having fun. And if I have to choose, I most definitely choose the second one...

But let me go on with my preparing. Next it's time to dry – first my body and then my long blond hair – and to choose a nice body lotion. I have several ones, all taken from nice hotels. Yes, I

ALWAYS take something as a souvenir from the nice hotels I'm staying. And most of the time it's the bath amenities.

I also have several perfumes to choose from – all presents of course. Mostly I choose the one I have gotten from the particular SD I'm seeing. I apply some on my wrists, my neck, between my breasts and – if I expect to receive oral delights – also on inside of my thighs.

One surprise that the Sugar World has given me, is how much many of these men like to please me. I never received so much oral sex before. Amanda – my ex-escort friend – more about her later – says men in the escort world are the same. It makes them feel utmost manly when they are able to please a woman.

Now before the Sugar World I used to be better in giving than receiving. So getting all this pleasing has been a good lesson. Lately I am receiving. And thoroughly enjoying.

You know, when I first became a Sugar Babe, I thought it would be all about pleasing men. Being submissive. But it isn't at all. As a Sugar Babe you have a power that surprises me. Most of these men treat me like a princess. Really. In 'normal' life men haven't treated me like this. Sugar Daddies – the real ones that is, not the Salty Daddies, the ones who think they are but have no idea what it takes – are true gentlemen and know how to make you feel like a lady. They bring a gift, hold the door and are utmost polite.

Outside the bedroom that is. In the bedroom all is permitted. That's also what they want from a Sugar Babe. She has to be a lady until entering the bedroom. In the bedroom starts the dream. According to Amanda it's actually what all men really want: a lady on their arm and a hooker in their bed.

So yes, the Sugar World is an illusion. It's like a different dimension inside the real world. It's the dream world of the Japanese geisha, as my visit to Mr. Japan has taught me. The flower-world.

No. Geisha weren't hookers. They were mistresses. For most people that might seem to be a thin line, but when you are living the life there is a big difference. Most westerners don't get the concept. The Sugar World does.

See, sex is not the most important part. If it was just sex, these men would go to hookers. Much cheaper. No it's the play, the illusion, releasing the stress of daily life. These men are interested in art, classical music, fine wine and dining – the best of life. And like a geisha, a Sugar Baby has to be educated and able to share it all. It's a good thing all my studying and my good upbringing are finally paying off! ;-)

But let me get back to the preparing. Next it's time to polish nails – toes red and fingernails pearl. And to put on my make-up. Now I'm a specialist in applying make-up that nobody even seems to notice. Sometimes I don't even know why I bother...

So when I am Sugar Dating – which is the only dating I am doing lately – I tend to use a little more. Not too much of course. I do like to look classy. I have this really nice Chanel travelling make-up case that I received from Mr. Viking which I love. It has all natural colours. *Some men just know exactly which present to choose...*

But back to preparing. Make-up is easy. Jewellery is easy. I usually wear the pieces Mr. Iran has given me in the Galleries Lafayette in Paris. Dressing is harder. I normally try on a whole range of dresses and send pictures for advice to my ex-escort friend Amanda.

We've been friends since we were five years old, and she is the only one who knows everything about me. Every. Dirty. Detail. She also receives all information about my dates. Date, time, SD name, and – when I'm traveling – flight, hotel and room number.

Why? Well, I am meeting these strangers through a website and I often don't even know their real name. I'm taking a risk there, I know. But I always listen to my instinct. To this gut feeling. And I haven't had any bad experiences so far, but you never know ...

In a way, Amanda is the reason I got into the Sugar World (keep reading, you'll understand). I need someone to blame, right? Now the escort world is not the Sugar World. Though there are similarities of course ...

Most of my Sugar Daddies used to book escorts. And if not, they are the same kind of men – extremely busy, successful, educated and used to the good things in life.

But there is a reason they are now choosing Sugar. Escort is too impersonal, they say. They like the low-maintenance connection of Sugar Life. As Mr. Yoga puts it: "I'm having Sugar Babies for the romance." As a Sugar Babe you're like a mistress. I build up a relationship with every single one of my Daddies.

What my typical Sugar Daddy is? Most of them are married. In their end-forties and fifties. And yes I have sex with them. With most of them. But only if I want to. See, I choose my own men. I don't get bookings. I don't accept all men who contact me, no matter how much they offer. In fact I decline most. And yes they help me out with an allowance. Normally £300 for PPM – Pay Per Meet – and £1000 for a weekend, though the first meeting is always free. And without sex.

I know from my Sugar Daddies that there are girls on the site who are different. Some charge £150 for a first coffee together. Some have lists of how much they charge for each different sexual action they perform. Some have a rate for every hour.

To me charging for hours or actions doesn't feel good. I'm happy that they are helping me. I like spending time with them. I love the gifts and the traveling. If I wouldn't enjoy being with them, they wouldn't be my SD.

Now according to Seeking Arrangement girls generally get allowances between £1.000 and £3.000, but I'm seriously wondering whether that's true. Maybe the younger ones get £3.000, I have no idea. But I do know that finding one for £1.000 is already hard enough. Most men offer escort rates. And I'm not talking top end escort rates. Would I ever consider £150 for a sex-date? Hell no.

But back to the clothes. Upon choosing I sometimes send pictures to Paul. He is a father at the swimming lesson of my youngest daughter. He's 39, damn handsome, but married with two kids. He knows about my Sugar Life. Sometimes we kiss. I know he'd love to do more, but I haven't decided whether I want to. *Why would I? I'm getting enough sex as it is.* But we will get to him later.

So with the tips of my two advisers I choose my dress. Now the underwear I need no advice for. It has to be just one thing: sexy. Though I do change in sexiness depending on the SD I'm seeing. This time I'm meeting a new guy called Oscar, so I'm going for it all. I'm choosing a pretty black negligee that used to be Amanda's, a classy string, suspender belt and stockings.

Most men appreciate nice lingerie. Though the thing that bugs me, is that with most men you're not wearing it for long. I like to wear lingerie. It shows my long legs, which I like. It shows my nice butt. And it makes my boobs look bigger – the ones I don't really like. Though I do have to say that since one of my SD's called them 'Happy Boobs' I do appreciate them better.

So I put the Happy Boobs in the lingerie, put on the dress Amanda recommended and finally I'm ready. I look at myself once more in the hallway before I leave. *Damn, I'm looking good.* And off I go.

When I close the door behind me, I can hear children playing outside at the school yard. *Maybe my girls are amongst them.* And I smile. Before school is over I'll be back.

CHAPTER TWO: FLASHBACK

I was born in Sevenoaks, in a large detached villa which my mother had inherited after my grandfather died. It used to be his office. My parents are still living there, though it's falling apart now. Once it was this white villa with Greek columns in front. Now it's a damp grey villa with green moss stains that would do well in horror movies. Most paint is coming off and one column has long since disappeared. And the garden is a complete jungle.

Though it doesn't show from the outside, on the inside the house is divided. My mother lives on the left side, my father on the right. Both are painters and the house is their studio. They do meet every day in the kitchen, which is shared by both. And sometimes they come and look at each other's art. But most of the time they live their separate lives.

They once used to live together, but after I was born my father started his long collection of girlfriends and they came up with this solution. Catholics don't divorce, you see. So in his part of the house, my father has his girlfriends. "Watch out for the sperm stains!" he loves to call out to any visitor who wants to sit on his sofa. His bookcases are filled with literature and porn. He has a drawer with a collection of love letters from former girl-friends – mostly his models, or 'muses' as he likes to call them.

And his part of the house is filled with huge paintings of their nakedness.

My father's moods have always been as unpredictable as the weather. He is either thrilled and fervently painting, or he is totally depressed and drinking whiskey. That's when you don't want to visit his part of the house. And now he has also been diagnosed with Korsakoff Syndrome, which isn't making things any brighter.

My mother paints nature. Her part of the house is filled with paintings of flowers, leaves and the stillness after a summer storm. Nature is all around her. She has a collection of butterflies, stones, and pine apples, anything that takes her fancy. She collects anything and everything. You have never seen so much stuff packed together.

Archives of long deceased – almost, though not quite yet, famous – family members. Newspaper clippings of all the exhibitions that are truly interesting but that she will never go to. Pen caps of long finished pens – you never know when they will come in handy. And antique furniture – family pieces that no one else wanted.

There are leather chairs stuffed with horse-hair that are falling apart. The leather is torn and horsehair is coming out, scratching your bum when you sit on them. French oak tables covered with white heat stains. Chinese cups with cracks. Persian rugs half eaten by moths. Now neither of my parents sells much of their art. So it's no wonder that they have spent most of the fortune they inherited.

Behind their house is the house that once belonged to my grandparents. It's huge. A large detached villa on one of the best streets. It's where I mostly grew up, since my parents were too busy with their art.

It's where my grandmother would read me stories in her mahogany easy chair in front of the open fire, while I played with the pearls of her necklace. Where I would help her open the shutters in the morning. Where we had walks through her estate – with her pointing out all the birds and flowers we came across. Always stopping to chat with Ken the gardener, who was also her driver and would give me big books about horses. Now my grandmother may have had a lot of staff, but they were all treated like family.

It's the house where I would bring Amanda to run through the many empty rooms or through the big estate to play hide and seek. Where we would polish the silver together with the maid. Where the cook, grandmother and I would whirl around each other making dinner. It was the same warm kitchen where I would later make my homework, grandma putting on her glasses and helping me as good as she could.

And there were always people visiting. My grandmother simply loved people. You never knew who popped up whenever the doorbell rang. Friends, family – there was always someone visiting. To chat with my grandmother in a comfy easy chair in front of the open fire. Or in summer on the terrace, with the maid bringing crystal glasses with jingling ice cubes in home-made lemonade.

This was in sharp contrast to my mother – who was shy and rather didn't see anyone. She locked herself up with nature in her studio and preferred to be alone. Maybe boarding school in all those foreign countries had made her like that. Oh, and she despised men. Her favourite saying was: "Darling, all men are bastards."

How could my mother be the daughter of my grandmother? My grandmother was warm, loving, open and simply adored men. My mother was this rather closed detached person who watched life from a distance and was scarce with the hugs she provided.

My mother looked like the real artist. She had short cropped black hair, red lipstick, smoked her thin cigarettes from a long cigarette holder and always wore black. My grandmother was half Spanish and showed it. She had long black hair, streaked with grey, was short, and had the tiniest feet ever and fiery black eyes.

My father was rather tall with wild grey curls and could be called handsome, I guess. But with my father it was like he had two faces. He was either real fun to be with, charming, running around the garden with me on his shoulders, doing everything that was naughty and teaching me not to be common. "Dare to live your own life," he would say. "Follow your own drummer."

But other times he would be totally occupied with his newest girlfriend, having no time for me. Or he would be in a big depression, making his part of the house this awful dark place to be.

Now I had a couple of friends, but Amanda was my Best Friend. Yes, Amanda the Ex-Escort Friend. Though obviously at elementary school she was not my Ex-Escort Friend yet, just the Best Friend with whom I shared everything.

And at high school she was the one who taught me how to shave my legs. The one I smoked my first cigarette with, coughing our lungs out. The one I shared boyfriends with – we held hands with the same boy, we both had our first kiss with another one. She was the first one I sneaked into a pub with.

But once we were on different high schools, we started to go our separate ways. I didn't do the drugs. I didn't do sex, yet. And when she didn't finish high school but went off to find adventure in Paris, I was the good girl and stayed behind.

Now is my past the reason why I am doing the things that I do? I'm not sure. But I'm sharing my life with you, so I will tell you all. When I was thirteen I was on this camp and for the first time a guy gave me attention. For the first time someone told me I was pretty. For the first time I felt special. He caressed my hair and told me how beautiful I was.

But he was the camp leader, way older than me. And letting him caress my hair didn't mean I had given him permission to lie on top of me that night. Naked. I managed to push him off and hid in the bathroom the rest of that whole damn night.

But nothing had happened, right? Not really? And it was all my fault, wasn't it? Because I let him caress me... And I didn't just blame myself. I also blamed a lot of others, though I never blamed *him* for some reason.

I blamed Amanda, who was with me on that camp, sleeping next to me, and never even noticed. I blamed my mother, when she came to pick me up on that windy station, the wind blowing leaves in big messy circles. *I was so damn sure that my mother would see that something had changed inside of me...* But she didn't. *And nothing had happened, right? Not really...* So life just went on, as it always does.

Four years later something did happen. A friend of my father was visiting from the US and told him that he wanted to take me to the movies. *Well, why not?* But the strange thing is that he asked me to come and pick him up at his sister's place. Looking back now, I wonder why my father didn't ask some questions. *Why didn't he come to pick ME up? Why didn't my dad tell him to?*

Fact is, we never went to the movies. He jumped right on me after he let me in. *And I never said no.* It was my first time. This was how I lost my virginity. He took me on the sofa, underneath the drawings of his sister's kids, with some stupid soap on TV. And I never said no. I never said yes either, but who cared.

I didn't do much, my first time. I was just lying there, on my back, while he entered me. I didn't even know what to do with my arms. They were just hanging there, open, in the air. Afterwards I did see the blood on the sofa, but I'm not sure he even noticed. "It was just like taking a little girl," he said, before he let me out and closed the door. *Well, hello mister, I WAS a little girl.*

I walked back home. Through the night streets. With all those bloody happy families behind all those bloody windows. When I got back home, my father was already on the phone with him. Did I tell anyone? Of course not. I had never said no … Did it change anything? Did it make me into who I am? Into how I view men? Sex? Who knows … ?

Soon after that, Grandmother died. It was just before I finished high school, and she left this big emptiness behind. The house was quickly sold, the money shared between her nine children. And I was left in the ghost-villa of my parents, watching from the attic how a new family moved into her house, changing the wall-paper of the dining room where we used to polish silver, removing the shutters, cutting the pines in the garden which grandmother had loved so much.

She left me three things, next to my share of the inheritance. Her diamond encrusted engagement ring. The necklace – gold with pearls – that I used to play with as a child when she read me stories in front of the open fire. And an antique hollowed-out Shakespeare book-safe which she had used in the war.

I missed her so much, when I entered Oxford University to study History. She would have been so proud. But I did love studying at Oxford. I loved the atmospheric, golden-stone colleges, the grandeur of Christ Church and Magdalen, the cosy intimacy of Corpus Christi. And I simply loved studying.

I loved delving into books and spent most of my time in the library. I loved following the classes of my favourite professor, Dr Tanning – who would one day be Robert to me, but let's not jump ahead.

A couple of girls became my studying friends, but Sarah was the one I spent most time with. We would study together, go shopping, go pubbing and basically had a lot of fun. She was from the same neighbourhood in Sevenoaks and she felt like a sister. Most people even thought we were sisters, even though I am blond and she is a brunette.

At Oxford I also fell in love with Giovanni. He was Italian, exotic, romantic – everything I longed for. He had such a different idea of 'manliness.' Like all Italian men, he dressed excellent. He took incredible care of his body and clothing. And wherever we went, he would carry my purse around.

When I received my degree, so did Giovanni. And I was sad. I knew this meant that he would be going back to Italy. And with my grandmother gone, it felt I had no home to return to.

But then one night he invited me to come to Venice with him. *Well, who says no to that?* I had nothing to lose and everything to gain. And Sarah was thrilled when I told her. "You're moving to Italy? That's so cool!! Yes, you should go! It's the chance of a life time!"

I didn't think about cultural differences of course. About the challenge of finding a job in a foreign country – I ended up teaching English. About the Italian mother-in-law, or whether he was going to be faithful. I just left. And since Giovanni was still living with his parents, he helped me to get my own small apartment which I was able to rent with my grandmother's inheritance.

The first few months, I attended the Istituto Venezia, a language school for foreigners. This gave me the skills and confidence to truly meld into Venetian society. Whenever Sarah had the chance she would visit me, and even Amanda came to visit a couple of times, when she was not modelling in Paris.

I loved Venice. I loved the wake-up call of gondoliers calling "Ooooeeeee!" Getting a morning *spritz* in a sunny square. Having lunch in a crowded *bacaro* bar with Giovanni's friends and at night walking along the edge of the canals, surrounded by 1,600 years of history enjoying fuchsia-pink sunsets.

I loved the green canals and the famous bridges. The warmly coloured grand *palazzo* residences and the narrow alleyways. The breath-taking openness of Piazza San Marco. The way Italians seemed to do everything in slow motion. The extreme attention to detail. If I would go into a shop to buy just four pieces of chocolate, they would spend fifteen minutes to make it gorgeous for me with paper, tags, ribbons…

I would stay for seven years. But fact is, pink glasses only remain for a certain amount of time. After a couple of years, Venice started to feel different to me. The fact that no cars were allowed, did give life a slower pace. But the vast amount of tourists clogged the tiny streets. And because of the maze of tiny streets and bridges, it could take up to an hour to cross the small island.

Also food was much more expensive than on the mainland and anything I bought I had to lug in a shoulder-bag from the market to my home. Also I didn't earn much with my teaching, but my rent was high so my inheritance was quickly slinking. And then there was Giovanni.

After a couple of years, I started to see Giovanni differently too. First there was his mother. I would see her every day and had to eat lunch in her house twice a week. And Giovanni was his mother's hobby. She lived and breathed him. She wanted him to marry – she made that very clear. But not to a foreigner – and she made that very clear as well. And yes of course she was the only one making spaghetti the way he liked it.

Also after our first year I started to notice that Giovanni had some traits of my father. He seemed to be very interested in women. There were always women around. And though he strongly insisted that they were just friends – that he would never ever cheat on me, that this was Italian culture and I had to get used to it – having grown up with my father, trusting was a very hard thing to do.

Of course, in the end, I was right. He got engaged when we were still together. And it was his mother who came to tell me, all happy and shining. "If my son was serious with you," she said with her strong Italian accent "Giovanni marry you long time ago, no?" When I confronted Giovanni, he just held up his hands. "Amore mio, you know my mother … What was I supposed to do?"

It didn't take long for me to leave it all behind me. Giovanni. His mother. Crowded Venice. So after seven years I was back in the UK. And with no place to stay, I moved back in with my parents.

I felt like a complete failure. There I was, thirty-one years old, unemployed, single and living in the ghost villa of my parents again. By now all my friends had moved on. Sarah had a husband, her own house and a kid. Amanda was traveling the world and I had no idea how she was making her money. Probably through modelling, I thought.

So I decided that all I really wanted, was to be normal. I had never been normal. I had always been the girl living with her grandmother. The girl with the crazy artist parents. I had always felt different. And now I was the girl living with her parents again.

So hereafter, I decided, I wanted a normal life. A normal man. Preferably with a house I could move into, since I was so eager to leave my parents. I longed for the family I never had. Or at least the family-feeling I had with my grandmother.

But since Giovanni had cheated, there was one thing I now believed. All Men Cheat. Though maybe – I hoped – if I could find a man who needed me, maybe he wouldn't?

I met Eric through an online dating site. When I first met him, I was thrilled, but for all the wrong reasons. Because the more I learned about him, the more I made up my mind that this was a guy who really seemed to need me.

He had no friends whatsoever, his house was a mess and so were his feelings. He was still bearing the scars of growing up with an abusive father. So one thing I decided: I was going to save him. That way he would stay with me forever.

Now Eric came from a totally different social class and my parents disliked him from the start, which made me even more enthusiastic. But, though his stepfather seemed to be okay with me, his mother obviously disliked me. She was the kind of woman who simply didn't like anything that she didn't understand. And she definitely didn't understand me.

Yes there were obvious social differences. His parents called lunch dinner and dinner tea. But I loved that. It felt exotic. Together we had to merge these two very different cultures. And I didn't want a man like my father again. I wanted someone different. Also I loved his lean, dark good looks. And I thought I loved him.

So we got kids way to early. Now if I had allowed myself some more time to get to know him, I would never have married him. But I was pregnant within half a year of meeting, and in such short time you are still wearing pink glasses.

I didn't know about his financial mess. I didn't know about the Borderline personality disorder. Had I known, no way would I have gotten children with him. But everything seemed rosy. And the moment I discovered it all, I was pregnant, we were married and I had moved from my parent's house in Sevenoaks to his damp little council house in a coastal village in Kent.

I did make one real good friend in the village. Barbara. Her marriage with a veteran was probably as miserable as mine. He had returned with mental and physical scars and had changed into an angry, disconnected person. Her oldest daughter was born right after Sophie and we spent time together with the girls, drinking coffee and trying to make the best of it.

Eric's Borderline started to show quite soon after we got married, though in those early days I didn't know about it. I did notice that he started to be very controlling. He started to control my friendships and got rid of anyone he didn't like by creating a scene.

Now living with a Borderliner is like living in a roller coaster. And I have never liked roller coasters in the first place. For some time Eric would be high on his own greatness, believing he had power and talents no one else had. Believing he was going to be a genius. But then all would come crushing down. He would get deeply depressed, feeling worthless, not taking care of himself. No showers, not brushing his teeth for months, changing his underpants once a week.

And if I tried to make a kind and loving remark to make him feel better, he would become furious. *Who was I to tell him what to do? Who the hell did I think I was? Just because I was from a better family, heh? Did I think I was any better?* He never hit me, but when he was in a depressed mood he would be verbally very cruel and cutting.

Soon he started to keep my family at distance. He hated my family. He hated the fact that I had received a degree from Oxford, while he had never finished high school. He hated my background.

Though in those days I never saw it that way, I now realize that my education and family background probably gave him an inferiority complex. He felt less, and therefore he was always trying to prove his worth. Anything that had to do with my family background he would spit upon. There was this constant tension in the air. So soon my world became a very small one.

After our youngest was born, I was so worn down that I didn't have the strength to fight any more. Whenever he was depressed, I tried to keep the girls at a distance. I knew he could lose his temper in a second and I hated them to be there when we had our fights.

Sophie was still too young to notice, but Lisa started to change. Since her father promised heaven on earth in his good days, but never kept his promises she stopped believing. There started to be this distrust in her eyes that hurt me deeply.

And since he could completely lose his temper with the girls – if they didn't react soon enough because they were preoccupied with their drawings, or if they still had to pee when he wanted to get out – I just tried to keep them out of his way. I liked my days best with the kids when he was not around. The moment he set foot in the house, something changed in the atmosphere.

Looking back on it now, I can only wonder. First there was Giovanni, who cheated like my father. Next I chose Eric, who had moods like my father. I guess in some way I was trying to deal with my relationship with my father. But I never saw it that way. I never stood back and looked. I was just trying to survive.

And it wasn't just his moods. There were also the money problems. I still don't know what he did with his salary – he had worked himself up, had a good job and earned well – but somehow it was always finished way before the end of the month.

When I asked about it, he would get angry and tell me that it was 'none of my business.' Also he didn't want me to work. I had to be a stay-at-home mom. I guess he just couldn't stand the thought of me working somewhere and being able to meet other men.

Eric gave me an allowance of £400 every month. For food, clothes, haircuts and everything else. Now juggling the money was very hard to do. There was always something that had to be paid. Either the washing machine broke down, or the car had to be fixed. And for £400 I just couldn't do it, so I secretly would ask my family to help out. They also helped me with clothes. They would give me bags with the hand-me-downs of cousins for the girls and me. For us this was a feast. These were nice clothes of expensive brands and for us they felt like new.

But when I would pass Zara or Mango, the shops I used to go to with Sarah, I couldn't even imagine how life had been. I couldn't even imagine how it would be to go into one of them, look around and just buy something, all for myself. I had never felt poor before, but now I really did.

Every time a new stack of bills dropped through the letterbox I freaked out. We had debts everywhere and would get letters threatening to send the bailiff if we didn't pay in time. I guess it is no surprise therefore that money became the root of our growing number of arguments. I hated opening the mail.

Now that I am out of it, I can only wonder. *Why did I put myself in this situation? Why did I stay?* And I have no idea. It just grew like that. Once the kids were born, I felt like I was caged. I wanted to stay for the kids. I was living this empty life in a cage. And the few occasions that I did do something with Barbara or Sarah, I made sure not to make myself too pretty because Eric was jealous as hell.

But then Eric became religious. And though I didn't know it then, his religion would become my ticket to freedom…

CHAPTER THREE: FREEDOM

So that's where my life was two years ago. I was a 'decent' married woman. Was I happy? Hell no. Then Eric became religious. He registered with a small sect-like church, which became more and more important to him. And suddenly all Eric's weekends were spent in church. The kids and I barely saw him. When he *was* home, he would be asleep on the sofa in the sitting room. And he started to talk about how he had actually always wanted to be a minister.

I wasn't so thrilled with his new church-thing. It meant he had even less time for the girls. But on the other hand, I did notice that the three of us seemed to enjoy ourselves much better when he wasn't around with his unpredictable moods.

Church also meant no sex, since ministers-to-be in his church apparently also practiced abstinence. But that wasn't a big change. Our sex-life was practically dead anyway. Fact is that I wasn't feeling that attracted to Eric anymore. He had grown real fat and the way he treated me wasn't very attractive either. I was rather left alone in my own room with my own fantasies and manual abilities.

Yes, we slept separately too. Eric had moved out of our bedroom and onto the sofa right after Sophie was born. She cried for one whole year, waking me up every hour and refusing to go to sleep for another. Eric said he needed his sleep, so he moved out and never moved back in. From then on the sofa was where he slept.

So basically, church meant the girls and I had to spend less time with their father. Now I would have loved them to have a nice relationship with their father. Really. It still breaks my heart whenever they return from him with pale unhappy faces. But considering the bright change of atmosphere in the house, church wasn't such a bad thing. And I had no idea of course, but it was going to give me the perfect excuse for a smooth divorce ...

Three things triggered my divorce. First there was my great-uncle's funeral. I had loved him dearly. He was a medical professor, very erudite, always wearing gold-rimmed glasses, a tweed jacket and an old-fashioned gold watch in a pocket of his vest.

We used to have philosophical discussions together, starting from when I was a small girl staying with my grandmother, or when we would visit him and my great-aunt in their huge estate. About life. Dreams.

Only great-uncle knew my big dream from when I was eight years old. I wanted to be a writer. So whenever we met, he would ask me how my novels were progressing – the ones I was always writing, but never finishing. I loved him so much. He always treated me as an important person. Not a child, but a person.

So I was in shock when my cousin called and told me that great-uncle had died. I knew I was going to miss him dearly. Needless to say, Eric refused to join the funeral. He hated my family, no need for him to meet them. So I dressed my girls in pretty black dresses and off we went, just the three of us.

Great-uncle's funeral was grand. And afterwards we had a big family gathering in this fancy restaurant that also used to be my grandmother's favourite. Now with Eric my world had become so small, that I just loved being with my big family.

Tears were being shed, laughs were being laughed. I loved the jokes, the thrill, and the buzz. I watched with awe how my cousins were with their kids. There was a naturalness with them. Things went easy. Smooth. With laughs and love. *Why couldn't Eric be like that with our kids? Why did everything have to be so tense at our house? No joy, no laughs, no friends.*

Sophie loved being amongst family. She was running wild with cousins in the big garden behind the restaurant. Lisa was staying close to me and observing me quietly. Suddenly she pulled my arm and whispered: "Mummy, you are so happy here at the funeral. Why do you never laugh at home?" Now that hit me hard. I had never realized that the girls noticed how unhappy I was. It was the first crack in my marriage.

Then, after the funeral, I decided to go for what my great-uncle had always encouraged. I started writing. And after three months I had finished my first book and put it on Eric's desk. I was so proud. I was beaming. I was thinking how proud my great-uncle would have been. My grandmother. How proud Eric would be. *I was finally living my dream...*

But as the days passed, I watched how my story was slowly covered with Eric's papers. He never read it. He simply just didn't care. Realizing that was a slap in the face. But also a good kick forwards.

Because someone else did react. He was a journalist called Ben. He contacted me right after my book was published and this guy seemed to know *everything* about me. He had googled me and found me on Facebook, Twitter, LinkedIn, all the sites I used to promote my book.

"You're beautiful," he wrote. Now that was the least thing I was feeling in those days. I was something that was simply there in the house. A piece of furniture. Hearing someone call me beautiful felt good. Real good.

Then Ben sent me an invitation for a hidden board on Pinterest with pictures on it. A hut in a snowstorm, a fire, a bear skin, the curves of a woman. And on messenger he wrote:

"We are in a hut in Antarctica. Outside an icy snow-storm is blowing, but inside a crackling fire is warming us. You are covered by a warm bear skin. Underneath it you are naked. I am lying behind you, feeling your warm body, your soft skin. My fingers are caressing you slowly. Following your curves. Feeling your shoulder, sliding down to your hip, flowing over your long legs, moving to the front now, going up, up, up …"

I couldn't help but react back:

"I can feel you. I can feel your strong fingers on my skin, touching me, caressing me, touching my breasts, moving down over my belly … Making me so wet … I can feel your breath on my skin. It's getting faster, I know you are getting excited. I can feel you are getting hard against my bum. Rock hard. And all I want is to feel you inside of me …"

We kept writing like that and I ended up masturbating right there, sitting at the kitchen table. *God this guy excited me. I hadn't felt that horny and desired in years.* And so we started what we called our 'Dream Travels.' We 'pinned' nice pictures on Pinterest, of places where we wanted to travel and then wrote about all the exciting and erotic things we would do to each other. It was fun. Sizzling hot mind triggering fun.

Now Ben was a journalist. He was skilled in asking questions. So apart from our Dream Travels he asked me questions. About me. My life. And he soon discovered I wasn't happy. One of his questions was: "If you are unhappy in your marriage, then what the hell are you still doing there? Life is short. You are gorgeous. Start to enjoy your life."

And I would come up with my big excuse: the kids. I would do anything to safeguard my children. I didn't want them to grow up in a split home. "Kids are stronger than you think," Ben responded. "If they see you happy, they will be happy. Is this the example you want to give?" Ben was the second crack in my marriage.

The third one came quite soon after that. One day I had to go to London to pay off another bill we had received. And afterwards I couldn't help but linger around. The kids were at school and it just felt so good to be in London again.

It was almost Christmas and everything was decorated, so I missed the girls to point at all the prettiness. Pulling my coat closer around me against the chill wind, I suddenly heard a familiar voice call my name behind me. "Monique!" I turned around to face Mr. Tanning, my favourite Oxford professor. It had been ages since I had last seen him, but he still looked the same.

He was wearing a tweed jacket, there was only a little grey in his black curls and his blue eyes were still mesmerizing. "How are you?" he asked me, beaming. "My favourite student ..." Now upon hearing that I felt both proud and awkward at the same time.

In a way I wished I could tell him about some great academic career, but here I was – a mother with a bad marriage and no money. "Well, I lived in Italy for a while ..." I told him, "But now I'm back, you know, the regular life. Kids, husband ..."

I must have looked miserable, for a look of sympathy crossed his face as he asked me: "Did you have lunch, darling?" I shook my head. *I had eaten a banana that I had taken with me.* With our financial situation, lunch in London was not a luxury I allowed myself to enjoy. "Please come and have lunch," he said. "I live real close by."

I made a quick calculation. *I had four hours before I had to pick up the kids. Maybe I could even ask Barbara to take them until I would be back.* So I nodded and said: "That would be lovely, Mr. Tanning." He turned around with an amused look and said: "Please, call me Robert."

His place was close by indeed. It was beautiful; huge, with big bookcases, art on the walls and antique furniture – exactly the way I would have imagined it. Mr. Tanning served me a glass of white wine and disappeared in the kitchen, chatting all the time with me while he tossed vegetables into a large bowl for a luxurious salad.

After my second glass of wine I was getting honest. Real honest. And just like Ben, Mr Tanning…, no, Robert, was an expert in asking questions. Eating opposite of each other at this big wooden table, he asked me: "Monique, why are you staying in this marriage?" His eyes drifted over my face, my body. "Darling, you can get any man you want. Do you know how well preserved you are at 39?"

I laughed. "Well so are you, at…" "Fifty seven," he said. I gulped. *He was way older than I had thought.* "Well, you are married, right?" I asked him. He nodded. "What is your secret?" I asked him. "Very simple," Robert said. "We have an open marriage." And I paused for a moment to digest that.

When I finished the salad, and another glass of wine, Robert came to my side of the table, put my glass down and kissed me. "You know, this is something I always wanted to do, all those years at university," he sighed when he finished. And then he started kissing again, pulling me up from the chair, up the stairs, into his bedroom. Or rather his and his wife's bedroom.

It had coral-red walls, big photographs of topless African women and a huge bed. Robert tore off our clothes and pulled me onto the big four poster bed caressing me, kissing me. Then suddenly he pulled away.

"I'm afraid I don't have any condoms, darling," he panted. "Neither do I," I laughed. And with a smile I imagined myself carrying condoms in my purse. *Of course I had no idea how things were going to be…*

So I sat on top of him and played with myself, while he watched below me and started wanking. I had never masturbated so openly before. Normally it was something I did secretly. Quietly. In my bed.

But it made me feel grand. Like a goddess riding him. His cock was ramrod hard beneath me and Robert murmured: "God, you're gorgeous ... You have *such* a sexy body ..." Not long afterwards we both came at almost the same time ...

Robert was the last crack in my marriage. Yes I was late that day. I had to call Barbara to keep my girls with her for an hour. But all the way on the commuter train back home I was smiling.

Of course Barbara guessed. She just *knew* something had happened, the moment she saw that big smile on my face. But she also knew what my marriage was like. "Good for you," she said and she hugged me.

And I didn't feel bad when I saw Eric that evening. It didn't feel like I had cheated. After Robert, I realized that my marriage had been over a long time ago. I just had to find a way to legally end it now. But with Eric's tempers I also knew I had to be real careful. I knew how explosive he could be and I didn't want this to turn into a huge scene.

First I told my parents. Now they had never liked Eric in the first place, so – Catholic or not – they were totally fine with it. Next I found a house. I loved the place from the moment I laid eyes on it. *This was it. My home. My First Home.* It had an open fire place where I could read stories to the girls, they would both have their own room, it had a beautiful attic and a small garden leading to an enclosed playground where all the neighbourhood kids would assemble.

Also it was real close to a good school – the village one which they were now attending was rather crappy- a supermarket, a doctor, a dentist. And it was close to my parents. To Sarah. To my grandmother's house, where I had grown up. And to my

In-Laws – though that was not something I was considering, yet. So my mother and I put a bid on the house. It was for the first time that I felt so close to her. I loved that feeling.

Next I had to find a job. Now most places turned me down. Either my CV was too good, or I had a gap in my CV so I wasn't good enough. But eventually I did find a job as a waitress at the airport. And I rather liked the idea of working at the airport. It would almost feel like travelling. Now the shifts were irregular, but my parents said they could help with the kids. And it was part-time, giving me enough time with the girls.

Only once I had arranged everything for a safe escape, I started to talk with Eric. But I didn't talk about the divorce quite yet. I knew he would explode if he knew the idea came from me. He would never accept it. And I didn't want to leave this marriage fighting. I was so done with fighting. I wanted it to be a peaceful affair.

Now I knew this could only work, if he thought it was *his* idea. So I talked with him about his church. How he wasn't happy with us. How maybe being a Minister was something to go for. I had followed my dreams with writing, I told him, now he should follow his. So he cried a little. He said: "I'm so sorry I'm not a family man." And then he beamed at the prospect of becoming a Minister.

He would never become one and in a way I guess I already knew. I figured it would be one of his famous plans that were never carried out. He had tons of those. But his Minister Dream worked well for me. We had a calm divorce and an easy agreement on the kids. He would see them every other weekend, we agreed, and he would pay some alimony for them.

But it was still three months before the girls and I could move into our new house. And those three months were the longest ever. Calmness was not a state Eric could be in for a long time. Soon he was losing his temper at everything. At me packing our boxes, wrapping up our china in old newspapers, piling books into boxes. And though his anger was red-hot, we still had to go to school events together.

Christmas-dinner at school was so beautiful that it broke my heart to know the girls were leaving. Meanwhile Eric was stamping around the school, his anger steaming out of him. It felt so weird, knowing this was our last Christmas together.

New Year was also bizarre – celebrating it together, knowing it was the last one. As the girls and I watched the fireworks from our warm home, sipping our alcohol-free champagne, Eric was a lonely shadow outside, firing off tons of fireworks we didn't have the money for and that no one had asked for.

That night, for the first time in my life, I wrote down my New Year's resolutions. Because one thing I had decided. 2016 was going to be my year. So I made a list and was hoping some of it would be coming true:

- Meet new people
- Earn money
- Become more confident
- Take some chances
- Meet interesting men
- Have better sex
- Adopt a cute pet
- Travel more and see the world

When I started to tell people about the divorce, most people were sympathetic. A mother at school even hugged me and said: "I never understood why you were with that guy in the first place."

The mover who came to check how many boxes I needed – an older man with a kind smile – looked around the damp house and said: "Darling, one thing I know. Wherever you are taking your children, you will definitely be better off." He patted my back sympathetically and gave me a huge discount.

Even my hairdresser looked me in the eye through the mirror and said: "Love, you should have left him a long time ago." He was this lovely bald gay guy, and as he cut further, he told me something very interesting that was going to change my life.

"You know, darling?" he said. "There was something about this website in the newspapers. It's free for women and you can meet interesting businessmen to have dinner with." And he smiled at me in the mirror.

"No *sex*," he continued and gave me stern look, "just dinner. But who knows. Might be something for you. Maybe it's good to remember! Hell, had I been a woman, I would register right now!" And he pretended to throw invisible hair over his shoulder while we laughed.

So freedom was coming nearer. I could feel it pulling. And I was so much looking forward to leave the cage I had lived in.

One evening I took off my wedding ring and replaced it with my grandmother's engagement ring. From now on, I promised my grandmother and myself, I was going to choose for the girls and myself. And whenever I drove the kids to and from school, I would play Elton John's 'Live Like Horses' real loud and feel this excitement rush through my body. Finally I would be free.

When the movers came, I had made sure the girls were staying with my parents. I didn't want them to see how their old home was torn apart. After the movers left, I just stood there, alone, in the house I had been so unhappy in.

I knew this was the last time I would stand here, though it would still be a part of my girls' lives. My eyes lingered for a moment on the table the girls and I used to make cookies on. The sofa we watched movies on. The kitchen Eric and I had so many fights in.

Outside it was a beautiful, crisp, sunny, almost spring day. And I left. Without a backward glance, feeling this rush of excitement running through my body. *Finally I was free…*

CHAPTER FOUR:
STEPPING IN THE SUGAR BOWL

For months I'm exhilarated and high on my new found freedom. I just feel so happy. I have wings. I'm free. The world has colour again. For the first time I am living in my own house, the kids are doing well and I live close to my family and to Sarah again.

And it doesn't take long for our little house to become a home. Since I've left most furniture with Eric – most was his anyway – we don't have much, but I can take some antique furniture from my parents' house and find the rest for real cheap through preloved.co.uk.

Our furniture becomes an interesting mix. I find this beautiful oak cloister table, really big, that becomes our centre piece in the kitchen, surrounded with a mix of different chairs I've taken from my mother. Our sofa is tiny, the three of us just fit on it. Our TV is even tinier, but it has a DVD player so we're perfectly happy with it.

I find a second-hand rocking chair to put in front of the open fireplace. And the girls get second hand beds, desks and closets. Only the mattresses, pillows and duvets I buy knew.

I really like looking for hard bargains, getting these nice pieces for a very low price. So soon we have a home. And it's such a cosy place. The girls love sitting at the table, drawing, making cookies or playing games.

But one thing is still missing. The girls had always wanted a cat, but with Eric's allergy it had been just a dream. Or maybe I should say Lisa wanted a cat. Sophie isn't a real animal person, but Lisa is. She is always finding animals, and animals find her. She can't go through a street without patting all the cats.

So on the first weekend in our new home, I take the girls to the animal shelter. They are thrilled, especially Lisa. And one of the first cats we lay our eyes on is Fuzzy. He is an old big striped cat who starts purring the moment he sees us and keeps nuzzling up against Lisa. So the moment Lisa has laid eyes on him one thing is sure: Fuzzy is coming home with us. And with the cat our house truly becomes a home.

Now the girls take the divorce much better than I had dared to hope. Their first years of life had been a roller coaster, but now life is steady and predictable. They love our new house and are quick to make friends in the neighbourhood and at school. They are thrilled about all the family, the cousins they had never met. And they are immediately close with Sarah's kids – she has two girls, just like me.

And then there is my new job. It starts off with a course and I love being in a work space again. I love being amongst people, meeting new people, being at the airport amongst the bustle of traveling people.

But the irregular shifts can be tough, especially since my parents find it hard to take care of the girls. They forget picking them up from school, and find it a hassle to take Sophie to her swimming lesson. But I remain positive. I'm sure they will learn. Or so I think …

And my household quickly settles down into a happy rhythm. This new house is the home I have always dreamed of. It's filled with children voices, whispers, games and laughs. I enjoy the happiness, the noise, the laughter. And every Saturday when the girls are with me, we cosy up together with Fuzzy on the sofa and have a movie night.

But then there are the weekends that the girls are with their father. And it's hard when the house is all empty. It's just so silent. I close the doors to the girls' rooms so I don't have to look at the emptiness inside.

On my first weekend, Barbara visits me. She leaves her kids with her husband and helps me with decorating the girls' rooms. Now I suck at any DIY project. I really do. But Barbara is a real handywoman, since she used to help her dad when she was young. So she fixes everything that needs to be fixed and then we go dancing all night.

It has been ages since I danced that much and it's so much fun. I feel like a teenager again. And one thing I notice. Robert was right. Men are still interested. Though we don't give the men much attention. Barbara and I chat even more than we dance and I'm happy to learn that her husband is finally doing therapy. It looks like at least their marriage will be saved. It's so much fun to have a friend over and I'm sad when Barbara has to leave again.

The second weekend that I am alone I try to make an appointment with Sarah. "Sure you can come over," she writes. "Andrew and the girls would love to see you!" But then I get second thoughts. I would love to see Sarah alone, but not with her family. It will make me miss my girls even more.

So I make myself a hot chocolate and settle down on the sofa to chat with Amanda. She is living in Australia now, where she has married a rich Australian banker. We chit-chat for some time, but when I write: "You know, I never understood how you did all your traveling!" it takes her a while to answer. And her answer is not what I had expected.

"You are writing books now, aren't you?" she writes. "Would you be interested in writing my memoirs?" "Well, sure I am," I reply. "If you're travels are interesting enough to write about…"

Again it takes some time before she answers. And the answer blows my mind. She writes: "I was a top-end escort for five years." *Bloody hell. What?* Now I *try* not to judge her. Really. But the thought makes me sick.

A top-end escort? Amanda? Why? So I write back to her that I greatly appreciate her offer, but that I know nothing about the escort world. It would be better for her to find someone else to write her memoirs. And I avoid chatting with her for a week.

So my weekends without the girls are damn quiet. I do a lot of sexting with Ben, and in our minds we fuck the world around. Also he starts sending me porn-links through either Pornhub or Redbox, which we watch while we help ourselves. But by now I am getting a bit tired of all the sexting. I need something real…

The third weekend the girls are gone, I am restless. I need *something*. A date or anything to have some fun and take my attention off the empty house. It's at that moment that I remember the site which the hairdresser talked about. *A site for dating interesting men.* So I open my laptop and do some research.

There appears to be a term for it. It's called Sugar Dating. And there are loads of sites for it. Several are British, but it's the international businessmen that I think I would be interested in. Those are the ones that might be lonely while travelling, I decide, and eager for some company at dinner. I have no idea yet how many lonely men are right here in the UK.

Now most sites talk about Sugar Dating as young college girls dating older businessmen. And I'm neither young, nor a college girl. But hey, I can always try. This seems way better than a dating site. See, at this point in life I'm not interested in dating with the goal of a relationship. All I want is something that is low-maintenance and high-fun to fill the weekends when the girls are gone.

Since Giovanni and Eric, I also don't really believe in relationships anymore. Next to 'All men cheat', I'm *not* carrying my mother's conviction that 'All men are bastards' quite yet. But in a way I do believe I shouldn't get too much involved with them. In the end, one thing is for sure. They will hurt me.

So if that's the case, I'd better enjoy something low-maintenance and high-fun. If I don't lose my heart, I can't be hurt. Also, I don't want any men to enter my private life with the girls. They are happy as it is. I don't want their lives to be uprooted. Again.

So I choose an American site that seems classy and offers free membership for women. It's called Seeking Arrangement. By now I'm all excited and I really want to share this new episode in my life. But who am I going to tell?

Not Sarah. She is happily married. She would never understand. Nor Barbara. She's married as well. But Amanda? Yes, she is a good one to share this with. With her own past I know one thing for sure: she won't judge me.

And I'm right. Amanda is all excited. When I'm filling in my profile, she keeps bugging me. Saying I should make myself younger and not tell anything about my kids. But I'm stubborn. I decide to go for honesty.

The first message I get is from an American. He writes: "My girlfriend and I love your smile." What? Now this is definitely not someone looking for a business dinner … But I do have to say that I'm intrigued, so I start chatting with him and it turns out he has a wife, two girlfriends and he wants me to be the third.

Now I have no girl experiences so far, so I open Pornhub and search for 'Lesbian Love'. The results are plenty. I choose one from Nubile Films showing three girls gently making love to each other. And though I have never thought about sex with a woman, I do have to say it greatly arouses me. I'm soaking wet and can't help but play with myself and come. Three times.

But as exciting as this all is, I'm not on Seeking Arrangement for new sexual experiences, as tempting as they may be. This is just sex and I don't want that. I want dinner dates. I want to have a connection. So the moment the guy starts sending me pictures of his girlfriends' pussies – and requests mine – I decline.

Next there is a millionaire who is looking for a lady to travel the world with. We video-chat. Something I have never done before. Now this is a guy loaded with money who is traveling the world. Still, he doesn't seem happy. Single, no kids, the guy actually looks miserable. And we will never meet. With my girls, traveling the world is simply not an option.

The millionaire reacts coldly. "It's just a matter of where you put your priorities, dear," he writes. Well, he is right. And my priorities are definitely with my girls. I prefer any day together with their hugs and laughter above him with his rich coldness.

His last words are: "People choose their own unhappiness" and he is right again. I guess it's intended for me, but fact is that since my divorce I'm not unhappy at all. Lately I'm bursting from happiness. It's the guy who seems bloody lonely.

A lot of other chats follow. Apart from the weekends when they are gone, I now also chat in the evenings when the girls are asleep. And I learn a whole new cyber dating code.

There are lots of acronyms: SD is Sugar Daddy, SB is Sugar Baby, SR is Sugar Relationship, SA is Seeking Arrangement, POT is a Potential Sugar Daddy, FWB stands for 'friends with benefits' indicating a casual, sexual relationship, PPM is Pay Per Meet and not allowed on Seeking Arrangement, LTA is a Long Term Arrangement, STA is a Short Term Arrangement, NSA is No Strings Attached – you get what you want as long as I get what I want and everyone is happy – and LMSO is Laugh My Ass Off.

There are also tons of terms. 'Sugar Bowl' refers to the Sugar Lifestyle in general or to the Sugar Daddy dating scene. An Arrangement is a negotiated relationship between a Sugar Daddy and a Sugar Baby. A 'Hook-up' is the opposite of an Arrangement; it's a random, and most likely indiscreet, sexual encounter with a stranger or sexual acquaintance. 'Road Sugar' are Sugar Daddy's who will only see Sugar Babies outside of their city of residence. Most of these are married. And a 'Salty Daddy' is a fraud. A person who is not generous or wealthy enough to be a Sugar Daddy.

Now I don't hunt myself on Seeking Arrangement. I don't want to be the one to chase. I prefer to respond to the men who contact me. With my age I must be ancient on the site and I know most men will be looking for younger girls.

But men keep contacting me. One guy who doesn't have a photo on his profile, does send me a picture of his dick so I block him right away. Another guy I never meet, but we chat for some time about our Sugar experiences.

Some men just go silent for no apparent reason. Some write long-rambling emails. And many men mostly seem to be interested in the thrill of online flirting and have no intention of meeting. Amanda calls them the 'Time-Wasters'.

One guy asks me whether I think he is really short. Now I have to check his profile to answer, since I just see this picture of a friendly looking guy. On his profile I read that he is 1.50. Well, I guess that's short. His profile also reads that he likes to take really tall women out shopping to make him feel real short.

Okay, so I'm tall, and I can wear heels to look even taller. But then he starts asking me whether I want to go out shopping with him – no sex needed – and totally humiliate him in public. He will pay me for doing so. I kindly decline. And I can only wonder what happened to him that he gets such a kick out of humiliation.

Next an American contacts me. He is 65 years old but looks younger, is retired, traveling the world and looking for a girl to join him. He is in London and wants to meet me that evening, but I don't have a babysitter for the girls that night so I decline.

I assume that's the end of him, but the next day I get a new message: "I'm in the plane thinking of you ... You're a gorgeous woman! You look and think splendidly! I desire you ... 😊"

And one day later:

> "Do you see some possibilities for us? Do you think you have one more relationship in you … or are you just putting together moments? It's important to know if you are seeking one last, easy and enjoyable long-term relationship, or are you infatuated with being an object on this site? You could work less and spend more time with your girls if someone stepped up to take care of you … Would you be interested in and capable of living anywhere else in the world or are you firmly rooted and already have an established support network? I'm sure there is much more … but that is a start …"

Ay, that's tempting …. 'If someone stepped up to take care of you …' Now that would feel so good. I have been struggling to keep my head above the water for so long now. For a moment I close my eyes and imagine some happy future with a rich guy and my two girls in the US.

But it's just a dream. Eric will never accept me taking the girls to the US. And, much more importantly, I made my girls a promise. We are not going to move again. I open my eyes and look around our cosy little home. *This is where I want to be.*

> But the American doesn't easily take no for an answer. He writes back: "Barring a significant paradigm shift in your thinking … and at this point, lacking any personal empowerment to change what you want for your girls … and yourself and where you can live, it sounds like your lot is cast and you are necessarily locked into UK for a few years … ☺ Or … is it … ? Can you visualize and manifest it any other way … ? C'mon … I know you have a fertile imagination …"

I write back: "I can visualize and dream loads of wonderful other ways…. But then reality kicks in ☹ Though the dream is beautiful…"

His reply comes fast: "Well good for getting in an effort…. Please let me know if you conjure up some possibility. You are a keeper so thanks for being so engaging! Wish I would have been able to gather you up in my arms and spend some joyful and satisfying time with you…"

I close my eyes once more to dream the beautiful dream… Then I move on.

Now I came on this site for dinner-dates. And so far I have gotten a lot of interesting offers, but nothing comes even close to a dinner date.

But then finally one guy stands out. He is 65 years old, from Denmark and calls himself The Viking. He is in London for business and looking for a girl to take out to dinner. I immediately set an appointment with him. And for the date I choose to wear one special item. I decide to wear my grandmother's pearl necklace, for good luck…

We meet in this charming Italian restaurant. It's a small but classy place, with candle light and soft music. It almost has the atmosphere of a living room. And I'm thrilled. *It's been ages since I've gone out for dinner. Especially to a nice place like this!*

Mr. Viking is waiting for me at the table. And I do have to say that when I first see him, I feel a bit uncomfortable. Now this guy is definitely much older than me, and I wonder what people will think. But I manage to put my hesitation aside as he gets up to greet me and we give each other a polite peck on both cheeks. *What do I care what other people think?*

Fact is, Mr. Viking is a true gentleman. He holds my chair for me, is charming and has this beautifully wrapped gift with him. I open it carefully. It's a bottle of Chanel. "I do hope you like it, dear," he says and smiles. *He hopes I like it? I haven't gotten a nice gift like this in years!*

When we get the menu, I take one look at the prices and gulp. It's a monthly changing menu ranging from three to six courses and the prices are mind blowing. Well, for me that is. And that's even before I have seen the wine menu ... But of course I have just come from taking bananas with me for lunch.

Mr. Viking doesn't seem to think it's mind blowing at all. He takes his reading glasses out of a tortoise case, puts them on and seriously studies the menu. "What would you say, dear?" he asks. "Are you hungry? Do we take the three – or the six course menu?" And he looks up to me expectantly. "You choose, darling," I tell him. "It's your visit to London." So Mr. Viking chooses the six course menu – so he can taste all – and the wine menu that goes with it.

Now I haven't enjoyed myself like this in a long time. Mr. Viking is funny, charming, making jokes and talking about tons of things. His life. Mrs. Viking. And soon Mr. Viking and I are talking about the Danish art of hygge. "I heard about hygge," I say, "But what does it mean exactly?"

He looks a while into the distance before he talks. "There's no English word to describe it I guess, but several can be used to describe the idea. Cosiness, happiness, comfort, simplicity and being content. You know, in essence, it means creating a warm atmosphere and enjoying the good things in life with nice people."

Mr. Viking gestures to the candle on our table. "The warm glow of candlelight is hygge," he says. "And friends and family are – there's nothing more hygge than sitting around a table, discussing the big and small positive things in life like we are doing now." He gives me a warm smile. "It's a feeling or mood that comes from taking genuine pleasure in making ordinary, everyday moments more meaningful, beautiful or special. It's is about being here, in the now."

"So it's a little like mindfulness?" I ask him. He thinks for some time. "Yeah, yeah. Maybe. But it's more than that. It's to recognize and acknowledge a moment or feeling when the ordinary feels extraordinary."

Now the moment the food arrives, I definitely acknowledge the extraordinary. I'm in heaven. The food is simply divine and takes me all the way back to my days in Italy with Giovanni. Now this is Italian food the way it's supposed to be. And I haven't eaten this deliciously in a long, very long time.

Our wine glasses are regularly refilled and we are well informed about the dishes and the matching wines. The wine is delicious too: supple, light and fruity, and all from northern Italy.

The crusty bread is homemade, the olive oil is splendid and each time another one is served it comes with an explanation of the oil. But what surprises me most is the unexpected and bold combination of flavours and dishes.

As antipasti there is squid filled with courgette and marjoram on a crispy Italian panissa chickpea pie with a typical bagna cauda Piedmont sauce and sweetbread in Milanese manner, with Jerusalem artichoke, scorzonera in red wine and parsnip-chips that come with a Pinot Bianco.

The primo piatto is homemade stuffed cappellacci pasta filled with mushrooms on a pumpkin foam that comes with a Barbaresco red wine. And the secondi piatto is veal roasted in Barolo that melts in the mouth, white polenta, seasonal vegetables, a waffle made of saffron risotto and a matching White Piedmonte wine.

We are quiet for some time as we enjoy our pre-desert with different preparations of citrus fruits with bergamot. And as desert we get pears stewed in red wine, homemade ice cream of gorgonzola cheese and crumble of Sicilian capers. Then Mr. Viking orders us an espresso with a homemade limoncello with it. And he gets back to his Danish Miracle.

"Hygge is more than a cosy room full of candles, company and good food, though," he says. "It's a philosophy, a way of life that has helped us Danes understand the importance of simplicity, of time to unwind and slowing down the pace of life."

Talking about slowing down, when I look at my watch I realize we have spent the whole evening in the restaurant. Time has had wings. Now when Mr. Viking gets the bill I hold my breath. I know he is going to spend a fortune. But Mr. Viking nods when he opens it and says "For such quality food the bill is very reasonable."

He calls me a cab, opens the door for me, gives me money for the ride and says: "Thank you dear, I had a lovely evening with you." I smile and say: "Thank *you* darling, I spent an evening in heaven. It was very hygge!" And I can still hear his roaring laughter as the cab turns the corner.

That night when I am lying in bed, I am still enjoying the memory of the evening. It has been lovely. Really lovely. I had an excellent dinner, wonderful company and I haven't had such a good time in ages. Seriously. And one thing I have learned. The Danish Miracle of hygge. And that's exactly how my home and my life with the girls is going to be.

The next morning Mr. Viking texts me. "How is my Princess of the Pirates doing? I truly enjoyed our evening. Hope to meet you next time I'm in London." And that's the first message I get from him. From that day Mr. Viking sends me messages every morning – wishing me a good day – and every evening – wishing me a good night. And we chat in between. He always contacts me when I'm down. For some reason, he just *knows* when I'm feeling blue. And yes, we will have dinner again.

But more about that later. For now, as I'm snuggling up under my duvet I realize Seeking Arrangement is turning out to be just as I had hoped. And of course I have no idea how it will all change...

CHAPTER FIVE:
MR. BIG

It's Wednesday afternoon, so the girls are free from school. We just had lunch and have decided to go to the playground, when I hear a familiar sound. I have a new message from Seeking Arrangement – SA messages now have their own tone on my phone – and I wonder who it is. It can't be Mr. Viking. He has already sent me my Morning Message. And Mr. Viking and I have moved to Skype for communication.

So I give the girls some paper to draw on while I check my inbox. It reads: "You have received access to private photos of Farshad4u." I click on the link underneath the text to see them. They are pictures of a bald guy with a friendly smile standing in front of the Eiffel tower, on Tiananmen Square and sitting in a small plane.

So I write to him: "Thank you! Nice pictures! Looks like you enjoy traveling and planes! :-)"And I give him access to my photos. He reacts back immediately:

"Thank you for your photos and your message. You look so pretty nice lady. I am in Frankfurt for some business meeting. I am a high educated engineer and international business man in fields of high technology precision equipment. Because of my work I have to go to many trips around the world. Are you interested to visit other countries around the world?

Really, I am new in this website and I didn't have experience of sugar daddy before, but I want to be a good daddy for my baby. I am following for a nice woman for kind and gentle friendship and dating. Please let us know more about each other. You can connect to me by WhatsApp or some other chat application."

And he gives me his phone number. But I can't message yet. The girls are impatient now. They are pulling my arm, asking me when we're leaving. So off we go.

When we are at the playground and the girls are giggling on the swings, I keep getting messages from him. He wants to meet this weekend, he says. *And that happens to be exactly the weekend that the girls go to their father.* Now I don't chat for long, because I want to give the girls my full attention. Normally I mostly keep my chatting for the evenings. So I let him know I will contact him that evening.

That night he is still enthusiastic. He wants me to come to Frankfurt, but I refuse. I'm not crazy right? I'm not going to travel to another country to meet a complete stranger! *And little do I know all the crazy stuff that I will be up to in the future...*

Now Mr. Iran is obviously not a man who hears 'no' a lot. At first he seems annoyed. But then he gives in and says that ok, he will come to London just to meet me. But he still has business in Frankfurt, so he can only arrive on Saturday evening and leave the next afternoon.

"Will you be able to stay with me, so we can spend our time most efficiently?" he asks. And I think about that for a while. *Well, why not? If I don't like the guy, I can always leave.* But just to be sure, I ask the expert. I ask Amanda.

Amanda is all excited. "Iranian men are very generous," she writes. "And very good in bed. Go for it!" "Hey, I'm not going to sleep with the guy!" I tell her. "Yeah, right," is her answer. "You're meeting him in his hotel right? Dream on! Just let me know the name of the hotel and the room number. I want to know you're safe." I grumble and think: *I'm NOT going to have sex with him.* But I don't want to argue with Amanda.

To Mr. Iran I text back: "That's fine. I can stay with you. We can chat all night. But I am not going to have sex with you." Mr. Iran remains silent for some time. Then he reacts: "Ok. Meet you Saturday evening." And I have no idea that this is going to be one of our big jokes together ...

So that Friday I drop the girls with their father. And Saturday evening I go all the way to Heathrow to pick him up, wearing my grandmother's necklace for luck. Now while I'm waiting for the guy to appear, I feel quite self-conscious. *Because what the hell am I doing?* Here I am, meeting a complete stranger – I don't even know his surname – and I have agreed to stay in his room ...

And I notice that when you are waiting for a bald guy you have never met before, the world seems to be flooded with bald men. With every dark bald men swishing out of the arrivals-door, I wonder whether it's him. It's the law of attraction in a funny context. The whatever you put your focus on you will receive.

But the moment Farshad comes out, I know it's him. He is my height, dark, with elegant glasses, sun-tanned skin and a kind smile. And the moment he sees me, he hugs me like I am a long-lost friend, grabs my arm and marches us over to the taxi stand, smiling and giving me a sideway look from time to time.

We take the cab to his hotel and share some formalities. Soon we are at the hotel and I gasp, because the place is simply stunning. As I walk through the hotel lobby, my jaw just drops to the floor. The hotel is such an elegant space. It's in sharp contrast with the bustling streets outside. And for a moment I pause in awe underneath a giant dazzling crystal chandelier. *Now this is life…*

But checking in feels very uncomfortable. Especially since Farshad keeps saying things like: "Honey, you are so much more beautiful than in your photo's," which causes the two guys at reception to give each other a knowing glance.

"I'm NOT an escort!" I want to shout, but I bite my tongue. Instead – since I still have no idea what his surname is – I do my best to check what name he is writing down. But I can't read it. *I guess at 39 I now need reading glasses too…*

To my surprise Farshad doesn't pay with some golden credit card, which for some reason I had expected with a Sugar Daddy. He gets a thick envelope out of his bag that is filled with a hundred pound bills to pay for the room in advance.

"Honey, can I first put my suitcase in my room?" Farshad asks, and with a quick glance he checks out what luggage I have with me. I am travelling light. All I carry is my handbag. "Yes of course," I say and follow him, which gives me the chance to further explore this luxurious hotel.

It's a Victorian building and much of its original design maintains in its window frames, the stair banisters and the ceiling decorations. Oak timbers are throughout the hotel, giving the place a warm ambiance. And my footsteps are muffled by the thick carpet. For a moment I feel like I have just stepped into a movie. *I have never been in a place like this.*

But by now, my nerves are also killing me. *If he jumps on me in the room, what do I do?* Well, I shouldn't have worried. Mr. Iran is a real gentleman. Once we are in the room, he starts to unpack his suitcase, humming some exotic song under his breath.

In the meantime I marvel at the decadence of his – or actually our – posh five-star hotel room. There is a comfy living area and the bathtub has a built in TV and stunning views over Trafalgar Square. It seems like ages since I stayed in a hotel and I have most definitely never stayed in a hotel like this!

The moment Farshad moves to the bathroom to unpack his toiletries, I flip over the hotel card to see his name. And I text his full name, the name of our hotel and our room number to Amanda. She gives me a thumbs up." Good luck!"

When Farshad has finished his unpacking, he holds out his arm for me. "Azizam, would you like to join me for drinks?" "What is the meaning of Azizam?" I ask him. "It's 'My Dear' in Farsi," he answers and I smile. "I would love to." So I take his arm and he takes me down to the hotel's al fresco Garden Lounge, which has two crackling fireplaces.

The moment we are seated, he asks me: "Do you mind if I smoke?" I smile at him. "Not at all." He gestures at the bar. "You know, this place has sixty-two varieties of whiskey, but more importantly it also has over fifty-three varieties of cigars. It even has its own cigar sommelier."

When the cigar sommelier has arrived, Farshad asks me: "Have you ever tried a cigar?" I shake my head. "Not yet ..." "Would you like to join me then?" I nod. "I would love to." *Sure. Why not. Posh hotels. Cigars. This is all turning out to be fun!*

Now I'm not sure whether the sommelier notices my discomfort, but he treats me like I'm always visiting places like this. And he suggests I try a cigar called 'Hoyo de Monterey Double Corona' – not that the name tells me anything.

We go pick it together, walking in their impressive humidor. Next he suggests a very nice white wine to pair with my cigar. Farshad takes the same and orders a piece of cheesecake with two spoons – to share.

Puffing on our cigars and sharing our cheesecake, we chat nicely. Farshad is very friendly and polite. He tells me about his life, how he is an engineer from Iran and occasionally visits Europe for business. Yes, at this time the UK is still Europe. Though not for much longer...

Farshad tells me how he divorced a couple of years ago and has two grown-up children – a son and a daughter – in Teheran. And for his work he is travelling a lot, not just to Europe. He loves his work, that's obvious. But I'm not sure he likes all the traveling. In a way he seems lonely.

I like him. He asks me sincere questions and shows he is really interested in me. He is also honest. "I have never met anyone through this site," he says and states very matter of fact: "Before I only had escorts in Europe." And there is no hint of shame here. "But I don't like escorts," he continues. "They are too impersonal."

I straighten my skirt. In a way it doesn't feel very nice to be the 'more personal' solution after escorts. But in a way, why do I care. I'm here in this posh hotel enjoying the finer things in life. There is no reason for complaining.

After we finish our cigars, we go back up to the room and Farshad takes a shower. I quickly slip in my beautiful-but-not-too-sexy nightgown and lie down under the duvet, waiting for him to appear. In a way I am afraid he will show up naked – *what do I do then?* – but Farshad is a true gentleman. He doesn't.

When he gets out of the bathroom I notice how hairy he is. And what he is wearing. It's a tight Calvin Klein boxer and just before he slips under the duvet with me I can't help but notice how big the bump in there is.

"Honey, I know you said no sex... but is spooning okay?" he asks me as he cuddles up against me. "I love to sleep like that and I never do..." I nod. *Sure. Why not.* So he turns off the light and spoons up behind me, softly caressing me.

Well, I know that you probably already expected it. Amanda most definitely did. Because the 'no sex' doesn't hold of course. With Farshad behind me, I can feel his cock against my bum. And I realize that it is *huge*. And it feels like it is still growing...

Now I know I told him no sex, but what the hell? I'm a single woman, I haven't had intercourse for months. Why shouldn't I have some fun?

So I turn around. And Farshad responds immediately. He starts kissing me. His sensitive hands cupping my breasts, then moving to cup my bum. And one thing is for sure. This guy has steaming passion.

While his hands are caressing me, *my* hand goes down to have an adventure on its own. To explore something that has greatly aroused my interest. And when I slip my hand in his boxer short, I can't help but gasp a little. Farshad laughs happily and peels off his boxer shorts.

Now I've never been really into dicks. Until now that is. Because Farshad's dick is Majestic. It's Glorious. And it's Huge. But it's not just Huge, it's also Thick. And thickness – I will soon discover – is what truly pleasures me.

He is circumcised, and his glans is soft and pink and just looks so soft and vulnerable on top of the veined greatness of the rest of his cock. Now as you might understand, I can't just let his cock stand there in all its greatness.

All I want is to feel his Majestic Greatness inside of me. I have never had sex with such a big dick. And I just *long* to know how he will feel inside of me. So I climb on top of him.

But then I realize something. "I don't have any condoms," I pant. But Farshad has a naughty sparkle in his eyes. "I do!" he says. "Just in case you'd change your mind..." And he grabs a package from the drawer of his nightstand.

It takes one split second for the condom to be out of its package and rolled over the Splendid Dick. And before I know it, I climb on top of him and start riding all his gloriousness.

Now I have no idea when I had intercourse for the last time. It must have been ages. And as I now discover I was simply starving. So our first fuck that night is just like that. It's a Fuck. But one with a capital 'F'. There is basically no foreplay, I just ride him until he comes.

After that we have more time for sweetness. I lie on his chest, crawling with my fingers through his chest hair. I never thought I would like chest hair, but fact is I'm loving it. It's so soft…

But I didn't come yet. And I'm still horny as hell. Soon I discover that I can get the Majestic Dick back up in no time. And this time Farshad is in action. He starts taking me from behind, since we were spooning anyway.

Then he flips me over and takes me doggy. Now doggy has never been this glorious. His Thickness and Hugeness are majestically inside of me. I have never felt so completely filled and I love the feeling. I'm amazed he even fits into me. And it's in doggy, while I help myself, that I come. But we are not finished yet. We fuck the whole night and part of the next day.

Oral is not the biggest success. Mr. Big doesn't seem to do oral and I'm fine with that, receiving oral makes me very uncomfortable. But when I try to give him a blow job, his dick is just simply too big to even think about Deep Throat.

Otherwise, we fuck in every single position I have ever known. I'm sure we've fucked our way through the whole Kama Sutra. In total Mr. Big comes eight times, I have a total of five.

When we finally do stop, it's because he has to go to the airport. So we dress and I join him in the cab back. I'm sitting huddled in his arm, like his biggest love. My cheeks are still flushed and rosy. And I forgot to bring a brush, so my hair is a mess. But who cares. I have just been in freaking heaven.

Mr. Big keeps looking at me and grinning. Then finally he says: "No sex?" and he bursts out laughing. The cab driver looks at us through his rear mirror, but who cares. I'm sure cab drivers experience things like this all the time.

At customs Mr. Big grabs me and kisses me like his biggest love. When he enters customs, I keep waving till he is out of sight. And all I can do is sigh. *Jeez. This was crazy...*

But the biggest surprise is still awaiting me. When I'm about to catch the train back home, a message pops up on my phone. It's Mr. Big. And he writes: "Honey, I've left you a little something in your wallet."

The moment I am in the train, I go to the ladies to check. And I gasp as I open my wallet. A whole bundle of fresh-smelling 100 pounds are tucked inside. I start counting them and ... *Jeez!* He has given me a thousand pounds!

Now if you had told me beforehand that I was going to have sex with a stranger and receive money for it, I would have definitely told you that it was going to make me feel bad. But fact is, it doesn't. Not at all.

A rush of happiness flushes through as I think of all that this money can do for us. New shoes for the girls. A handyman to finally get some safe locks on the doors. Maybe a dinner at the girl's favourite pizza place.

That evening I put the money in my grandmother's antique hollowed-out book-safe. And I contact Amanda. "See!!" Amanda cheers. "That's what I'm talking about." So I also let her know something else. I have made a decision. I tell her that I will start writing her memoirs ...

CHAPTER SIX: KARMA

It's funny how soon adventures seem like a dream once you are back in your daily routine. It's a rather warm spring day in the beginning of April and I am sitting with Sarah in her garden. Our girls are running around together blowing bubbles and whatever I did with Mr. Iran seems like a vague distant dream.

Still it's something that makes me smile within. I feel this big bubble of laughter inside of me. But it's also causing a distance between Sarah and me. Normally I share everything with her, but now I can't. She's my best friend, but she is happily married and I know one thing: if she knows she will judge.

To make things even worse, I'm now telling her lies. And I'm really struggling with those. I'm not very good in lying and I don't feel comfortable doing it. But Farshad wants to take me to Barcelona when the girls are with me and I really want to go. So I've made up a story. I am telling people I might have a project in Venice for two days. And I have just told Sarah that I need to find a place for the girls to stay.

Sarah looks at me with a frown. "They can always stay with me, you know that. But do you think you will get this opportunity more often?" I think about that for a while and nod. "Yes, maybe." "Well, then you need to find a more permanent solution."

Thing is, I never got the job. After my training was finished, they sacked me because I wasn't 'dependable' enough. And they were right. I wasn't. Having my parents look after the girls turned out to be a mistake. They can hardly manage taking care of themselves, let alone two little children.

Thing is, with my father's Korsakoff he tends to forget everything. He's living in his own little world. Making up whole new versions of the truth in which he totally believes himself. And my mother, well she just locks herself up in the house. Bringing kids to school is not her cup of tea.

So I kept getting calls from the school. "Why weren't the girls there? Why weren't they picked up?" Of course I thought of other options, like a paid baby sitter. But truth was that I simply wasn't making enough. So I lost my job and now I'm struggling to get by.

But with Farshad's financial help, I suddenly see a new option. I realize that Sugar Dating can become my way to survive. I know from Amanda that there are quite some men willing to have paid arrangements. And this might be my solution. Meeting Farshad in Barcelona means that we can most probably survive for another month…

Sarah doesn't know anything about Sugar Dating of course. But she knows I lost my job. And she knows I need extra income. So we go through a whole range of options. Eric has to work and I don't consider my parents an option anymore.

Picking up the girls in time, dropping them off at school is not something I seem to be able to expect from them. To have the girls for two whole days is unthinkable. So I know one thing. *If I want to have this secret adventure, I will have to find another solution…*

"Can't they stay with Eric's parents?" Sarah then asks, stretching out in the sun. I winch. She opens her eyes and pats me on my hand. "I know how you feel about them … But the girls

like it over there, don't they?" I nod unwillingly. "Yes, they do."
"Well, it might be an option?"

Now my Ex-In-Laws and Sarah's Stepmother have been amongst our favourite subjects when we feel like complaining. Thing is, my Ex-Mother-In-Law and her Stepmother are quite similar. They both are simply toxic. They are controlling, judgmental, critical and overbearing.

I haven't told you much about her yet, but Wilma, my Ex-Mother-In-Law, would do well in fairy tales. She would make a great stepmother too. And I had thought Giovanni's mother was bad ...

First of all, Wilma is always right. Without exception. She'll never admit being wrong, and she will never apologize for anything. In her eyes, I am the only person ever to blame. Especially since the divorce.

When I make a remark about the tons of candy she gives them, she replies that candy is not unhealthy. Next she tells the girls they shouldn't eat the whole grain bread I give them, since white bread is much healthier. Her reasoning is: why would they otherwise sell candy and white bread at the supermarket.

Fact is, when she comes for a visit I feel constantly on edge. I clean like crazy, but whenever she comes she will always find something. Dust on top of a closet – pulling her finger over it and showing me – a little spot on the stove, a toy that is not stored away ...

And then there are all those remarks ... "Don't you think Lisa should do her homework by herself?" "Why can't Sophie choose her own outfit?" "Why can't they have another piece of cake?" "Why do they go to bed so early?" "Why do you have dinner so early?"

It's no surprise that she hates my alternative parents. She just can't understand the different way they approach – and live – life.

She doesn't get it how my parents are not living up to middle class etiquette. In her eyes, anyone who fails to do so is wrong.

See, Wilma's way is clearly the best. And since I obviously didn't get the appropriate upbringing, she had expected me to learn *her* way of taking care of Eric: her way of cooking, cleaning and just about everything else under the sun. Since I failed to do any of that, she now has a right to complain about me to anyone who'll listen.

Fact is, our relationship was troubled from the start. When Eric introduced me to her, she suggested that I needed some highlights in my hair. Next our wedding was too simple. When invited for dinner, she would advise me how – or what – I should cook next time to make a better meal. And it was a shame that I simply didn't know how to iron Eric's clothes decently – and especially that I didn't iron his socks and underwear.

Then I got pregnant. And she changed into a Monster-In-Law. My whole pregnancy she kept telling me how huge I was. And that my breasts were simply tiny. "Where are your breasts?" she would screech in the middle of restaurants or shops. "Why don't you have any breasts? *I* had lots when I was pregnant," patting her own sagging bosom. "See, I still have lots."

Now you might remember that my breasts are not what I have on my list of things I love about myself. I would have loved them to be bigger. And though I *knew* I shouldn't let her hurt me, it still hurt.

Then there were the children … Apparently, I'm an idiot and she is Dr. Spock. Of course I breastfed Lisa too long, and Wilma would wonder aloud why I had to nurse so often. Also it wasn't natural that Lisa didn't want a dummy. Whenever Wilma would push a dummy into her mouth, Lisa would frown, suck on it for a few seconds before spitting it out as far as possible.

To Wilma – for reasons that I still don't understand – that was simply unacceptable. Whenever Wilma was outside with us, she would go to other parents with children happily sucking on their dummies and ask them how their child accepted the dummy, pointing a bony finger at me saying: "See *that one* can't make her daughter suck on one." When Lisa didn't walk on her first birthday, something was definitely wrong with her. When she had tantrums in public, it was because I didn't raise her well.

Then Sophie came. And the first year all my little baby did was cry. Whenever Wilma saw her, she would have a frown on her face. "Children should be quiet," she would say. "You are not their slave. Babies need to fit around your own schedule."

Whenever I would pick Sophie up to sooth her with my In-Laws around, Wilma would pull her out of my arms and put her down forcibly in another room saying: "You make your children needy if you pick them up when they are upset."

I believed differently. I believed that by meeting Sophie's needs I was making her secure. But of course only Wilma was ever right.

When Lisa was three years old she was afraid of Wilma. She wouldn't even come near her. She was always going to Fred, my Father-In-Law. Playing with him, hugging him – and pissing off Wilma even more.

Now Fred is Eric's stepfather and I really like him. Though sometimes I just wish he had some more backbone, for his sake. He met and married Wilma when Eric was eighteen, right after Eric's abusive father died.

Fred is the opposite from Eric's father. Fred is kind, caring and – since he never had any children of his own – he just loves my girls. He wrestles with them, comes to their school events, and does all the things their father isn't doing, because Eric is too busy working or going to church.

But I'm not sure Fred is appreciated by Wilma. He is like her butler. He does everything for her. Since Wilma sleeps in every day till twelve, he brings her breakfast – and her Prozac – in bed when she wakes. Since the rheumatism hurts her hands, he cleans the house, cooks, and takes care of the gardening.

Not that this makes her treat him any better. She is always nagging on him. He's not cleaning well enough, he is not giving her enough attention … How he manages to stay in that marriage is a mystery to me.

But Wilma is not judging everyone. She throws herself on her two children, Eric and his sister Josephine. Since our divorce she has taken over my 'wifely duties.' She cleans Eric's house, brings him food and does his laundry and ironing. And no doubt she praises herself on doing such a better job than I did.

Then there is Josephine, Eric's sister. Sarah and I call her 'Holy Josephine'. She has three kids, a rich dominant husband and works part time as a teacher. Whenever Wilma judges me, she will include some praise about her. *Now Josephine knows how to treat her husband. Josephine knows how to raise her girls. At least her girls are well behaved.* Fact is, anyone would behave well with her controlling husband around.

So as our four girls are playing and Sarah is stretching out in the sun, I sigh and say: "You know, Wilma just has this way of getting under my skin." I sigh once more. Sarah puts her hand on my leg. "Maybe you should try not to let her get under your skin anymore. Fact is, she is nothing to you anymore." I gasp. Now *that* is a revelation. She is right. But then I realize that she is still something to my girls. And if I am going to let them babysit, I'm about to become dependent on her …

"You know there are 'good days,'" I tell Sarah, "When Wilma is on her best behaviour and everything appears normal. I am sometimes even tempted to think that things are getting better. Then, out of nowhere, she will turn on me again. And I will be reminded that she will never accept me, and I can never have a relationship with her."

Sarah looks at me. "Is that a bad thing?" she asks me. "You know, I have been thinking about this. And as you know my Stepmother is just like Wilma. She has just this disapproving way of looking at my kids that makes me fume. She keeps judging me for not smiling on their wedding pictures, right after mother died. I hate the way she keeps hurting me."

I can see tears welling up in her eyes, and Sarah looks away for a second, blinking a few times before she continues. "But then sometimes I think maybe it's our Karma. Maybe these women are in our lives for a reason. Maybe we should look within and find out what it is. I know if my mother was still alive that's what she would say…"

That's right. Her mother would have said that. And for a second I think of Sarah's mother, the way she was before the cancer wore her out. She was a short woman with a grey bob, very alert and assertive, but also very alternative. She used crystals for healing. She believed in karma. And she could say things that just hit you right on the spot.

Sarah swallows hard before she continues. "See, my mother used to say that whenever someone pushes your 'buttons', it's a good indication that there's inner work to be done. We shouldn't fall into the victim mentality. If we blame everything on them, it won't bring us anything but bitterness, anger and a sense of helplessness. Maybe we have to accept part of the responsibility."

I stir. I don't feel like taking *any* responsibility for my toxic relationship with Wilma. "The worst part is that they make us question ourselves," I say. "Our self-worth. They make us wonder why we aren't good enough." Sarah nods and says: "But we shouldn't lose faith in ourselves. If they can't appreciate us, it's their loss."

She stares into the distance for a while before she continues. "See, there is one thing we can be sure of. They will never accept us. We can never have a healthy relationship with them. Maybe we should just accept that. My mother would say that maybe we should take our situation philosophically. Treat it with humour. And find comfort in the fact that other people love and accept us."

As I watch the girls I ponder on Sarah's words. *Maybe she is right.* If I look at my own part in the relationship, it's that I don't always make more effort to communicate. I react emotionally, and I shut down. In other words, I act like a child.

So maybe I should take responsibility for that. Maybe I should make an effort to be more direct. But also be aware of my "triggers" that Wilma pushes. And maybe I should cultivate a philosophical mind-set that allows me to brush things off, rather than become hurt and defensive.

Maybe she *is* my karma. Fact is that if I can handle her, I can handle any difficult person in my life. So right there and then I decide to sign a pact with the devil. I decide I will ask my Ex-In-Laws to look after the girls the two days I will be in Barcelona...

So the next day after school the girls and I head off to Fred and Wilma. Fred is inside polishing the silver with jazz on the radio. The moment he sees the girls he gets on his knees to hug them. The girls cheer, climb on his back and he crawls around with them.

And for a second I wish it could be just like that. For a moment I hope Wilma isn't home. That I can just ask Fred and have it over with. But when I ask him: "Isn't Wilma in?" he answers: "Yes she is. She is upstairs." And all my hopes of a peaceful time without her go crushing down. With lead in my shoes I go up to meet her.

Upstairs in the guestroom she is ironing, a bunch of Eric's shirts are dangling on the door. The moment she sees me, she gives me a piercing look with her ice-cold blue eyes and I winch inside. "So," she says as she continues her ironing. "You decided to finally pay us a visit."

She tosses some hair to the side. "You never come," she says. I nod and start: "I'm sorry, it's been busy..." *And I hate how apologetic I become when she's around. I'm a single mom raising two kids on my own, for fuck's sake. Why do I have to defend myself?*

But I put on my nicest smile and do my best to stay nice and smiley. I know she hates me when I'm not around, but I now notice that I throw her off a bit when I act all kind and smiley. Apparently it confuses the image of me that she has created inside of her.

I hug her and she answers with a wooden hug back. Or to be more precise, she doesn't hug back. She lets me hug her, while she stiffens. Next she sighs, puts the iron down and comes downstairs to meet the girls.

When she comes down, the girls ignore her. They are running after Fred, who is all flushed and smiling with bright eyes. Wilma throws me an icy look. "Girls, come and say hello to your grandmother," I tell the girls.

They don't listen, of course. They are in the middle of their game with Fred. So I have to ask them two more times before they come. And I can almost *hear* what Wilma is thinking as she sniffs. *Josephine's children do listen...*

But that's not what she says, as she holds out her cheek for them to kiss. *She doesn't kiss or hug them back, I notice.* "You shouldn't have to tell them, Monique," she says. "They should be doing it out of themselves. By now they should have been taught at least *those* manners..."

And I wince inside. But then I think of Sarah. And I do my best to brush it off. I realize that I am a tight ball of stress, visiting Wilma. The thing is, I really want my girls to make a good impression. And it's like the girls can feel my stress, which makes them behave even worse. And for a second I wonder. *Why do I even care what she thinks about my kids? Why does she have that power over me?*

Wilma points a bony finger at Lisa. "You know who I saw yesterday?" Lisa shakes her head. "No grandmother," Wilma says. "No grandmother," Lisa repeats neatly. "I saw your friend Jessica," Wilma says.

Lisa looks at Wilma with a blank face. I know that Jessica is not her friend. She is just a bossy girl in her class who can be real nasty to Lisa and who happens to live close to Fred and Wilma.

As I watch Lisa, I realize that for some reason Wilma makes Lisa retreat in herself. It's like before Lisa says anything to her grandmother, she first checks it a couple of times in her head to make sure her grandmother will approve.

"You know what Jessica was doing?" Wilma continues. "She was carrying empty bottles and paper to dispose of them." Wilma pauses for Lisa to reply, but Lisa still has her blank face on and just watches her.

"Do you ever do that?" Wilma then asks Lisa, annoyed because she didn't get any satisfying reply. Lisa shakes her head. "No grandmother," Wilma says. "No grandmother," Lisa repeats.

"Girls should help out, you know…" Wilma continues. And I see Lisa's face drop. I jump in. "Lisa always helps me," I tell her. "And so does Sophie. They just don't do it alone, we always do it together."

Wilma starts to oppose. "Girls should learn on their own…" "Yes you are right. And we like to do it together." And with that I finish the conversation. And quietly feel proud for having ended this myself.

"Now what a lovely flowers you have," I continue changing the subject. And Wilma is easily distracted. "Yes, aren't they? You see, *Josephine* brings me flowers when she visits…" And she keeps talking, but I don't listen to the rest she is saying.

I vaguely notice that her story moves from flowers, to a friend who needs their help, to a vacation on Ibiza, and to how to bake good cakes. Following her line of thought is a challenge on its own. But I do realize something. I realize how easy it is to make her change the subject of her conversation. And if she is someone I have to deal with, that is a good thing to know ...

Instead of listening to her, I look at my girls. For a moment I wonder whether leaving them here is something I should do. For a moment I want to cancel that whole trip to Barcelona.

But Lisa is beaming again as she is running with Sophie behind her grandfather. And I realize that I can never cut Wilma out of their lives. She is their karma too. She is their grandmother. Whenever they are with Eric, they have deal with her.

Now Sophie doesn't seem to have any real problems with her. For some reason Sophie is a master in brushing things off. If something bothers her, she will scream and cry, but after that it's out of her system.

Lisa is like me. And I'm afraid Wilma is getting under her skin. But all I can do, is give her the tools to deal with it. When Lisa goes to the toilet, I take her apart for a moment. "Do you really like it here Lisa?" I ask her. "Would it be okay if you stay here when mommy has to work?"

Lisa nods. "It's always cosy here mommy. Grandpa is always playing with us ..." "And grandma?" I ask her. Lisa shrugs. "I just ignore her when she is nasty," she says. "Or I change the subject." And I smile inwardly, realizing how wise my daughter already is.

So when we have our tea with a slice of home-made cake, I ask The Ex-In-Laws: "Remember I was living in Venice?" Wilma gives a little nod. *Living in foreign countries is not something she approves of.* In fact, anything foreign is not something she approves of. But Fred nods with a smile. "Well," I continue, "I got a job offer for a project for two days ..."

"Really?" Fred says. "How wonderful!" But Wilma just looks at me. And I realize I have to win her over. So I make a quick calculation in my head. *Fact is, I know exactly the thing that will win her ...* So I say: "And you know the girls can't possibly stay with my parents ..."

In a way I feel bad, talking like that about my parents. But now Wilma is nodding fervently. "You are quite right, darling. I'm happy you realize that," she says. And I don't even have to ask her anything. Even just the thought of my unfit parents makes her jump in. "They will stay with us," she says decisively, ending the conversation. "Are you sure?" I ask her. "Would that be all right for you?" Wilma nods fervently. "Darling, at least *I* know how to raise children ..."

And with that the babysit thing is settled. The girls will stay with Fred and Wilma. Which means that *I* will be going to Barcelona. With Farshad. With the Man with the Majestic Dick. And I feel a bubble of joy rise inside of me. Needless to say all kinds of problems will follow. But for now I am still in a happy ignorant bliss ...

CHAPTER SEVEN:
ROSES AND DRAGONS

It's a grey dull day in the middle of April when I drop off the girls with their suitcases at Fred and Wilma's. Sophie jumps on her grandfather and barely notices me leaving, but Lisa keeps waving with a tight little hand until I disappear around the corner.

In a way I don't want to leave. My heart is hurting to leave them behind. To see my big girl waving at me until she doesn't see me… But I make myself strong. *Mothers are also allowed to have fun.* And who knows? Maybe I will end up with money again. So I make myself think of all the things the girls need.

Farshad is waiting for me at Heathrow airport. He has come all the way from Munich to pick me up and travel together. Now I haven't slept most of the night, I just kept thinking that maybe I was doing something really stupid. *Meeting a stranger in a foreign city, he can do anything to me…*

But I forget all that the moment I see him. I feel a surge of happiness the moment I spot him and he throws me one of his big smiles. He's traveling light I notice, like me, with just one carry-on suitcase.

In a way it's strange to travel with a stranger – because that is what Farshad still is to me, even though I spent one night fucking the living daylight out of him. And he is someone who I would never have dated in my normal life. So somehow it feels like everyone around us knows what I am doing.

Once we are in the airplane he starts making jokes about Turks in a very loud voice, increasing my discomfort. These jokes might be incredibly funny when you are Iranian, but they do sound different here. So I do my best to get him talking about different subjects.

But when he orders us drinks and snacks I feel good again. As a kid my dad never allowed me to order anything in an airplane. "Too expensive," he'd say. And – though I didn't take that many flights after that – I kind of adopted his lifestyle.

So ordering things on board of the plane feels like splurging in a lovely way. *I'm already loving this lifestyle!* And in a way I still can't believe I'm doing this – traveling with a Sugar Daddy to another country. I'm just a regular single mom. No one even knows what I am doing. *Am I really doing this?*

When we are landing, I can see the sun beaming down on the planes. Spring has already started here. I just love it. And once we are out of the plane, the airport is spacy and modern. It must have been ages since I was last in a plane and on a foreign airport. In a way I'm amazed with the amount of people traveling. *How are all of them making a living? How can they afford the traveling?*

Farshad is a real gentleman. He lets me go first everywhere and I'm not used to this at all. But when I tell him so over my shoulder, he laughs. "Better get used to it," he says. "I will always let you go first. I respect you." He is silent for a second before he continues: "And I *love* watching your bum. It's too much beautiful…" And he bursts out laughing.

At the sign 'rental cars' he asks me: "How about renting a nice little car for our adventure?" And I don't even need to answer. He has rented us a really nice black Mercedes sports car in no time, paying out of one of his envelopes filled with cash. And when he starts the engine, the car buckles up automatically almost entangling my purse in it.

The moment we whizz out of the airport, we are in the Mediterranean. It's sunny, there are palm trees…, it's just absolutely lovely. And the moment we drive into Barcelona I fall in love. Because this place is gorgeous. It's like Paris in a Mediterranean way. I love the old stately buildings, the fashionable people in the street.

Right in the city centre Farshad asks me: "Are you hungry?" and he steers the car into a parking garage. When we get out we find ourselves in a bustling fashionable street, which Farshad says is called 'Las Ramblas'.

Walking through Las Ramblas we pass lots of shops. And Farshad keeps stopping in front of them asking me: "Can I buy you a little something?" Now I'm so not used to men buying me 'little somethings'. Especially not since Farshad keeps stopping in front of really expensive jewellery shops. So I feel rather uncomfortable and tell him: "Thank you darling, but I'm fine. Aren't we going for lunch?"

For a second, Farshad looks surprised. It's obvious that he isn't used to women refusing offers of jewellery. But then he nods. "Yes honey, of course." We don't need to walk for long before Farshad finds us a lovely place, airy with a Parisian elegance, where he orders us spicy tapas and sweet Sangria.

Now I had tapas before, but I never had tapas in Spain. Which is no surprise of course, since this is the first time I am in Spain. And I have to say they are stunning. Farshad orders us blue cheese and walnut salad, spicy patatas bravas, sardines, exquisitely flavoured mushroom bruschetta, lovely manchego cheese with honey and thyme and spicy chicken strips.

And Farshad is charming company. He talks about his airplane – yes *his* airplane. It turns out he has his own little airplane stored away somewhere in Rome. He talks about his family. And about his failed marriage.

"You know," he says. "No matter what I did or how hard I tried to make my wife happy, she would always find something to nag about. All I did was work and take care of her and our children. I wish she had just seen how hard I tried." He sighs and looks into space for some time. Then he smiles, grabs my hand, kisses my fingers and says: "I guess I just married the wrong one…"

After lunch Farshad drives us to our hotel. It's just outside Barcelona's centre, and it's fabulous. The lobby is fashionable and a friendly guy checks us in and receives the cash from Farshad's envelope. But it's not until we enter the room that I gulp.

Apparently Farshad has booked us a spacious Jacuzzi suite with a beautiful ocean view. And the room has everything you might ever want: a bathrobe, slippers, an amazing range of bath amnesties and free access to the Spazio Wellness spa.

While Farshad fills the tub, I run around the room checking out all the luxuries. "You know honey," I call out to him, "I can get used to this lifestyle!" When I'm done with my cheering, I stand in front of the window and enjoy the view of the ocean. *This is just so amazing. I feel like I am in heaven.*

But Farshad doesn't let me stand like that for long. He wraps his arms around me and kisses my neck. "Honey, you like it?" he asks me. "I thought I book something special for my special lady." "Like it? I LOVE it! Thank you so much darling."

He turns me around and pulls me towards the Jacuzzi. I slowly strip down and undress him while he kisses my neck, my breasts, and my belly before he pulls me into the hot water.

For one second I realize how much my life has changed. Only two months ago I was a married woman struggling to get by. Now I'm in this mesmerizing city in a beautiful suite with a charming guy and his Majestic Dick. And nobody even knows

I'm here … But Farshad doesn't let me think for long. I gasp when he pulls me on top of him.

His cock is so huge that he can't go in all the way. I have to move up and down on top of him, feeling him slide in and out of me, each time a little deeper and deeper until he fills me thoroughly.

It turns out that there are only a limited amount of positions you can do in a Jacuzzi. So I stay on top of him and move faster and faster, thoroughly enjoying the length of his whole Majestic Dick until he eventually comes.

Afterwards we just lie soaking in the tub. It feels like ages since I have felt relaxed like this. Normally there is always something that still needs to be done. Something I didn't finish. The laundry, ironing, groceries. Or when I finally relax the famous call comes: "Mommy!!" And I'm up for another Barbie rescue or finding back missing socks or whatever else mothers are good for.

Not now. I can feel all the stress slide of my body. Farshad and I just lie there, soaking in the water, while night falls over Barcelona. Outside there is a bright moon. We're both not hungry – our lunch was so fulfilling. But finally Farshad pulls me out of the tub. "Come," he says. "Let's go to the beach."

It's dark outside, but the temperature is still lovely. *And for a moment I can only imagine how cold it must be in the UK now … But my girls will be inside, cuddled up underneath their duvets.* Farshad puts his arm around my shoulders and pulls me close while we walk.

The moment we are on the soft sand, I kick out my shoes, run towards the sea and splash my feet through the lukewarm water. Farshad lights a cigarette, puts his other hand in his pocket and watches me with a broad smile on his face. When I come back to him for a kiss, he grabs my waist and carries me to the restaurant right there on the beach.

The place itself is closed, but there are still chairs outside. He pulls me on one of them and strokes all the sand off my feet, kissing them before he kisses me again. And I am so totally there with him, so in the moment. I can hear the waves rolling. I can smell the salt. The tobacco on his hands. I feel the sand itching on my skin. And I realize I haven't felt so happy in a long time.

Back in the hotel Farshad puts some music on. It's music from our youth, Gloria Estefan, Tina Turner. Then he slowly takes my clothes off, lies me on the bed and gently enters me. It feels so warm and loving, that all I can do is close my eyes to feel it all even more. I love how he totally fills me.

I'm not as sex-starved as I was in London. Back in the UK we were fucking, now we are making love. And our lovemaking is shifting to a warm, loving rhythm. He moves slowly, caressing me. My face, my neck, my breasts. His eyes are warm, loving. Missionary becomes something intimate and special with him.

After a while I pull myself up and sit on his lap while we move gently. I love to go all the way up until the tip of his cock is almost out of me, then going down real slowly, feeling the full length of his cock as it penetrates me.

I ride him for a while. Then he flips me over, pulls my hair in a tight ponytail, his other hand on my hip and takes me doggy. He's moving fast now. Fast and real hard. I can feel his balls bouncing off my ass. This is just so sexy, that I start playing with myself. And it doesn't take long before we both come.

Afterwards I'm lying in his arm, caressing his chest hair. He kisses the top of my head. I look up to him and follow the line of his lips with my finger. There is a scar underneath his lower lip. I follow it with my finger and ask him: "Did you have an accident?" He nods, while he takes my hand and kisses my fingers. "I had a motor accident when I was a teenager. It was all damaged. You shouldn't have seen me then. Lucky for me, it all got cured."

He kisses my fingers again, then puts my hands at some distance to look at them. His hands are so sensitive, so elegant in a way. I just love men with beautiful hands. But Farshad is already having a naughty twinkle in his eye.

"Are you sure you are not married?" he asks, touching my ring. I laugh. "Yes, I am sure. This is my grandmother's engagement ring. I've been wearing it since my divorce. To me it means I am choosing my own little family now. Above all else." Farshad kisses my hair. *And I smile, remembering my grandmother.*

But then Farshad totally freaks me out, when he says with a warm and loving voice: "Jigaram. I want to eat your liver." *Bloody hell!* I pull away, seeing Hannibal Lecter in my mind's eye and I'm all ready to plan my escape.

But Farshad laughs. "Don't worry honey. That is a Persian way of saying I love you." And he kisses me. Now that kind of relaxes me, but for one split second I could see how this could go all wrong. *And I don't even want to think about what I could have done...*

Farshad pulls my chin up and kisses me lightly on my lips. "Thank you for coming to Barcelona with me Azizam," he says. "You're special. It feels like I have known you for ages. I can be so lonely. But with you I enjoy life."

I softly bite his lip. "Why are you lonely?" Farshad trails the line of my hip with his finger. "I love my job. But I don't like all the traveling. Being alone in hotel rooms, I can feel so lonely... Sometimes I wish my life was different. I wish I could just have a normal family life..."

He's yawning now. "Honey," he says, "Let's get some sleep." And he hugs me until he sleeps. I lie awake in his arms for some time. It just feels so good to be hugged again. It feels like ages since I was lying in a man's arms. It just feels so safe. Like nothing in this world can harm me. But I don't sleep much that night. Farshad is either hugging me, or holding me. And whenever I try to roll away, his long arms find me and pull me back into an embrace.

The next morning I wake up on his chest and he is holding me tight. The moment he feels me stirring, he murmurs something, kisses my shoulder and hugs me even tighter. I smile and just lie for some time. *It's so nice to be cuddling. I feel warm and safe and loved.* It's a feeling I haven't had for such a long time. It's this fuzzy feeling and I want to enjoy it a bit longer.

When Farshad finally gets up, we have a shower and go down for our buffet breakfast. Now the moment I enter the buffet area, I realize that I just *love* buffet breakfasts. It's just great, having all these options without having to prepare anything myself. Normally I don't even have breakfast until after the school run.

Anything I could desire is here: fresh bread, meats, vegetables, a lot of Spanish specialities and there is even cava – Spanish sparkling wine, as Farshad explains to me, produced in the same way as champagne but with different grapes.

And whereas normally I'm running around at breakfast, here I don't even have to get up. Farshad tells me to sit down and gets me everything. Hot lemon tea. Cava. Scrambled eggs …

There is another couple at the buffet who also must be in some kind of arrangement. But they are quite different. He is way older, she wears a lot of make-up and a bored look on her face and they seem nothing but polite strangers to each other. I can't even imagine what they will be like in bed together … It's different with Farshad. We are really enjoying our time together.

After breakfast we get back into the car and while Farshad drives through Barcelona, I decide that I am *definitely* in love with this city. It's colourful, playful and unique. It bubbles with life. The Old City is full of winding lanes that emerge into secluded squares with palm trees. The waterfront bristles with life. It has the chic neighbourhood Eixample, the narrow Barri

Gòtic alleys, and our Las Ramblas – the colourful pedestrian boulevard.

Here people seem to really enjoy themselves. The cafés are filled. Families are strolling around. And suddenly, with a pang, I miss my girls. For one split second I feel sad about being divorced.

Not about being divorced from Eric, I still cheer about that every day. But just the thought of this new stigma saddens me. 'Divorced Woman.' It's not what I had dreamed of being. My dream had been this. All I had wanted was to be like one of these families that I see strolling around.

Somehow it's like Farshad has picked up on my feelings. He takes my hand and starts talking to me in Farsi. "Khoshgelam, azizam, nafasam. I will take you to a treasure." And he kisses my fingers. "What are khoshgelam and nafasam?" I ask him. Farshad smiles. "Khoshgelam means 'my beautiful one' and nafasam means 'my breath.'"

He parks the car, takes my hand, leads me through the streets and it doesn't take long till I see where he is taking me. It's the Sagrada Família. Now I have only seen it on pictures, the real thing is simply huge and impressive.

"This is Gaudí's most famous work," Farshad tells me. "His masterpiece. And it's still in progress." Well, I can see that. There is still construction going on. "But he died a long time ago, how do people know how to proceed?" I ask him. Farshad smiles and says: "They base it on models he left."

I marvel at the big church. The façade contains biblical elements and scenes from the nativity, the spires represent the apostles, the Virgin Mary, the four evangelist and Jesus Christ. *My grandmother would have loved this.*

The front of the façade depicts Jesus's last weeks and watching it, Farshad seems to be lost in thoughts for some time. "You know how Gaudí died?" he then asks me. I shake my head. "It's a too much sad story, really," he tells me.

"He got struck by a tram. And because he was dressed in rags, people mistook him for a beggar. No taxis would pick him up." "Why was he dressed in rags?" I ask him. Farshad shrugs. "He was a real artist, more busy with his work then with his looks. And he never married, you see…" And he sighs while we head back for the car.

Next Farshad takes me to another Gaudí building, to Casa Milà. And the moment we get out of the car he is talking. "Casa Milà is also known as La Pedrera, the stone quarry, because of its rough outer appearance. See, it looks like an open quarry."

But the first thing *I* see when we enter is the price. It's 22 euro to go in. So 44 euro for both of us. To Farshad that seems to be nothing. He pays – without wincing – out of his envelope. Inside it's not too busy and a lift whisks us up to the top terrace level.

Now the roof is amazing. The view over the city is spectacular and it's full of curves, shapes and chimneys moulded into weird statues. "What do you think?" Farshad asks me, standing in front of a weirdly shaped chimney. "You think Star Wars got the idea for Darth Vader here?" And we both laugh. The roof is just so futuristic, that it seems unbelievable that Gaudí created this a century ago.

From the roof we slowly make our way down the stairs. Now there are a lot of stairs to go back down. First there is an exhibition on how Gaudí created this building. It shows how he preferred to build 3D models of his buildings above drawing plans, so he could create a more accurate portrayal of what he was seeing in his mind. And Farshad is fascinated.

Next he pulls me to a section which shows how Gaudí used the natural world to develop architectural techniques. He analysed plants and animals to see how they naturally supported shapes and weight. For instance, the orbit of the stars was used to design columns. And Farshad keeps murmuring: "This man was a genius. A genius."

Along our way down, we visit an apartment that has been styled as it would have been years ago. It's fascinating to see. And the tour ends at the beautiful ground floor courtyard where Farshad takes my arm and leads me into El Café de La Pedrera, located on the ground floor of the building. We get a bench table, he sits down next to me and orders two lemon tea and an apple pie to share.

Farshad pulls me into his arm and kisses my hair. "How did you like it, honey?" he asks me. "It was beautiful," I tell him. He smiles. "Yes. Too much beautiful. I'm happy you like it. It's a place very close to my heart. As an engineer I just love Gaudí."

I look around the café. It's lovely. Very elegant, with big windows which give beautiful views of the avenue. And I notice that the avenue is covered with little stalls selling books and roses. Many women are strolling around with roses, and many men with books. Farshad follows my gaze. "Is it any special day?" he asks our waiter when he brings our lemon tea. "Oh yes," the waiter beams. "It's Saint Jordi's day!"

I frown. *Grandmother had tried to raise me a Catholic and I know many saints, but I don't know any Saint Jordi…* The waiter sees my frown and says: "That's the Catalan name of Saint George, the patron saint of Catalonia." He smiles. "St. Jordi's is our most romantic day of the year. It's our version of Valentine's day."

I ask him: "Saint George slew a dragon to save a princess, right?" He nods and adds: "Then a rose bush grew on the exact spot where the dragon's blood had spilled and he plucked a red rose for the princess."

Farshad looks happy with all this romance in the air and the moment we get out of the café, he sprints towards a little stall with an old toothless woman and buys me a red rose. And I have to confess that it warms me inside. I kiss him and promise him one of the books I have written the next time we meet.

But when he looks at his watch, we have to hurry. We have a flight to catch. We pack our bags, drive to the airport and drop off the car. In the lounge we have one last drink together. From here, Farshad will take a flight to Istanbul and I will go back to the UK.

Now I promised you to be honest, so I will be. Let me confess this. One thing I do on purpose. I excuse myself to go to the ladies, but I leave my bag with my wallet with him. *And I can only hope that he will be as generous as he was before…* If not, it won't be a drama either. I still had such a lovely time with him. But I also know how happy I will be if he does…

I don't check my bag right away of course. Farshad brings me all the way to customs, apologizing for not flying with me and kissing me goodbye before going to his section of the airport. And as he walks away he keeps turning and waving.

The moment I am through customs I go to the ladies, lock myself up and check my wallet. And I cheer inwardly. There is a whole bundle of pounds in there again. And when I count them I feel like cheering even more. It's another thousand pounds. *Back home I will spoil the girls with something fun…*

When I'm waiting for boarding I get his message. "Thank you for joining me Azizam. I left you a little something." I smile. *I know.* And I text back: "Thank YOU darling. For everything. Thank you so much."

Both girls jump on me when I'm back, while Wilma fills me in with how they spent every second of their day and how she has taught the girls better manners. But I don't really listen. I just focus on my girls. It's just so lovely to hug them again. And in the back of my mind I am planning to do something special with them. In a way I still can't believe it. I have received another thousand pounds…

That evening, after I have read the girls their bedtime story, tucked them in and stored my pounds safely in my grandmother's book, I deactivate my account on Seeking Arrangement. Because I have found The One. Or so I think…

CHAPTER EIGHT:
THE CITY OF LOVE

A week after Barcelona Farshad keeps sending me messages, telling me how much he misses me. How I am his little flower. How he wants to introduce me to his mother. Then he suddenly becomes silent again. Very silent. And I have no idea when I will see him again ...

May passes and soon it's June. Summer is approaching and life goes on as usual. I'm job hunting like crazy, but to no avail. I'm also working hard on Amanda's book and I do some copy-writing on the side to survive. The girls are a happy bunch most of the time. They enjoy going to their new school, Sophie goes to her swimming lesson every Wednesday evening and every other weekend they spend with their dad.

Now on a personal level not much exciting is going on. I chat with The Viking every day, but my contact with Ben is starting to fade. I'm getting tired of all the erotic chatting and I am reacting more slowly each time. I don't have time for erotic fantasies, I need to make money.

Sophie's swimming lessons, on the other hand, are something I'm starting to look forward to. I am starting to dress nicely when I go to them, putting on some extra make-up and having a final rear mirror glance at myself in the car before I get out. The reason is no surprise of course. The reason is a man.

See, there is a father there, tall, dark and handsome. He has a lisp that melts my heart. And sometimes he gives me this deep look that makes me hot inside. But I do my best to ignore him, because I'm now Sugar Dating. I have no place for normal men in my life. I do notice though that just the thought of meeting him brightens up my Wednesday evenings.

Since I have no intention of dating him, I do my best to keep my distance. But with Sophie's last swimming lesson we know we will never see each other again. So he sits down next to me and starts chatting and I just melt at that lovely lisp of his. He tells me his name is Paul, that he is married and has two boys. Now it might be strange, but that first thing is a relief to me. It means this is not a normal guy courting me. He has a private life he needs to keep private. So when he asks me for my phone number I give it to him.

That evening we're chatting nicely on WhatsApp and he asks me whether he can take me out for dinner. I hesitate for one second, but then I think: *Well, why not?* I have all these weekends without the girls, I'm not hearing anything from Farshad, so why not? Amanda is all excited when I let her know. "Good. Have fun. Take some lovers as well. If you don't hear from Farshad, why are you waiting for him?" And she is right, *why am I?*

So that next weekend Paul picks me up. He has reserved at a restaurant close by. It's a nice, fashionable place and I almost feel like I'm Sugar Dating again. I have even done my whole Sugar preparation for Paul. I had a mask the day before and a nice hot bath, polished my nails and I am wearing a short skirt with a tight top.

As Paul's eyes go over my body, I can see the fire in his eyes. *He wants me. I just* know *he wants me.* And with him being married and obviously prepared to live a double life, it feels safe to be wanted by him. He's not a guy that might want to intrude into my private life. He will not interfere in the nice balance the girls and I finally have. And then suddenly a thought comes up. *Maybe he can be a Sugar Daddy? He fits the profile...*

So when he asks me what I am doing, I'm totally honest. "I'm a Sugar Babe," I tell him. "You're a *what??*" He nearly chokes, starts coughing and his eyes almost burst out of their sockets.

I kindly wait until he has finished coughing before I continue: "Well, men take me out for money." Paul turns as red as a tomato, starts pulling at his collar and murmurs: "So sorry, I have to excuse myself" as he rushes off to the restroom.

So there I am. All alone in the restaurant. And I kind of wonder what direction this dinner is going now... *Will he return? Has he fled?* So I take out my phone and text Amanda. "At the restaurant. Guy just ran off..." Amanda asks me: "What did you do? 😄" I chuckle as I type: "I told him I'm a Sugar Babe... 🐶 " "You did WHAT?" "Well, I thought he could be a good one too..." "LOL. So what happened?" "He ran off to the restroom. No idea whether he is coming back. Oh, wait his phone is still here. He'll be back." "LOL girl you are crazy!" "Oh here he is again. I'll keep you posted."

Paul is still red and flustered when he returns to the table. He mutters: "Sorry darling, I didn't expect that," and sits down again. *Well, apparently he has survived the news.* He is the first 'normal' person whom I have told about my new status. And though he is obviously shocked, he soon gets his shit together. As the evening proceeds he relaxes. We order food and a nice wine. We talk and laugh.

In a way it's almost like a Sugar Date. Paul talks about his empty marriage. How he is the one who has to do everything in his house. He is the one who looks after the kids, the house and all. His wife is not doing anything, he says.

It's a nice evening. We are having fun. I have a really nice meal, Paul is great company, he pays afterwards and he brings me all the way home. Just before I get out he leans over and kisses me. And he is passionate, I notice.

So when I'm in bed that night and I go over the evening in my mind I make one note. Apparently men are different from women. Apparently they can accept and don't necessarily judge Sugar Dating. Luck is on my side again. Because the next day Farshad finally contacts me and he asks me whether I want to join him in Paris. I check the date and I see that I can. The girls will be with their father.

But I'm a little pissed with him, since I didn't hear from him for quite some time. So I don't reply immediately. Only after he sends me a couple of messages apologizing I tell him that sure, I'd love to join him in Paris.

Fact is, by now I'm looking forward to two things. Foremost I'm looking forward to seeing Farshad again. I love spending time with him. But the truth is that I'm also looking forward to the money. It will make me survive another month. I need it...

So one week later Farshad is waiting for me in the Searcys St Pancras Champagne Bar at London's beautiful Victorian St. Pancras station. I spot him immediately. He is standing with his back towards me, taking in the panoramic view over the entire station terminal, with the glorious wrought iron and glass ceiling overhead. *If he wasn't bald, he might even be considered handsome...*

The moment he sees me, he starts to beam. "Azizam, how have you been?" he calls out as he grabs my waist and kisses me. He holds me at arm's length saying: "You are still as beautiful as ever." I smile a bit uncomfortably and I give him a copy of my book, as I had promised him in Barcelona on Saint Jordi's. He beams.

But after not seeing him for all this time, I need to get used to him again. To his voice, his baldness. *Is this the guy I was getting a crush on?* It seems different for Farshad. I guess that's a difference between men and women. Men can just take off where they left it, women need to warm again.

Kissing me once more, he hands me the menu asking: "Shall we have a nice glass of champagne together before we leave?" So we order a glass of Searcys Selected Cuvée Rosé and as we toast Farshad says: "Azizam, I am so happy to share another little adventure together. This time I selected the train for us."

And he shows me two train tickets. "See, it's only two and a half hours," he continues. "I figured by plane it will take around the same, with customs and all ... Now by train we arrive right in the centre." He looks at me for a second before he continues: "You will return by plane though, since I will not be able to join you then. So sorry ..." I kiss him lightly on his lips, murmuring: "That's fine darling, thank you ..."

After our champagne is finished, we stroll towards the trains. And not much later we are rolling in the Eurostar towards Paris. The train is quite crowded, so we sit next to each other. Something Farshad seems happy about, since it gives him the opportunity to caress and squeeze my long legs. A rather snobbish French couple sit opposite of us and do their best to ignore us. And in a way I wonder how we look together. *Could we be a normal couple?*

Farshad is not wondering much. He is chatting along all excitedly, telling me how he just did a course about personality types. "See, there is the Aphrodite type like my daughter," he says. "They like to be in the spotlight and they like material things ..."

Farshad pauses for a second and looks at me from over his glasses. "Sometimes you could be a little more Aphrodite, you know ..." He chuckles. "But don't worry. I'll make you. Just wait and see ..."

So Farshad talks about personalities for the next two and a half hours. Until we arrive at Gare du Nord, right in the heart of Paris. And the moment we get out of the train, I can feel Paris wrap herself around me. Even the scent at the station is Parisian. It's the sweet smell of baked croissants with a hint of freshly brewed coffee mixed in. And for a second it feels bizarre, how easily I can move between countries and cultures with this new lifestyle. But for most Sugar Daddies this is their way of life…

We take a cab to our hotel, which turns out to be in the pinnacle of Paris's luminescent splendour. The plush hotel is all in creams and pink pastels and soaked in the scent of lavender. It has glass chandeliers and over-the-top classical 19th-century grandeur.

We have a room, not a suite, but still it is all kinds of fancy. It has classical furniture, damask curtains, embroidered bedheads with in the bathroom a gilded swan tap and peach-coloured towels and dressing gowns. It also has a TV which magically appears in the mirror, concealed plugs and a touchpad to control air conditioning and heating. I sigh. *Now this is life!*

I could have spent the rest of the afternoon in that room, but Farshad has his mind on something else. "Honey," he says once he is finished unpacking, "Let me take you somewhere." And he leads me out of the hotel and calls for a cab.

While we have elegant Harrods in London, Paris shows its sophistication with Les Galleries Lafayette. And that's where Farshad takes me. I want to soak in the beauty of the window displays, but Farshad takes my elbow and leads me in. And inside I'm in awe. The place is all neo-byzantine style with stain glass windows and an amazing dome roof.

"Let's get you something for your girls," Farshad says as he leads me to a Pierre Hermé counter selling macaroons. And I smile. *I love the fact that he thinks of them.* At the counter I close my eyes for a second and breathe in the exclusive scent of sweetness, fruits and spices. The line isn't too long and soon we are selecting macaroons for my two little monkeys.

We select the 'Infiniment Rose' with rose and rose petal, the 'Plaisir Sucre' with milk chocolate, praline, apricot and crunchy pistachio, and the 'Mogador' with milk chocolate and passion fruit.

They are simply beautiful and packed in a charming little box. Now I'm not even supposed to *be* in Paris, so I know I'll have to give these with a lie. Still I'm already looking forward to giving it to them and seeing the joy on their faces.

Farshad gives me a sideway look and then asks me: "Have *you* ever had macaroons?" I shake my head. "No, never." "Ah, well then my little flower needs some too," he says and orders a bunch for us.

Before I bite into them, I hold them carefully in my hand. They are tiny and soft with a delicate shell and – once I bite – the perfect amount of crisp inside. I marvel at their taste. They are not too sweet and the flavours are so rich and so authentic. I just love the interesting flavour combinations.

First I try the 'Infiniment Rose' which is a nicely perfumed pink macaron that really tastes like rose. Next the 'Arabesque' with apricot and crispy pistachio nuts. Then the 'Mogador' which has a surprising taste and has pieces of passion fruit in it. Finally we have a 'mint' which has a real mint herb flavour.

When we have only a few macaroons left, Farshad closes the box and says: "And now it's time for your Aphrodite side." And he laughs for some time. "This time," he tells me, "I'm getting you a little something."

So he takes my arm, marches me over towards the jewellery counters which are soaked in strong perfume from the perfume counters close by, saying: "Go ahead. Choose a little something."

Now when I look at the prices I gulp. There are no 'little somethings' here. Not that most people walking around seem to care. A whole group of Japanese line up in front of Louis Vuitton.

A well perfumed lady with a mask of make-up walks around with a bored look on her face. And I just feel so totally out of place …

Suddenly I become insecure. I feel like I'm underdressed and I just feel so very self-conscious with Farshad by my side. So I just walk around aimlessly, too polite to make a move towards buying anything. Though I do notice that wherever we go, the salesclerks have one look at Farshad and then practically jump on us.

It takes me a while before I realize why. It's not until at one counter he points at an elegant watch and I see it's the same he is wearing. Now I always knew it was nice, but I never had a good look at it.

Apparently it's Swiss. And it's over 3000 euro's. *Gulp!* Farshad smiles. "You want one?" he asks me. "We can have matching watches?" I'm getting all flustered and hot. *How can I accept a watch of over 3000 euro's?* I thank him kindly and speed away to the next counter.

But from that moment I realize what the salesclerks are looking at. They jump on us the moment they see his watch. And I also realize something else. I *have* to choose something. It's obvious that Farshad is going to stay here until I have chosen my 'little something.'

So when he asks me whether I like a beautiful Dior necklace which is 'only' a couple of hundred euros, I tell him that I do. But apparently that's not enough, Farshad also chooses a matching watch with it.

The Asian salesgirl takes them out of the counter and hand them over to me to try. When Farshad has put them on, he kisses my cheek. "They really suit you, honey. You like them?" And when I say I do, he nods to the girl and she starts packing them.

Farshad gets a phone call, so he hands me his calfskin Mont Blanc wallet and gestures me to pay. And I can feel myself blushing, but the girl behind the counter is very friendly. It's like she can feel my uneasiness. *And probably she can.* I guess it's not hard to notice that this is obviously *not* something I normally do, but she does her best to make me feel at ease.

"Are you paying cash?" the girl asks. I feel all hot again as I open his wallet and peek inside. *There is not an awful lot of bills in his wallet...* But Farshad jumps in and hands me a thick envelope with hundred euro bills. So I smile at the girl saying: "Yes, apparently..." And she smiles away my uneasiness.

Next I count out and hand her a thick bunch of hundred euro bills. Farshad's 'little something' is costing him over a thousand euros... And I am just *so* not used to this. I feel flushed, embarrassed...

But I also feel happy. Really happy. It feels so good to get something special like this. I have never gotten expensive jewellery from a man before. And since Farshad is still calling when we are outside, I text Amanda. And she is cheering. "See," she writes. "This is the life I was talking about..."

Outside dusk is falling. And Farshad – who is still on the phone – gets us a cab to the Notre Dame. Outside a little bistro, up a quiet street off the river bank with views towards the Cathedral, he chooses a covered table.

We both have a pot of lemon tea for over six euro. Farshad is still busy with his phone calls in Farsi, so I overlook the Notre Dame. It seems to magically spring forth from the Seine River and soar towards heaven with its towers, spire and flying buttresses.

When business is finally finished, Farshad says: "Honey, I have booked a little something for us." *Another little something... This man is full of little somethings...* So I wait while he pays the bill. He takes me to the Seine River. And when he leads me towards a group of boats, I know what our 'little something' will be. He has booked us a dinner cruise.

Now there must be no better way to discover the City of Lights than from the Seine. I marvel at the city's beauty after the sun sets, when all the city's landmarks are illuminated. We cruise past the impressive Notre Dame Cathedral, admiring its imposing Gothic architecture. We continue to Ile St Louis, an ancient and tranquil spot in the middle of the Seine. Then there is the Hôtel de Ville, the Louvre Museum, the Musée d'Orsay, Place de la Concorde, and the dazzling Eiffel…

But we don't just enjoy the view. As Paris' night time panorama drifts by, we enjoy a three course meal, prepared by a top Parisian chef. As a starter we have a glass of champagne with creamy soft butternut velouté soup with mushrooms and roasted squash. Then as a main course there is a juicy Viennese chicken supreme with herbs, spelt and lemon jus. And as wine Farshad chooses a nice round French Bordeaux.

The desert is a pear poached in spiced red wine and a nut and almond croustillant, but before we start with it, Farshad kisses me and asks: "Shall we go up for a little fresh air?" I nod, so he takes me up to the roof.

The roof is deserted. There is only the two of us, underneath the stars, with an almost full moon. "Wait a minute," Farshad says and he sprints back down, reappearing a few seconds later with our deserts. And while we enjoy our desert, with a warm Parisian summer breeze in our hair, the nightlights so close by, the stars blinking above us, I just feel so damn happy.

Back in our plush room he assertively pulls me towards him as his hands slip around my waist. I can feel that he is already hard. And huge. So I gently undo his buttons. I feel the lust heat up my body. I feel the adrenaline surge through. He strips off my dress, while I'm fondling his balls and his Majestic Dick.

Farshad doesn't even take the time to appreciate my fancy black underwear – my bra, pretty knickers, suspender belt and stockings. They all go out in a second. And as he kicks off his pants and lets his shirt drop to the floor he pushes me with my back against the wall. I wrap one leg around his waist as he enters me.

God, he is just so big... Soon I wrap both legs around him, while he pushes me hard against the wall, his hands holding my hips as he thrusts his cock deep and hard into me. I just *love* his long thrusts in and out. I *love* feeling the whole length of his cock inside of me.

Then he turns me around, gently stroking my ass while I push my hands against the wall. I slowly bend and thrust my ass towards him. *I want him. I want him so badly. Inside of me. All of him.* And soon he pushes himself into me and takes me hard, holding my hips as he thrusts his dick long and deeply inside of me. I help myself and it doesn't take long before I come.

But Farshad didn't come yet. He throws me on the bed, crosses my arms above my head and holds them with one hand while he rides on top of me. I can't touch him, I can't do anything. I'm all in his control. And it feels marvellous.

After he comes he lets go of my hands and I caress him. He is soaking wet from the sweat, but the sweat is cooling down fast so I cover us with the duvet and soon we drift off to sleep. I wake once, when he is getting too heavy on top of me. I push him off, roll up in his arm and drift back into a lovely deep sleep.

The next day, the sheer luxury at breakfast takes my breath away. It is sumptuous and luxuriant in every way. And it is going to costs more than my groceries for a whole week. But I'm here to enjoy, so I decide to avoid looking at the prices. The food is out of this world – delicious, beautifully presented and in abundance.

We have an omelette, garnished with black truffles and caviar, with a glass of champagne to wash it down. Farshad is beaming as he makes me sit down and gets me everything. And the moment we have finished he says: "Today I have a special surprise for you, Azizam. Today I am taking you to the Palace of Versailles."

Now the moment I lay my eyes on the Palace that early afternoon, I understand that it's all about extravagance. It's of a mind-boggling opulence. Gold accentuates everything – from the gates, to the statues and to the furnishings inside.

And inside the Chateau is huge. Rooms bleed into rooms, from ceilings hang opulent chandeliers and every inch of wall and ceiling is covered with gorgeous frescos, massive paintings and tapestries.

We wander around for what seems like ages. And when we have finished with the Palace, Farshad takes my arm and leads me out into the gardens. It's a real summer day – sunny and hot. And sun is flooding the garden as we walk all the way down to Apollo's Fountain.

"Are you hungry?" Farshad asks me. Well, our luxury breakfast feels like ages ago, so I nod. He leads me to a restaurant right in the garden where we have lunch outside. We both have a delicious pizza and a glass of red wine.

"You know, I just realized something," Farshad says, while he takes a bite of his crusty pizza. "This palace is actually a valuable life lesson." He takes another bite before he continues. "Just because you're wealthy and powerful, that doesn't mean you live happily ever after." He takes one more bite. "You know, King Louis XVI and Marie Antoinette had ultimate power. They had every luxury they could think of. But what happened?"

He makes a chopping movement with his hand on his neck saying: "They were killed at the guillotine during the French Revolution." For some time he looks into the distance, before he continues: "I prefer to have less wealth, more happiness." He chuckles. "And keep my head."

After lunch we go back to Paris, to our beautiful plush hotel. But we have little time left. I have a flight to catch, while Farshad will stay another night before he leaves for the South of France the next day.

This time he doesn't hide money in my wallet. The moment we are in our room, Farshad opens the safe, takes out an envelope and gives me the money directly. He hands me a thousand euros with a kind smile. "I'm sorry you have seen me so little," he says. "I hope this little something will help you."

Now of course I kiss to thank him. And with the kiss, my lust for him returns. We don't have much time for love, so I unbutton his fly, take off my knickers and climb on top of him. We are fully dressed for the rest, but who cares. I'm too busy to think about clothes. I ride on top of him until he comes and then I help myself to an orgasm. It's a short fuck, but damn delicious.

After that he joins me all the way to the airport. At customs, when I look behind me to wave, I realize that Farshad has somehow managed to sneak in behind me. Now it may not be a great sign for security that people can just sneak in like that, but who cares. I'm happy he is with me.

He is right with me putting all his valuables on the band and he walks me all the way to the gate. He buys us a drink and sits down next to me waiting. And when it's boarding time, just before I get on, I have one last look at him. He is smiling and blowing me a kiss. And just like last time, I feel a pang of love for him. And a slight sensation of tearfulness. *I know one thing. I'm going to miss him…*

Little do I know that it will be months till I next see him. And little do I know what other adventures await me…

CHAPTER NINE: THE PROPOSAL

Time flies. Two months have passed since I last saw Farshad and I haven't heard a word from him. So now it's the second half of the endless summer holiday. The girls are staying with their father and the house is steeped in silence.

I miss our routine. Making lunch boxes in the morning, plaiting the girls' hair. I don't miss the school run, but the house is just so damn empty. I miss the noise of children, playing and squabbling. The kitchen table, normally crowded with kids, is now deserted. Only Fuzzy is there to keep me company. And The Viking. My loyal Viking. He keeps texting me every day.

But then one day I get an interesting email from Mr. Tanning – or Robert as I should call him. He tells me he just got a new position in Berlin and is moving. But that is not the most interesting part. The interesting part is his proposal. He asks me whether I would like to join him for two days – all expenses paid.

Well, why not? In a way this is interesting. Robert is not from SA, and I have never before gotten offers like this from 'normal' men. Apparently something has changed. Or maybe my vibe has changed. Maybe I am now more open to receiving.

So the next day he is waiting for me at Heathrow airport. And he is looking the same as always, wearing a tweed jacket, with only a little grey in his black curls and his blue eyes still mesmerizing.

"How have you been?" he asks, beaming. "You are looking splendid." "I'm fine, thank you," I answer and smile back at him.

And we board an EasyJet flight to Berlin's Schönefeld airport together. It's a short flight and Robert talks a lot, so time flies. He chatters away about his new job, his interesting new research and how much the press loves him.

But Robert seems to have changed. Success seems to have changed him. And I'm not sure I'm thrilled about the change. He seems to be so full of himself. It now all seems to be 'just me, myself and I.'

We take a train from the airport into Berlin and a tram to his new apartment. There is a market right in front of his apartment, so Robert buys some bread, cheese and sausages for lunch. The apartment is in a stately East Berlin Art Deco building. It's beautiful and airy. And everywhere are traces of his family who will be joining him soon.

The moment we get in, Robert is busy preparing lunch. But before we start, he pushes me hard against the counter, pulls down my underwear, zips open his fly and tries to take me, right there. Now I'm the last person to reject being taken at unusual places. But I *am* all for condoms. Especially since Robert has an open marriage. So I murmur: "Only with a condom."

That turns out to be a big turn down. He zips up again and we have lunch at the little table, while he watches an interview he has given for German television on his mobile phone. Forgetting all about me sitting opposite of him.

During lunch I manage to cut myself with my knife and start bleeding badly, so I go to the bathroom to get a Band-Aid and return back to the table, without him noticing one thing. He is too absorbed with his own interview.

After lunch, and after watching the interview, he gives me a light kiss on my lips and says: "I have a press conference, darling. Here is the key. Enjoy Berlin." And with that he leaves.

Now this is NOT the way I had envisioned joining him in Berlin. Here I am, all alone in his huge apartment. I walk around for some time, looking at the books in his bookshelves and the little things that remind me of his wife.

Fact is that I don't really feel like exploring the city by myself. I prefer to do things together with someone. Doing things alone makes me feel insecure, I don't know why. But after some time I gather all my courage and go out. Googling Friedrichshain, the neighbourhood I'm in, I discover that it used to be East Berlin. And that I'm just steps away from the Berlin Wall.

This neighbourhood is where the artsy and free-spirited people choose to live, work and play. And it has an atmosphere of its own. Buildings are painted with street art and graffiti, while squatters hang out on the streets with their dogs, listening to music from ghetto blasters.

Everywhere around me people seem to be enjoying life. They are hanging out in bars, cafes, parks, chatting, laughing or smoking joints. People dance, smoke, drink, paint, play music and ride bikes. There seems to be no judging here. Everyone does what he wants to do. And I love that atmosphere.

But when I have wandered around for a couple of hours, I get a message from Robert. "On my way home. Are you ready for dinner?" So I head back to the apartment.

Robert is already home. He is sitting on the sofa with his reading glasses on, flipping through a magazine. I don't even have to ask him anything. "It was a marvellous interview," he says the moment he sees me. "People just *love* my new research." And he continues to talk about himself and his research while we go down, go to the Thai next door and have a nice Thai dinner on a picnic bench outside of the restaurant.

I'm not really listening. And I don't have to. He keeps talking anyway and he doesn't ask me any questions, so there's no need to answer. I just look at the people around me.

Of course – in the back of my mind – I do realize something. I realize that Robert has no interest in me whatsoever. Maybe he is interested in the sex – though he doesn't seem to be that sexual either – but he has no interest in me as a person.

Last time he saw me, I was still married. So I must have been going through a lot, right? Divorce, being a single mom … But he really doesn't care how I am doing. Robert has just one interest. He is only interested in himself.

After dinner we go back to the apartment and I know what's coming. Now I'm not really into having sex with him, but he has gotten me here, paid my ticket and all, so in a way I feel obliged.

So I do kiss him and let him climb on top of me. But I still refuse to have sex without a condom. "Can we do anal then?" he asks and I gulp in surprise. "Anal?" "Yes, then you can't get pregnant …"

I laugh for a minute, thinking he has just made a joke. But he is dead serious. "Darling, what about Aids?" I ask him. But Robert gives a dismissive flick of his hands. "You're worried about *that*? My god that is so nineties …" Well, nineties or not, I'm not going to have anal sex and the guy has to use a condom. But since he doesn't want to, we end up helping ourselves again.

He falls asleep quite fast after that, snoring a little. I lie awake for some time, watching the Berlin city lights coming through the white curtains. *What has happened with the professor I had a crush on. Was I just liking an image I had of him in my head? Or has he really changed so much?*

Well, one thing I decide. From now on I'm all into the real Sugar Dating. If these are dates with 'normal' generous men, then I prefer the ones on SA.

The next morning Robert is up early. He kisses me on my lips and prepares to leave for another press something. I won't see him anymore, since my flight is late afternoon and he won't be back before that. Just before he leaves he calls out: "Enjoy Berlin! Just leave the key inside." And he closes the door.

Only after he is gone I get out of the bed. I take a nice long hot shower, using his wife's shampoo. And I put on a nice summer dress. Then I make myself some strong coffee, have breakfast with the hump of bread and small piece of cheese that Robert has left behind and ponder on my options for this brand new day.

I'm in Berlin, and I love it here. I have a whole new day to explore. But I'm done with enjoying Berlin by myself. I need some company. And I do know that signing up with SA won't help, you don't get dates on SA that last minute.

But I did read about sites where you can meet people that are in your neighbourhood. So I check on my phone for apps and register with one of them. It's called 'Skout' and claims: 'with millions of users all over the world, Skout gives you the ability to connect with people no matter where you are.' Now that sounds promising…

The moment I log in, I find lots of people in my Berlin neighbourhood. Or, to be more accurate, they mostly find me. But most of them turn out to be men looking for sex. *No surprise there of course.* One guy sends me a message that he is so horny, whether I can help him and sends me a picture of his dick. Others are similar.

But the moment I'm ready to delete the whole site, a Pakistani contacts me. His name is Jamal, he is twenty-five years old and he asks me whether he can show me the city. Now he seems nice and polite enough and his picture shows a rather handsome Pakistani, so I make an appointment with him.

Next I pack my stuff, take my suitcase and roll it out of the apartment, closing the door with the key inside. I know one thing, I won't be coming here anymore. Next I take the tram to Alexanderplatz where Jamal is waiting for me.

In real life, Jamal is even more handsome than on his pictures. He is tall, with broad shoulders, is wearing jeans and a polo and has a handsome face with full lips, beautifully arched eyebrows, large almond-shaped eyes, wavy black hair and a mahogany skin. He smiles the moment he sees me. "Nice to meet you Monique. I'm happy I can be your guide for the day."

Jamal is polite. Whereas Robert let me carry my own bag, Jamal takes my suitcase and rolls it to the lockers, puts it in and gives me the key saying: "I'm looking forward to enjoying Berlin together." Smiling a ravishing smile that makes me melt inside.

Jamal checks his phone. "We're in Mitte," he says and he shows me a map. "This is the historical centre." And he reads from the phone: "There are numerous important sites to see here. Like the Museum Island, the Holocaust Museum and Checkpoint Charley." He looks up at me and asks with a shy smile: "Where would you like to start?"

"Let's start with the last," I say. Jamal nods. "We will take a train then. That's quite a walk." And he guides me into Berlin's subway-system. "Have you ever been at Checkpoint Charley?" I ask Jamal, while we wait for the train. He shakes his head. "No never. But I am quite happy to explore with you."

The train is rather busy, so we are pushed against each other. But I don't mind standing close to his handsomeness. "How long have you been living in Berlin?" I ask him. "One year," he answers and then he smiles. "But this is the first time I am doing anything touristy."

He looks at me and asks: "Why are you in Berlin?" I shrug. "I came to see a friend." And he must hear something in the tone of my voice, because he suddenly looks worried and asks me: "So where is your friend now?" I shrug. "He is busy." "I'm sorry for you," he says, but I smile. "I'm not. Thanks to that I'm now spending a day with you." And Jamal chuckles.

When we have changed trains, I notice he is looking at my hands. And he looks shy when he realizes that I have noticed.

"Are you married?" he asks me. "No, I'm not. I'm divorced. I have two little girls." And Jamal seems to digest that for some time.

"Are *you* married?" I ask him. "No, no." he says. "I have never even had a girlfriend." He stares in front of him. "I would like to have one though," he then says. "I would like to meet a love in my life." "Well, aren't there nice *younger* girls on Skout?" I ask him as we climb up the stairs.

Jamal shakes his head. "I'm Pakistani," he says. "And I'm illegal. Most girls don't want to date me." Then he looks at me and says: "You are such a nice woman. Your husband should have taken better care of you. If I had a nice woman like you, I would take good care of her." And I smile.

We have reached Checkpoint Charlie on Friedrichstrasse and Jamal checks his phone again as he reads: "This was the only crossing point between East and West Berlin until the wall was torn down in 1990."

Next to it is the Haus am Checkpoint Charlie. It's a museum covering the cold war and the Berlin wall. "Shall we go in?" I ask and Jamal nods. Now the cold war and the Berlin wall must be mostly Western history, and Jamal is way too young to remember the fall of the wall, but he is interested in everything.

In the museum it's remarkable to see how innovative people were in their attempts to escape the communist regime of the DDR. And to see how desperate they were. But it's sad to see how many people were killed trying to get to freedom.

Jamal is very quiet in the museum. When we get out, we walk quite some bit before he starts talking. "I also fled," he then says. "I fled Pakistan." I look at him. "Why did you flee?" He shrugs.

"My brother got killed in some land dispute and the assassins had links to the Prime Minister. They wanted me dead too." "Couldn't you go to the police?" I ask him. Jamal laughs a dry ironic laugh and just says: "In Pakistan? No way. They are as corrupt us it goes. No, I had two choices. Either I go into hiding or I leave the country."

"So how did you get out?" Jamal gives a dismissive flick with his hand. "There are lots of travel agents who send you abroad. They take large amounts of money. My uncle knew one of them. So I took a bank loan of 3000 dollars and gave it to him. In a week he gave me a visa for Dubai and I left right away. I stopped over in Dubai and then moved onwards to Libya."

Jamal kicks a stone with his shoe as he continues. "In Libya there were already lots of other Pakistani refugees. But the security situation was worse than I had imagined. It was a nightmare, as the militias were fighting against each other."

For a second Jamal is quiet. He seems to be remembering. But then he continues. "So when I got an offer to be transported to Italy for a 1000 dollars, I took it. We started around three o'clock in the morning in a small wooden ramshackle boat. It was crammed with people."

Jamal watches a little girl that rides her bike past him. "There were around ninety people on the boat," he says. "Also women, children and old people. We came from Syria, Africa, Pakistan, Afghanistan and Bangladesh. But it was a shabby boat. And it was definitely not suitable for the long journey. There were these gigantic waves, which would flood the lower part of the boat where the engine was. And the smoke coming from the engine was suffocating. Suddenly our boat broke at sea and we all thought we wouldn't survive. Fortunately another ship came to our rescue and fixed the boat's engine. In total the journey was sixteen hours long."

Jamal brushes his forehead with his arm and says: "When we finally landed on the Italian shore, we could barely walk. We were so weak and tired and the salty sea water had damaged our skin. I stayed in Italy for a few days, then I came to Germany by car."

"Why Germany?" I ask him. He shrugs. "People told me that in Germany the refuges got a better treatment than in other European countries." "Do you?" Jamal shrugs again. "I have no papers. But I have work. And friends. I work with other Pakistani in a factory. Life is good." And he smiles.

As we walk past a lush green park, Jamal changes the subject. "Would you like to do some relaxing?" he asks me. "Sure," I tell him. "That would be lovely." Jamal puts out a handkerchief for me to sit on, while he sits in the grass. And I look at the people around us. People are doing yoga, running, riding their bikes, playing music, reading books and smoking weed.

Jamal watches two small brothers running after each other. "You must miss your brother," I say and I can see tears welling up as Jamal nods. "I do," he says. "I really do." "You had a hard life," I tell him. "And you are still illegal ..."

Jamal shrugs. "I also have a beautiful life," he says. "It's however you look at it." I look at his handsome face. "How can you remain so positive?" I ask him. Jamal shrugs and answers: "You know, life is what you make out of it." "What do you mean?"

"Well, right now, in this moment, you can find all the evidence you want to prove your life is miserable, depressing and a terrible burden," Jamal says and he looks at me. "Go ahead, try it. What are all those things that prove what a horrible life you have?" And he gives me some time to ponder over that. *Well, there are lots of things I can think of. My divorce. My financial situation. This trip with Robert.*

"Now change your mind-set," Jamal says. "Focus on finding all the evidence to prove that your life is a plentiful, happy adventure. Look around for all the joy in your life." *Well, that's easy too. My girls. My new freedom. The fact that I'm writing – I'm finally doing what I always dreamt of. Being here in Berlin with Jamal ...*

"If I look for problems, I will find loads of them," Jamal says. "But when I don't get what I want, rather than waste time and energy explaining why I don't have it, I rather find another way to get it. Inshallah."

"Inshallah?" I ask him. "That means 'God Willing'," Jamal says. "Ah, that's another thing that makes me feel happy. I take every day some time to find something to be grateful for. I express gratitude to Allah for the opportunities and gifts that I receive."

I smile. "My grandmother was like that," I say. "She was a Catholic. And she always made me thank God for what I received. I quit it though, since I don't consider myself religious. Spiritual maybe, but not religious." I sit back and let the sun caress my face. Then I say: "But maybe being grateful is something I should pick up again." I smile at him. "Thank you, Jamal. For making me remember."

He smiles back and we just sit there for some time, enjoying the sun. But time flies. And when I check the time, I need to hurry to catch my flight. Jamal takes me back to Alexanderplatz, gets my suitcase out of the locker and rolls it to the trains. He finds the train to the airport for me and waits with me for it to arrive.

While we sit and wait, he becomes shy. "Monique," he says. "You're special. You don't care about nationalities, race and religion. You see the person underneath. I wish you would have an easier life. With your girls and all. You shouldn't be divorced." He then clears his throat before he adds: "Would you be interested in a marriage with me?" And I gulp.

"Jamal," I say once I have found my voice back, "I am honoured. Really. You are a wonderful man and you will make a wonderful husband, one day. But I'm not the woman for you. I'm divorced, with two kids and I'm way older than you are. You will meet a nice girl of your own age. I'm sure of that."

Jamal nods sadly. He helps me get into the train and then stands in front of the window to wave. He is so handsome, as he stands there. His beautiful lips smiling a shy smile. And as the train rolls away, he runs a little with the train until we pick up speed and leave him behind.

Jamal. The Positive Pakistani. I will never see him again, I don't have his number, but his words will definitely influence me. From now on, I decide, I will focus on all the good I have. And be grateful for it.

CHAPTER TEN:
THE CITY OF LIONS

T hanks to Jamal, Berlin was unexpectedly nice. But it was just
two days. It's still summer vacation and the house remains
damn empty. So I'm really happy when The Viking is in the
UK for one night and we have another lovely dinner in our Italian
restaurant.

He's still the gentleman, holding my chair and bringing me
a lovely gift – a Chanel travelling make-up case. He chooses the
six-course menu again and we chat nicely about life.

Now the Viking seems such a relaxed and happy person.
And since Jamal I'm interested in what makes people tick. *What
is the secret that makes people happy?* So I ask him: "How do you
remain so positive and happy? Apart from being hygge, that is."
The Viking laughs at that. "Very simple," he says. "I don't give a
damn about what other people think about me." And he laughs a
bit more, while he pays the bill.

"You know what the problem is with most people?" he asks,
as he calls me a cab. "They care way too much about what other
people might think of them. Truth is that most people are not
even thinking that much about others. Most people spend most
of their time thinking about themselves."

As he opens the cab-door for me and gives me money for
the ride, he continues: "See, caring too much about what other

people think is just a waste of good drinking time." And I can still his roaring laughter while the cab turns the corner.

But Mr. Viking is just one date. I still have what feels like ages without the girls in front of me. I really want to do something... And since I haven't heard from Farshad for so long, I decide to get back on Seeking Arrangement.

I had hoped Farshad was the one. I really like him. But I'm not hearing anything from him. And I still want nice dates when the girls are with their dad. Also – let's be honest about it – I'm running out of money...

So I have several contacts, but many men don't seem to have any intention of meeting. They suggest to move to messenger to chat. Or to Telegram or KIK. There are loads of messaging sites that I had never heard about. Some want to video chat. But most of them just seem to enjoy sexting. They try to get my picture in lingerie – or even naked – and love to talk erotic.

So this morning, one week after Berlin, I'm sitting at the empty kitchen table with the sun pouring in the window, eating my yoghurt for breakfast, when I hear a familiar sound. I have gotten a message. From Seeking Arrangement. And the first thing I think is: *Oh no, not another one of those guys...* So I reluctantly check my phone. But the message reads:

> "Hi you sound great. I'm from Singapore, love baths, nice looking, fit, fun, single, well to do and generous. I like company of women not girls. Best, Sam"

I check his profile. Sam is a Singaporean of 48 and his profile reads:

> "Smart, fun, genuine, handsome, fit, well to do, generous by nature. Seeking attractive lady for no stress dating.

Please be educated with pleasing manners. Sex is not the most important thing to me. I am looking for a great friend and potential travel partner. Thank you."

Now Sam and I chat for some time. We talk about the UK, Singapore, architecture and about baths. Apparently we both really enjoy baths. And I can picture him in my head. A handsome Asian floating in scented bubbles. But I am surprised when he sends me:

"Would you like to come to Singapore for a few days? No allowance, but your trip and all other expenses will be well taken care off. Grateful for your interest, Sam"

What? Fuzzy jumps on the chair next to me, purrs and starts licking his paws. I absentmindedly scratch him behind his ears while I consider the offer…

Singapore… I have never been to Singapore. Fact is that since Farshad I do like to get financial help, but now that it's the summer holidays and I have all this time by myself, wouldn't this be great? A free vacation?

So I reply back that yes, I would be very interested in coming Singapore. His answer is fast. "How about tomorrow." It takes one split second before I answer: "Sure, why not?"

Great, he replies. And I have to send him a copy of my passport. His secretary will arrange the rest. Then one hour later I receive another message. Would it be possible to leave tonight? I take one look at the empty kitchen table. At the empty house. And it doesn't take me long to answer.

That means it's the end of my quiet day. Suddenly I have to hurry. I call the cat-sitter to see whether she can feed Fuzzy the coming two days. I go to the library to lend a book about Singapore on Lisa's free library card. I start packing. And I'm on the train to the airport by the time the summer sky starts darkening into deep blue.

It's not until I'm in the air that I give myself time to think. *I am flying thirteen hours, all the way to Singapore, to meet this guy I have never met, in a country I have never been to, to be there for two days. Have I totally lost my mind?*

I know I'm taking a chance here. The guy might be crazy. But I don't give myself a lot of time to think. I open my guidebook and start reading about Singapore. And the more I read, the more enthusiastic I become.

Sam is waiting for me at the airport. He is of Chinese descent and has black hair sprinkled with grey and Asian eyes behind gold-rimmed glasses. For a moment I think I can see a hint of sadness in them, but it's gone before I can place it.

Sam is a bit shorter than I am, but who cares. For a guy of 48 he's still looking good. He introduces himself politely, takes my suitcase and leads me to the taxi stand. Now the moment we get outside, the heat and humidity hit me. *God this place is hot.*

In the cab Sam is rather silent. Then he turns to me and asks: "You know the meaning of Singapore?" I shake my head and say: "I'm afraid I don't" Sam smiles. "It means Lion City. So welcome to the City of Lions!" And he laughs.

Now I loved the pictures of Singaporean shop houses in the guidebook, so when the cab enters a street with them I am thrilled. "This is Joo Chiat," Sam tells me. "Once it was a coconut palm-filled seaside retreat for the rich." Now it's full of colourful ornate shop houses and I am even more thrilled when the cab stops in front of one of them and Sam says: "This is where I live. This is my house and my studio."

His house is simply beautiful. It has French double-shuttered windows and a sheltered corridor at the front. "In Singapore's first town plan, those corridors were called for by Sir Stamford Raffles to protect pedestrians from rain or hot sun," Sam explains.

The moment he opens the door, his dog comes to greet us. It's a little Chihuahua called Kai Kai, who follows us everywhere. With Kai Kai following on his heels, Sam proudly shows me around.

We enter into an internal open-air courtyard containing a pond full of goldfish, with open stairways and skylights to bring in light and air. In the back is the kitchen. "This place belonged to my grandmother," Sam tells me. "Traditionally the ground floor was used to conduct business."

Upstairs is his bedroom, another room – which he doesn't open and seems to avoid – and a bathroom with a huge antique bathtub. He winks at me and says: "We're going to take nice hot baths together." But not yet, obviously, because he tells me he is first going to show me Singapore.

Once we are strolling through his city, it doesn't take me long to decide that I just love it here. I love all the different cultures. Little India with Hindu temples, secretive alleyways, flower garlands, hand-woven silks draped around and infused with incense. I love the heat, I love the atmosphere.

I take some pictures of the famous Singaporean prohibition-signs like 'no skate-boarding', 'no littering', including the fines you have to pay when you do until one in particular catches my attention. It says 'no durian'.

"What is a durian?" I ask Sam. He chuckles. "Wait, I'll show you." He pulls me into a fruit shop and points at a green, spiky fruit. And I don't even need to come close to notice its pungent smell. It's a mixture of sewage, rotting flesh and ripe cheese. "Wanna try it?" Sam asks and winks at me, but I fervently shake my head. "Come on," he says. "You are in Singapore. You should try. I dare you!"

Now people should not challenge me. Somehow I always take the challenge. So I nod and he orders the shop woman to give me a piece. Both the woman and Sam think this is a lot of fun. The woman is even chuckling behind her hand. But I don't. I shut my nose while I put the piece in my mouth.

To my surprise the flavour is sweet. It's not something I'd crave for, but it has sweetish, custardy flesh and the taste isn't far off an overripe banana. But one thing I know for sure. It's definitely not something I need to eat more of. So when Sam asks me: "You want more?" I shake my head and both he and the shopkeeper laugh.

Next Sam takes me on Singapore's MRT system and I'm impressed. It's modern, sleek, efficient, and spotless. Now as an architect, Sam has plenty to show me. He shows me the theatre buildings of Esplanade. "You want to know their nickname?" he asks me with a smile. "The durians," and he laughs. "For their spiky exterior!" And I wrinkle my nose remembering.

The other places he takes me to, are each special in their own way. The ArtScience Museum resembles a giant lotus flower, the Marina Bay Sands looks like a spaceship that dominates the skyline and he shows me the mind-boggling Gateway buildings, which look like they're only 2 dimensional and from a certain angle they look like they are paper thin.

Next, Sam takes me to the beautiful lush Singapore Botanic Gardens, where he explains everything to me. And when I say everything, I mean *everything*. How the gardens are 156 year old. That they stay open until midnight and are home to the largest orchid collection in the world. He even shows me one particularly delicate species named after Margaret Thatcher; the purple flowers are twisted and spiky, with two horns on top of it.

Sam is nothing but kind, but for some reason it feels like some places make him sad. Like the ArtScience Museum. And the Botanic Gardens. But whatever he is feeling, he is a master in letting it disappear. Sometimes I think I see tears welling up, but the next moment he is all smiles again.

Dusk is almost falling when Sam takes me to the Raffles Hotel. And this place stuns me. It has a magnificent ivory frontage, an – according to Sam – famous Sikh doorman and lush, hushed tropical grounds. There are white marble colonnades throughout the hotel and they encircle an atrium that soars three floors up. The last rays of sunlight pour through illuminating polished teak verandas that lead to the suites.

Sam is still sharing his facts to me. "In 1902 a Singaporean tiger managed to creep into the billiard room and cowered under a billiard table," he tells me, while he puts a string of hair behind my ear.

"After its presence was discovered, the tiger was shot at least five times before receiving a fatal blow." He takes my hand. "That tiger was the last of its kind ever to be shot in Singapore."

Next, he takes me up to the Long Bar to sip on a famous Singapore Sling. Now though I did have a Singapore Sling before, I obviously never had in Singapore. "And the Raffles Bar," Sam tells me, "is where it was first invented in the early 1900s."

The bar is dark and inviting. Palm-shaped fans give a cooling breeze, while guests lean back in wicker chairs. Most of them are sipping from a pink Singapore Sling.

The waiter shows us our seat, and as we walk peanut shells crunch under our feet. "Would you like me to clear the table for you?" the waiter asks. And with one big swoop of his arm he brushes peanut shells off the table, which fall to the growing pile on the floor. I stare at the waiter with mild horror, but Sam is laughing. "No worries," he says. "This is tradition." And he points to a sign:

Quite possible the one place in Singapore where littering is actually encouraged. Never would we suggest you to break the law. But at the Long Bar at Raffles, feel free to brush your peanut shells onto the floor...

As I scan the room, I notice that piles of peanut shells are littered around all the chairs and tables at the Long Bar. But soon my focus is elsewhere. Because when the waiter returns with the menu, I gulp when I read the price.

It's $27 for one Singapore Sling! I try to hide my shock as Sam orders one for both of us. The drink comes in a hurricane shaped glass. And it's gorgeous: a punch of pink with a foamy top, garnished with a Maraschino cherry and a slice of pineapple.

After our Singapore Sling, Sam tells me it's time for dinner. He has made reservations at the Imperial Treasure Super Peking Duck Restaurant on Orchard Road – which is a seemingly endless boulevard filled with shopping centres.

From the outside the place looks oriental chic, inside it's buzzing. And the moment we are led to our table, Sam starts to choose. He chooses roasted pork belly. "My personal favourite starter," Sam says. "And my s…" But he doesn't finish that sentence. Whatever he was going to say, he lets it disappear in thin air while tears well up in his eyes again. He winks a few times before he continues.

"Like the duck, I had to pre-order it at booking time, because it sells out fast!" he continues, as if nothing has happened. Next he orders Peking duck, saying: "This is one of the best – if not the best – Peking duck in Singapore."

And he orders double boiled Three Treasure Soup, mushroom tofu, crab and veggies in egg white, and some crocodile claw dish. Yes, crocodile claw. *Now this is going to be exciting.* Next he lets the staff recommend our wine.

Even though the place is really busy, we don't have to wait long for our food to arrive. Sam is talking a lot, about Singapore and architecture, but I'm not really focussing. He has given me so much information the whole day long that my head is full with facts. I nod kindly and smile, but I focus on the food. I have to say the Peking duck is my favourite. It has crispy skin and moist, tasty meat.

Sam needs to dare me to try the crocodile claw, but I have to say it's an eye-opener. It is really tender and well cooked. Then I have a herbal jelly for dessert. After dinner, I assume that we will go back to his house, but Sam has planned otherwise. He takes me to the Gardens by the Bay for a nightly light show.

By now I am exhausted. I barely slept during the flight, I spent the whole day in Singapore and I know I will most probably have sex with this guy as well. But at the light show all I can do is stare in awe as the super trees are lit up and the tribal soundtrack of the Garden Rhapsody transports me to the world of Avatar.

And it is with the night show that Sam finally breaks down. He takes off his glasses to dry his tears. "I'm sorry," he says. "This reminds me of my son." I look at him surprised. "You have a son?" He answers with one word. "Had." And for one second I have no idea what to say to him.

Then I take his hand. "I'm so sorry," I say. *And I really am. I can't even imagine what it must be like to lose your child...* Sam puts his glasses back on and focuses on the super trees. "It was an accident," he tells me. "We were all in the car. But only Joshua didn't survive."

I hold his hand and stand next to him. *Now what do you say to a guy who is carrying such a big loss with him.* "I'm so, so sorry Sam. I can only imagine the pain you are in. If it were my girls..." And my voice breaks with even the thought.

Sam shrugs. "It was the end of everything," he tells me. "My marriage didn't survive. We separated last year." And he shrugs again. "All I can do is live on. And keep his memory alive."

He squeezes my hand and we silently head back through the hot humid Singapore streets. So many questions whirl in my head. *Did it happen in Singapore? When did it happen? Is that why he is now going for arrangements?*

But I don't think it's appropriate to ask any of them. So when he finally breaks the silence with his whisper: "Are you ready for our bath?" All I do is nod. I guess trying to forget is all he wants to do now …

Kai Kai the dog comes to greet us when we open the door. And for a moment I wonder whether Kai Kai was maybe Joshua's dog, but I don't ask. Sam pours me a glass of white wine and goes up to prepare our bath.

When he calls me up, I'm a bit surprised. There are no bubbles whatsoever in the bath. And there is no nice exotic scent. In fact, it smells like … "A Dettol bath," Sam says proudly as he is already stripping. "I take one every night." And as he steps in, he holds his hand out for me. "Come, join!"

Now my idea of our bath together had been way more romantic than this. When we were chatting, I had pictured the guy in some perfumed bubbly bath with maybe some candles for even more atmosphere. But as it usually is in life, reality is way different from your imagination. And the Dettol smell strongly turns me off.

Still, Sam has been nothing but nice to me and the in-bath-together part is something he really seemed to be looking forward to. So why would I disappoint him? I slip out of my dress, out of my underwear and step into the hot water of his antivirus bath as the strong pungent scent fills the room.

In the bath Sam doesn't make any move. We just sit there opposite of each other, soaking in the stinking water while he lightly caresses my leg. When he finally gets out, he gives me a soft white towel to dry. I slip on a sexy nightdress, while he gets into the bed naked.

When we are in bed, Sam starts kissing me. And without his glasses, his Asian eyes are mesmerizing. They give him a beautiful exotic look. This whole day in Singapore has been so nice. Maybe Sam talks a lot, but I do like him. So I am preparing for more. But then suddenly Sam pulls away and starts wanking.

I'm surprised, but he seems to be greatly aroused by his wanking. "Can you help yourself?" he asks me, breathing fast. "I don't like intercourse. I prefer it like this." So there we are. In his big bed, in his beautiful shop house. Lying next to each other, helping ourselves to our climax.

We both come quite soon after each other. "That was marvellous," Sam says as he kisses me on my lips. Then he turns around and falls asleep. And I can't help it. At that moment I really miss Farshad.

The next morning on my way down I notice one thing. There is a small nameplate on the door of the room Sam avoided. It reads 'Joshua.' And I wonder what is hidden behind that door. *Has Sam kept the room intact? Are his toys still there? His little bed?* But I know I will never find out.

We have breakfast in Sam's cosy kitchen. And Sam has locked all his sadness inside of him again. He seems joyful. Only his eyes give him away. "I have a surprise for you," he says as we eat toast with scrambled eggs. "Hope you are in a sportive mood."

Not much later two of his friends are in front of the door. One is Indian, the other Chinese and both must be around Sam's age. They are both polite and smiley to me, as we follow them out and jump into their jeep.

"What is the surprise?" I ask Sam. He chuckles. "We go wakeboarding," he says. "On the North Eastern shore of Singapore facing Malaysia. It's a short drive." *Wake-boarding? Wow... Now this is the way to enjoy life...*

It is a short drive indeed. We get out of the jeep at a stretch of calm water between the lush greenery of an island – Seletar Island as Sam points out to me – and Singapore. It's simply beautiful. It's lush, green and tropical.

As the three men take me to a motorboat and start loading equipment inside, Sam is explaining to me. "See," he says, "wake-boarding consists of two words. 'Board' is the platform you stand on and 'Wake' are the waves created by the motorboat." He caresses my cheek. "This is going to change your perspective of wind, water and waves."

Well, it turns out it won't do any of these for me. But let me not get ahead. Singapore is one of the few places in the world where you can go wakeboarding all year round. And apparently Sam and his friends are doing this all the time, so no wonder they are really good. It is something they have done millions of times before. But I never have. And I utterly suck in it.

While Sam and his friends are making spectacular moves behind the motorboat, when it's my turn I can't even get up. With my feet strapped on the board and the rope in my hands, I am just pulled along with my ass hitting the waves of the motorboat … So I'm quite happy when the wakeboarding is finished.

Sam's friends take us home, where I pack, say goodbye to Kai Kai and all three of them take me to the airport. "Thank you for coming to Singapore," Sam says as he kisses me goodbye. "Thank *you*! I loved being here" I answer him.

Sam smiles. "It was such a pleasure to meet you. I'm sure we will meet again. I really liked it. Really. It felt like I could be myself with you." He swallows before he continues. "Take care of those two girls of you. Enjoy every single moment with them. Realize the precious gifts you are holding." And I can see he is fighting back sadness again.

And when I'm in the airplane, I know what I will do the moment my girls are back home. I will give them the biggest hug ever. And for a moment I wish I never have to leave them behind again …

CHAPTER ELEVEN: BIRTHDAY MAGIC

Summer holidays are over and the autumn term is in full swing. The girl's weeks are full of school, play dates and sports. And now it's one week before my birthday and I don't have any plans whatsoever.

I haven't heard anything from Farshad and – to make things even more splendid – when I drop off the girls, The Ex tells me he has a new girlfriend. Apparently Mr. Minister went on a dating site the moment we talked about divorce. I google her the moment I'm back in my car and she is the total opposite of me. *What the hell did I waste all those years of my life with this man for?*

For some reason I feel tears welling up behind my eyes. Now I am NOT going to ruin any tears on the guy. *All I need is some ass-kicking music.* I rumble through the glove compartment – noticing with annoyance that my hands are shaking – and find my Alanis Morissette CD crammed in the back. I put it on, real loud, and shout with her 'You Oughta Know' at least three times before I'm home.

Now this is obviously NOT the way I was expecting to celebrate turning 40. And fact is, I have no idea why this news hurts me. I was *so* finished with the guy. She can have all of him.

Maybe it's his words when I left him. "I'm so sorry that I'm not a family man." The fact that he wanted to be a minister. And there he is now. Moving on. Having no responsibilities for his girls, except for one weekend every two weeks. The guy can do all he wants to, while I have to carry the full responsibility for our girls. Now I love my girls. Deeply. Truly. Madly. I love every moment with them. But somehow it just doesn't feel fair that I have to carry their responsibility all by myself.

Back home I close the doors of the girl's rooms, so I don't have to see how empty they are. I put on some comfy pyjamas and my fluffy sheep slippers – thank god no Sugar Daddy ever sees me like this – while I pour myself a big glass of Riesling, take out a big bucket of ice cream and curl up on the sofa.

Fuzzy always knows when I need him. He settles down next to me, looking me straight into the eye with his big green eyes and purrs loudly. I scratch him under his chin and wonder what I am going to do.

Watch a tearjerker? Listen to my 'Ooh child things are going to get easier' playlist on Spotify? Yes, some singing and dancing will do. And maybe I'll have some Oreo's with milk and watch Johnny Depp movies afterwards. Somehow watching that guy always makes life seem more bearable…

I have just turned on Gloria Gaynor real loud, dancing all around the living room on my sheep slippers, screaming with her I WILL SURVIVE!!!- using my wine glass as a microphone – when suddenly my phone makes a familiar sound.

I have a message. From Seeking Arrangement. And it couldn't come on a better time. I fumble with my phone to open the message. It says:

"You look gorgeous on your photos and your profile highly appeals to me. Smart, classy, beautiful. You're making me curious…I hope you will send me a message back. This might be the beginning of an exciting adventure, something to look out and long for…"

Though I'm in the middle of my dance, my glass still in my hand, I react immediately. I tell him I'm all in for adventure. A second later a new message pops up.

> "What's your story? What are you looking for here on SA? I was here a couple of months ago, but I was kind of put off by the high amount of escorts. Nice to meet YOU this time. I'm very curious about you. Will tell you my story tomorrow. It's quite a story … X"

Now it's getting interesting. I sit down on the sofa next to Fuzzy and check out the guy's profile. He's 49, in an open relationship, really tall and damn handsome on his pictures. Forget Johnny Depp, George Clooney is calling! And the guy even lives in London!

I react straight away and tell him all. How I'm divorced with kids. Happy with my life. Would like an interesting man in my life, though I'm not looking for a regular relationship. And how I do hope to find someone who can help me with a monthly allowance, since it can be tough to make ends meet as a single mother.

I take in a deep breath before pushing the 'send' button. *This is the first time I'm openly asking for a monthly allowance.* But I now know from experience that most men on the site are not willing to. You better be clear about it from the start.

Then I put my phone away and decide to watch some Johnny Depp anyway. Maybe I'm not feeling blue anymore, but I will always find an excuse to enjoy his handsomeness.

The next day Mr. Handsome's message is waiting for me in my mailbox:

> "Ok, as promised: my story. I'm Rudolph, married with four kids. And I live close to you – in London. Last

Christmas I discovered my wife was having an affair with my best friend. And not just that – they had been having it for two years.

It felt like the ground under my feet collapsed. Those first months my life was like a roller coaster. I was overwhelmed by all these different emotions: red-hot anger, deep sadness, panic and overall I was just feeling so confused.

I tried to save our relationship. I wanted my old relationship back, our family and the way it was. But eventually I discovered it will never come back. The relationship I had, my family, it doesn't exist anymore.

I now know that we won't stay together. We're still living together for the kids at the moment, but that's it for now. Maybe we will find a form of being a family again, but we won't be lovers anymore. We are now trying to give shape to our new situation. It's still hard to see how things will turn out and I'm mostly worried about the kids.

The reason I am on SA is mostly because I'm looking for excitement, distraction and to feel desired again. I want an anonymous love, an adventure, no strings attached. An adventure with excitement, desires, discretion and sex. Amazing sex. Love, X"

While I am reading, I feel sad for him. I can feel his pain through his words. Then I ask him whether he wants to meet and he reacts immediately. He has time next week. On Tuesday. My birthday.

So we make an appointment for lunch and the rest of the week he keeps texting me. Telling me how much he is looking forward to our meeting. Being used to Farshad's silence, I immediately warm to this guy. It almost feels like I am normally dating him and he is doing all he can to court me.

Saturday night, before I go to sleep, I smile with his message:

> "Surfed this morning at Joss Bay and am now danc-
> ing. I was just thinking about you, even though I don't
> really know you yet. I was thinking you should actually
> be here. I would have loved to dance with you. I truly
> wonder how that will be. How will you move, smile and
> look at me ... ?
>
> Now drinking a gin-tonic at a bar stool and send-
> ing a message to my Mistress-to-be. It's such a strange
> thought, it's making me all warm inside. I'm so much
> looking forward to your birthday. Hope you are looking
> forward to it in the same way as when you were a little
> girl. To the Birthday Magic. Not so much to the pres-
> ents at breakfast, but to me at lunch. Hope you are truly
> excited. Hmmm ... genuinely looking forward to it. Now
> going to enjoy the view. I can see the waves and the set-
> ting sun. Only you are not here. Wish you were here to
> dance with me ... X
>
> Ps if I am writing strange things it's the alcohol. X"

And so the Tuesday arrives. My Birthday. The day I turn 40. The
girls wake me up with cuddles and self-made drawings, while
Fuzzy meows in my ear for breakfast. Downstairs the girls have
prepared the breakfast table, decorated it with some flowers they
have cut from our garden, and they have made me some interesting sandwiches with peanut butter, chocolate paste and honey.
Now I try my best to look like it's the most delicious thing I've
ever eaten.

When they are at school, I have the whole morning to prepare. And I'm actually quite nervous. This guy really seems nice!
So I keep sending Amanda different pictures of dresses until she
totally gets fed up with me.

Finally I choose a black dress. Maybe it's way too overdressed for an afternoon lunch, but who cares. Throwing one last look in the tall mirror in my hallway, I close the door behind me. In the bus I see Mr. Handsome has sent me one more message:

"Hip Hip Hooray my dearest Mistress. Congratulations! And we are going to meet, what a party! See you soon! X"

I smile with a warm feeling inside. *This guy is special.*

I spot him the moment I enter the restaurant garden. He is sitting at a table in the back. Tall, nice suit, ravishing smile. My own George Clooney. And I can't help but smile.

He has kind eyes and looks at me warmly, but he also exudes this air of importance. I love the way he takes control. He orders everything – wine, food. He orders a glass of Riesling and a delicious salad for me – a quinoa salad with roasted sweet potatoes, feta, dates, fresh figs, tomato, cucumber, paprika, and balsamic cream – but I hardly eat one bite. I just nibble on some lettuce. *For some reason I'm still nervous…*

We talk during the whole lunch. Not about his family situation, we delicately tiptoe around that sensitive subject. No, we talk about relationships in general – we both don't believe in regular ones anymore.

We talk about traveling and scuba diving – which we both love. About kids. And he has brought me a present. A notebook with a leather cover for writing, since I wrote to him that I am a writer and he has remembered. *I smile inwardly.*

But I hardly notice the time. Especially when he asks me for a kiss, and I slowly bend over the table towards him. We kiss for what seems like ages, right there in the restaurant garden. And his kiss tastes like more…

But then I hear the church bells ringing and I realize that I *really* have to go. *I have to pick up the girls from school!* Feeling a bit like Cinderella – I should have lost a shoe somewhere – I run to catch the bus, leaving him there in the garden with the bill to pay.

Driving off in the bus, I spot him when he is coming out of the restaurant. I almost knock on the window and wave, but something stops me. It's his look. I would have expected him to look happy. Excited. But the guy simply looks miserable…

The bus is fast and I'm just in time at school. Sophie jumps on me, Lisa beams but keeps a cool 'I'm-too-big-for-mothers' distance walking home. And to our surprise The Ex is waiting in front of my door, he has come to drop something off.

He's forgotten all about my birthday of course. *The guy never remembered when we were married, so why would he now?* And the times he did remember, he would buy me something as unromantic as scissors. See, I have no regrets for no-birthdays-with-husbands whatsoever.

"You're shining," he says. And I beam "Yes, I just had a wonderful date." He looks at me sideways. *And in a way I hope it hurts him.* "Sure, you should," he mumbles as he leaves. "You are a healthy woman." I laugh, perhaps a little too loudly, as I call after him: "I'm not only healthy, I'm also beautiful. There are enough men I can get, you know."

At that moment I spot the neighbours from across the street, returning with their groceries and looking at me with a frown. I give them a polite nod and quickly close my door. *OOPS.*

Well, who cares anyway? If there is one thing I'm learning, it's not to care so much about what other people are thinking. The Viking would be proud of me. My life is a freaking soap opera, so I might as well save myself the effort. People think anyway.

In a way I expect not to hear from Mr. Handsome again, because of that sad look on his face. But he sends me a message that afternoon, telling me how much he enjoyed our meeting, our kiss and how he would like to see me that Thursday. In two days, that is.

"So we can continue where we had to finish so suddenly," as he describes it so nicely... And the whole day I walk on clouds. Especially since he keeps sending me messages to let me know that he is thinking about me. His last one makes me smile.

"That image of you walking away in your pretty black dress... it's a wonderful image to remember. As I write this, it makes me smile again..."

On Thursday I drop the girls off at school and Rudolph stands in front of my door at 9. He's the first (and will be the last) Sugar Daddy whom I'm meeting home. And it does feel a bit uncomfortable at first. I make him some tea and we sit down at my table chatting. But there is this strong sexual tension in the air. Soon he pulls me on his lap and we are kissing again.

I'm not really into the kissing this time though, because I know we haven't agreed on an allowance yet and *this* is the time to start talking about it. "Make sure you agree upon an allowance before you do anything with him," Amanda wrote to me. But I have never talked about this subject before.

Farshad helped without me asking. And Rudolph is the kind of guy I would be intimate with without any money. But I met the guy on SA, he knows I want an arrangement and fact is that I need the money. So how do you bring up the sensitive subject of money?

When he suggests we go upstairs, I first ignore him and keep kissing. And it takes some time before finally I pick up all my guts and say: "We still need to agree upon an allowance." He stops kissing and looks at me with a serious look now. *Oh, oh,* I can't help thinking.

"Ah, yes," he says. "The allowance. How much did you have in mind?" *Jeez, how am I going to say this?* "Well, Mr. Iran helped me with a thousand pounds a month," I say. And I just *know* I'm getting all red.

But Rudolph gives a dismissive flick of his hand. "Ah, sure. No problem." And he assertively pulls me towards him again. I sigh inwardly. *I have just made my first real arrangement.*

After kissing some more, I take his hand and lead him up, to my bedroom. Upstairs he slips his hands around my waist as I gently undo his buttons and unzip his pants.

He is already hard I notice. Rock hard. He pulls my dress over my head and lets it fall to the floor. I lean my head back as he kisses my breasts and I feel his hands cupping my ass.

After he has taken off his shoes, I softly pull him towards the bed, push him on and climb on top of him as we passionately kiss. Then I slowly go down on him. Now this guy has a beautiful body. There is no inch of fat on it. And I love exploring every single part of him.

But as confident as Mr. Handsome is in public, in bed he becomes insecure. His wife's affair must have really dented his ego. When I go down on him, he gets soft again. And he becomes quite agitated about it.

"I'm so sorry," he whispers. "I do find you really attractive …" I hush him. "I know. Don't worry. I will get it up again." So I softly take his dick in my mouth and it reacts immediately.

Now giving this guy a blowjob is a feast. He REALLY responds. He simply can't keep still. I'm just loving it. I love it when men react. It's such a treat. And it doesn't take long for him to get rock hard again. And to come.

He comes in an instant and I swallow all, lick a bit more and then climb back up, but now he is all upset again. "I'm so sorry. I'm all rusty. I normally don't come so fast. But it's been a while …" I hush him again. "Don't worry. We have enough time."

First it's time to relax. So I lie in his arm. He caresses my back, my hair, kisses my breasts. "I love your breasts," he says.

"They are such happy breasts. Happy Boobs. They are beautiful." I toss a little. *As you know, my breasts are not exactly on my Things-I-Love-About-Myself list.* But having Mr. Handsome say that about them does feel nice. In a way they suddenly feel different. So from now on, Happy Boobs they are.

We spoon up and finally he talks about his wife's affair. His worries for the kids. And I truly feel sorry for him. *When you have a guy like this, why the hell would you cheat on him?*

When all is out, all his anger, his worries, his sadness, he starts caressing me again. And this time the hard-on stays. He slips on a condom and takes me from behind, taking me with hard thrusts, then flipping me over and taking me in missionary. He thrusts his dick into me with so much force that afterwards we discover he has moved the whole bed from the wall.

I don't come. I normally don't come the first time. And I don't need to come to enjoy sex. For me to be able to have an orgasm, I need to feel more comfortable with a guy. And I normally need to help myself. But suddenly I realize with a shock that I have totally forgotten the time. I dress fast and hurry him out with a passionate kiss. *I have to pick up the kids for lunch!*

Walking to school, my cheeks are still flushed and rosy. *It's nice to have a secret like this. It gives some spice to my normal life.* And at the school yard the cute dad nods at me with a smile, making my day even more.

That evening I deactivate my account on Seeking Arrangement. Again. It looks like I just found myself an arrangement. This might be The One.

CHAPTER TWELVE: ONE MORE TIME

It's a rainy November day. The girls are at school and I'm in London, shopping with Sarah. These months I've been writing so much on Amanda's story and copywriting for companies on the side, that it's nice to allow myself some fun time.

It has been a long time since we went shopping together. In fact, it's been a long time since I could *afford* to go shopping together. So I'm enjoying every minute of it. I just bought myself a nice warm winter coat at Zara's and Sarah is trying on a dress for Christmas when I see that I have an email in my mailbox.

Since I'm waiting for Sarah anyway, I get out my phone and check my mail. To my surprise there is a message from Farshad in my mailbox:

"My dear, how are you? My WhatsApp was not working in Iran because of filtering! I miss you too much. Fadaye to besham. Three times I plan to come to you to see you, but every time I couldn't make free time.

I will go to Milan 8th to 11th of Nov, after Italy I will go to Spain to Bilbao for 12th of Nov. After that go to France 13 till 15th of Nov. From 16th evening till 17th I will be free in Europe. Please let me know how we can meet each other. Big kiss, Farshad"

In a way I knew I would hear from Farshad again. Whatever it is that we have together, I know it's mutual. I know he must have other women and I'm quite sure he knows I have other men, but still there is some undefinable connection.

But now that I'm with Rudolph, he has moved into a corner of my thoughts. Rudolph is most definitely in the centre. As a matter of fact, I fear that I'm getting a crush on him. So I'm not sure whether I should meet Farshad. Truth is I'm not sure I will be able to have sex with him.

That evening I send Amanda a message for advice, though I could have known what her advice would be. "Of course you should see Farshad! You like him! And he helps you well."

I sigh. But she is right. I am really quite fond of Farshad. Getting a crush on Rudolph doesn't change that. And it will be nice to have a little trip again. So I reply to Farshad. *Sure, I'd love to meet him. Where would he like to go?*

In the meantime I arrange the cat sitter, because the girls will be with their father. But when the 16th comes, I realize that I'm actually quite nervous. *What will it be like to see him again? Will I be able to sleep with him?*

As usual, Farshad is waiting for me at Heathrow airport. This time he has come all the way from Paris to pick me up. And when I see him, I know I've made the right choice. I feel a pang of love for him the moment I see him. And in a way I am surprised. I always thought I was monogamous, but apparently I can have a crush on two men at the same time. *How interesting…*

Farshad is traveling light again, with just one carry-on suitcase. But this time he is also carrying a small blue bag that looks like a beauty case. And I wonder what it is, but I feel too shy to ask.

In the plane I now know how to handle him, making sure to talk about philosophy, avoiding his jokes about Turks. And once we have landed, Barcelona airport just feels so familiar. It's like a déjà vu. Especially with Farshad making sure he keeps a clear view on my bum. Of course he leads me to the rental cars and gets us our nice Mercedes – a white one this time.

The moment we whizz out of the airport, were are back in the Mediterranean. And even though it's in the middle of November, it's still sunny here. I sigh and lean back in the seat taking in all of Barcelona. *Now this is life...*

It's just so wonderful to be back. I love the palm trees, the old stately buildings, and the fashionable people in the street. And in a way I feel this strong affection for the man sitting next to me, giving me warm yet horny sideway looks from time to time.

Our hotel is the same and it's as fabulous as I remember. A friendly girl checks us in and Farshad gives her his blue beauty case, whispering something to her. The girl leaves with it and Farshad gives me a mysterious little smile... *I do wonder what I am up for...*

Of course Farshad has booked us our spacious Jacuzzi suite again. And while Farshad fills the tub, I stand in front of the window enjoying the view of the ocean, past the offices where I can see people working. *I missed this. I missed the traveling. The nice hotels...* But Farshad doesn't let me stand like that for long.

Soon I feel him behind me. He wraps his arms around me and kisses my neck. Then his hand slides down, fondling my breasts, going down to my bum, kneading it softly until he lets his hand slide underneath my skirt. He pushes my slip to the side and puts his finger inside of me, pulling it in and out, while I feel his ramrod dick against my bum.

He doesn't have much patience. Soon he takes off my knickers. I'm still facing the ocean – and the people in their offices in the opposite building who can most definitely see me too – while I hear him open his flies, tear open a package and know he is rolling on a condom.

Before I can even turn, he enters me from behind, right there in front of our ocean-view window. With all those people still working in the offices opposite of us. And I can see one guy who is most definitely looking at us, while his face breaks into a naughty smile.

I flash him a smile back. But I don't look for long. I close my eyes. *My God.* I just love his dick. I love the way he is filling me completely. So far, no man has been able to compete...

Next he turns me around and leads me to the bed. He doesn't even take the time to undress me. It has been so long since we last fucked together... He throws me on my back on the bed, pulls me real close to the edge, and as he stands in front, his jeans still at his knees, he enters me and fucks me hard. Real hard.

I bite the duvet not to scream from his force. Since he doesn't enter me slowly it hurts a little. He's just so big. But it's a nice pain... See, one thing Amanda already told me I would learn during my Sugar Dating. Pain can be nice...

Afterwards, when we undress and get into the tub my pussy feels all raw. *And we only just started...* But this time we don't fuck, we just soak in it. And as we watch night fall over Barcelona, I can feel all the stress slide of my body. I watch the sliver of a moon outside. *God I missed this. I missed* him...

When it's all dark outside, Farshad comes out of the tub, puts on one of the soft white bathrobes and the slippers and calls room service. I slip in a bathrobe just in time before a boy comes in with Farshad's little blue bag on a rolling table covered with white linen. While the boy leaves, Farshad says: "Honey, I brought you a little something from my country. It's from Iran."

When he opens it, the beauty case turns out to be a cooling bag. It contains a jar with silvery and black Beluga caviar. And by the careful way Farshad treats it, I just know how expensive it is...

"Wait, we need something with this," Farshad says. He gets up and calls room service once more for some toast and Cava. When everything is brought, I carefully try some of the caviar he has scooped on a square little toast.

He studies my face while I taste it. And I have to say it's just lovely. It has a creamy taste with a very delicate structure. "You like it?" Farshad asks. "Darling, it's heavenly," I answer him. "It's the first caviar I ever had…" Farshad beams. "Well, the first should be the best."

So there we are. And nobody even knows where I am. Who would even imagine that I am in Barcelona – for the second time – with a wealthy Iranian? Life is sparkling when you have nice little secrets like this… Sipping from our ice-cold cava, sitting in our bathrobes on our sofa, with behind us the black Mediterranean ocean, we take a long time to finish it.

Next Farshad calls room service again for dinner. *Apparently we are not leaving our room tonight.* He orders us a nice Bordeaux and a typical Catalan dish called 'arros negre' which we share. It's a soft rice dish with garlic, green peppers, sweet paprika, crab, shrimp and squid ink colouring the dish black. And as a desert we share a cheesecake.

When we have finally finished eating, Farshad has recovered his energy and he leads me back to the bed. We take our time now. We make long and lazy love. In missionary, sideways, in doggy. We already have our lust out of our system. We are already sexually satisfied. So it's a long and lazy lovemaking until we drift off to sleep.

The next morning I wake up on his soft hairy chest and for some time I just smile and lie in his arms. *I missed this.* But after a while Farshad gets up, we have a shower and go down for our buffet breakfast.

The hotel has the same selection of fresh bread, meats, vegetables, a lot of Spanish specialities and cava. And Farshad gets me everything. Hot lemon tea. Cava. Scrambled eggs…

During breakfast Farshad says: "Honey, we have two options. Either we go sightseeing in Barcelona again, or we take the car and go seek adventure." Well, it's not hard to choose. Last time was lovely, but this time I'm all in for adventure…

So after our sumptuous breakfast, Farshad jumps into the car calling out: "Where do we go, honey?" "Anywhere," I answer. "Find some new place. I'm sure it will be lovely." He smiles, takes the challenge and pushes the gas. And soon we leave beautiful Barcelona behind us.

For some time Farshad follows the highway along the coast in southwest direction, then he gets off the highway and starts driving the winding lanes along the coast. He stops in a lovely Mediterranean coastal town hidden between the sea and the dark folds of hills. The signboard tells us that we have arrived in 'Sitges.'

Farshad types the name in his phone. "It looks like I am a good treasure hunter!" he says proudly. "This is a famous place!" Well no surprise there, it is simply charming. The town snakes around a bay and up the mountains. It has large avenues, narrow streets and gorgeous beaches.

Farshad parks the car and we first cross the historical part of Sitges, which has white-painted walls and cute narrow streets. Next we cross some old caste leftovers, go past a church and take a big stairs down to walk over the seaside promenade. Farshad stops at a little restaurant where we both have a Sangria and enjoy the view of the beach.

It's not until dusk is falling, that we arrive back in Barcelona. Farshad parks his car in an underground parking place near Las Ramblas. "Are you hungry?" he asks me and when I tell him I am, he smiles. "Good! Just wait honey, you are in for a surprise…"

He leads me to an outdoor covered market just off Las Ramblas. Above the entrance is the name: 'La Boqueria Market'. Now the entrance doesn't look like much, but inside a food mecca awaits me.

As soon as we walk into the market, we are welcomed by the sweet smell coming from the crepes. And Farshad gets us plump cherries to eat while strolling through. It's a fun atmosphere. The floors are slippery with melted ice and fruit skins and some stall holders market their products loudly, but this all adds to the charm of the experience. Here all my senses are appealed to. In every corner there is something new to smell.

As we walk on, there are endless colourful displays of almost everything a culinary heart may desire. There are sweets, honey, cheese, refined oils, olives, spices, beers, local and exotic fruit and vegetables, meat, Iberico hams, and so much more. And all fresh and in a huge selection. The middle of the market is made up of a roundabout with a variety of marine animals, many of which are still living …

Farshad buys saffron, olives, spices, fresh fruit and candies. We stop by an Iberico Ham stall to try – the meat feels like butter and tastes great. But I do look at him questioningly, when he takes a bite off the ham. "Aren't you Muslim?" I ask him. Farshad nods. "I am. But outside of Iran I eat ham and I drink alcohol. Islam is my religion in my heart, not in my food." And he laughs loudly.

Next, we stop at a food stall with pull up stools. It's really crowded with tourists and locals ordering food. "Let's have a little something here honey," Farshad says. And we get a glass of sangria while we wait. It takes a long time, but finally we get a stool and Farshad orders an amazing selection of authentic Spanish tapas dishes.

We have fresh olives, fried small green padron peppers, spicy Spanish potatoes called potato bravas, crusty bread with creamy aioli, sweet dates wrapped in bacon, juicy tender meatballs, lightly fried seafood, mouth-watering garlic prawns in chili oil and a tasty seafood paella, all washed down with some excellent Sangria.

After our sumptuous dinner we're walking on Las Ramblas again. "Shall we do some shopping?" Farshad asks. Now I still feel shy when he suggests the shopping, but I also know how happy his presents made me in Paris. So I nod and say: "That would be lovely darling, thank you." And with a smile he leads me into an expensive looking shoe store. I close my eyes for a second after we enter, inhaling the rich scent of leather.

"Honey buy yourself some nice booties," he says. Well, I linger around in the store and marvel. The boots here are simply stunning, all made of beautiful expensive leather. It doesn't take long before a friendly girl has one glance at Farshad's watch and comes over to help me. And she brings me arms full to try. Finally I choose a beautiful pair made of cognac coloured leather.

"Thank you darling," I tell Farshad when we are back outside and I'm proudly wearing my beautiful new cognac booties. "They are lovely. Now whenever I am wearing them I think of you." He gives me a sideways glance. "Only when you are wearing them?" he asks with a naughty smile. "Of course not. Always."

But we don't have much time left. We have to catch our flight. Back in the hotel Farshad takes his money from the safe and hands me 1600 euros with a kind smile. "I hope you don't get any bad feelings with me giving you money honey," he says. I smile warmly at him. "Not at all honey. How can I feel bad? You are helping me. That makes me happy. Nobody has ever helped me before." And I add the Iranian 'I love you' – Fadat Besham – while I kiss him.

We take a cab back to the airport. Farshad is going back to Teheran, I'm flying back to the UK. And as always he has booked our flights so he has the time to see me off. He kisses me in front of customs and is waving at me until I am out of sight. And right there and then I feel a pang of love for him again. And a slight sensation of tearfulness...

CHAPTER THIRTEEN: SWEET DECEMBER

Over these months, my relationship with Rudolph has settled into a routine. He sends me messages every day, visits every week, we make love twice during our meeting – the second time always after spooning up – and he is the first one who makes me come without me helping.

By now Christmas is fast approaching and life is sweet. For the first time since ages I don't have to worry about money and Rudolph loads us with gifts. Now the girls will never know of course, Santa is especially good this year.

When Rudolph invites me for a fancy early-Christmas dinner, I'm all excited. Especially since it's in Sushisamba, one of London's top-notch Japanese restaurants. I send Amanda tons of pictures while picking a dress, then put on my hold-ups but no knickers. In my bag I'm carrying a mirror, a lipstick and a variety pack of condoms. For one thing I have decided: this dinner is going to be an adventure.

As I slip the condoms in my bag I smile a naughty little smile as I remember. *Wasn't I once smiling at the thought of myself carrying condoms in my purse? And that was only a year ago…*

Rudolph is waiting for me in front of Heron Tower and as he kisses me I guide his hands down to my bum while I whisper in his ear: "What am I wearing underneath?" He looks at me surprised. "I don't know?" Then a look of understanding crosses his face. "You're wearing..." I nod. *Nothing...* His cheeks flush.

A panoramic glass elevator whisks us from the ground to the 39th floor – and make my ears pop. "We might bump into Hugh Grant," Rudolph says as he kisses me lightly. "He is a regular here." Fact is, I'm quite excited about going to Sushisamba. I first heard of the place on an episode of 'Sex and the City', but I haven't been there since it has opened in London.

First we pass through the bar area, featuring one of Sushisamba's three kitchens. The main dining room has dramatic ceilings with bamboo and offers gob-smacking views of London with floor-to-ceiling glass on three sides. The views are stretching towards Canary Wharf and the Olympic Stadium. A grid of lights hang through the open bamboo ceiling at varying heights and create a magical intimate dining experience.

We are shown to a semi-booth facing outwards with views over East London, including the Olympic Stadium. Now when I take one look at the menu – and the prizes – I decide I am not even going to think about it. I will let him choose.

I love that about Sugar Daddies. Well the four I've had so far at least. They always select the wine and I let them choose most of the dishes. I also love the fact that they always pay. Especially after The Ex and his never-ending money problems, it gives me this warm feeling of being looked after.

As he opens his menu, Rudolph leans towards me. "This is one of only a handful of UK restaurants licensed to import Kobe beef," he states with importance. I must look puzzled, for he explains: "That is the most premium form of Wagyu available."

Sushisamba delivers a unique blend of Japanese, Brazilian and Peruvian cuisine and the cocktails are as experimental as the food. As I sip on a Padron pepper margarita – chosen by Rudolph – I watch how he prepares our culinary adventure.

He orders a wide variety of dishes. They are a unique combination and each is rich in flavour in their own individual way. The Rock Shrimp Tempura is served with snap pea julienne, spicy mayonnaise and black truffle vinaigrette.

The totally sumptuous Chicarron De Calamar – Calamari with less oil and thinner batter than usual, leaving the flavour of the squid come through – fuses nicely with the fried plantain, tomatoes, onion, mint and tamarind.

And Rudolph keeps choosing. *This dinner is going to cost him half a fortune.* The Peruvian skewers come with silky salmon, orange miso and Peruvian dark chocolate giving a fusion of savoury and sweet. I brace a mouthful of yellowtail sashimi with jalapeno. Now these are some of the best things I've ever eaten and they make me want to savour their deliciousness.

We also talk a lot during dinner. We don't talk about his wife. Nor about any of our kids. We just talk about love, sex and relationships. I'm not really my true self though. I'm acting like this flirty mistress, and it's fun to be in that role. When I excuse myself to go to the Ladies, I know he is looking at me as I walk away, knowing I'm not wearing anything underneath.

After dinner he offers me a ride home. And as the elevator whisks us down, he pulls me towards him and kisses me, his hand fingering over my dress, making sure I am really not wearing any underwear.

Now I always thought Volvo's were just decent family cars, but his Volvo XC90 is huge and feels grant. There is nothing family-like about it. Though Rudolph seems to think otherwise. "My wife thought I should be the one with the family-car," he sighs. "So now I'm driving around in this tank to all my business meetings, while she has the nice sports car." And I can only imagine what his wife's 'nice sports car' must look like ...

When we're driving on the highway, I remember I was going to make this dinner an adventure. So first I caress his dick for some time. It's rock hard. And then I open his zipper and take it in my hand.

It's so nice – hard and warm. I lick my hand and start jerking him off. As usual, he reacts strongly. Getting even more in the mood, I bow down and take his dick softly in my mouth. First licking it, sucking, then moving slow, faster, faster. The guy gasps as he drives on.

Close to my house, he lets the car slip into an empty parking lot and pulls me on top of him. We both glance around to check no one is there. *I'm not wearing any underpants so this is going to be easy…* And I have loads of condoms in my purse…

I've never had sex in a car before and neither has he. Now it might seem all nice in movies, but in reality it kind of sucks. I have basically no space for my legs, as I sit on top of him. On one side is the door, on the other side the clutch. It's highly uncomfortable. I do manage to make him come and then quickly slip off.

I make two mental notes. *It's a nice memory to have had sex in a car. It's also not something I necessarily need to repeat.* But I will remember this, that's for sure. It's a place I will pass with a smile, every time I drop off the girls with their dad…

For our next adventure, we decide it's time for the world of bondage. I've never tried it before, but being a Sugar Babe, I guess I'm allowed to explore my kinky side.

I prepare our session very carefully. I choose some soft shawls to bind and blindfold him with, and I select items that are all different to the touch – and try them out with my eyes closed to see how they feel.

So I end up with a spiky hairbrush, a soft feather duster and ice cubes ready in the freezer. Amanda also suggests clothespins as nipple clamps, but I decide to leave those for now.

Next I put on some music – so he won't know where I am – and light scented candles all around the room for some extra atmosphere. It's 9 in the morning, but who cares.

I open the door for him in just my kimono, wearing nothing underneath. Rudolph smiles as I take him up, help him out of his clothes, ask him to lie down naked on my bed, softly bind his hands and feet with my shawls and put a shawl around his eyes.

For a moment I watch him as he is lying there. All in my power. His beautiful body slightly shaking from excitement. Then I go down to get some ice on a tray, leaving him there waiting.

Back in the bed I slowly draw the ice on his body, leaving a trail of goose bumps behind. He reacts strongly. Especially when I put the ice on his nipples and the inside of his thighs. He just can't stay still. I put the ice in my mouth and take his dick between my lips, softly letting the ice cubes touch the tip from time to time.

Next is the feather duster. He has no idea what I am touching him with, but he is squirming underneath me whenever the soft feathers touch his skin, his nipples, the tip of his dick…

The brush follows. Its spikes are quite rough on his skin, they turn it red and leave another trail of goose bumps. Using the music to hide my sounds, I make sure he never knows where I am. I want to surprise him, as he is lying there expectantly, wondering what I will do next.

I tease around with the kissing. Licking his lips, almost letting him kiss me, sometimes kissing passionately, sometimes pulling back. I tease his dick. Sitting down on it, rubbing it softly with my pussy, almost letting him enter me, then pulling away.

When I finally take away the scarves, he is ecstatic. He flips me over and takes me hard in doggy, while I help myself to orgasm. We both come fiercely. As we lie panting next to each other he kisses me on my nose. "Next time it's your turn, dear."

And so it is. I have everything ready for him. He makes me strip and lie down naked on the bed. *Now this is exciting…* He kisses me one more time before he blindfolds me and ties my hands and feet to the bed.

I'm all in his power. And it's highly arousing, lying like this. He can do anything with me ... And with the music on I have no idea where he is going to touch me. All I can do is wait.

As he touches me, I gasp. Not being able to see, it feels like all other senses are dramatically heightened. His hands are softer then I remember them to be. The feathers are so soft and fluffy, they give me the shivers each time they touch my skin.

First he uses a light touch to heighten my sensitivity and pleasure. Next he uses the soft tip to gently caress my skin all over. He uses a combination of barely-there touches and pro-longed strokes, paying attention to how I react to each of them.

The spikes of the brush hurt a little, but in a nice way. They leave an intense tingling feeling on my skin. My body is tingling from head-to-toe and I am left with an extra sensitive skin. Not being able to see him is thrilling, taking me to new levels of euphoria.

Suddenly he drips something sweet and sticky on my lips. Licking it off, I whisper: "It's honey ..." The sweetness and sticki-ness linger on my tongue. He starts teasing me with it, putting some on his tongue and pulling away every time I try to suck.

Then he drips some on the Happy Boobs and licks them until there is no trace of honey left. He does the same with my pussy, almost making me come. I normally don't let him go down on me, but what I am to do? I'm all in his power ... Next he drips some on his dick, holding it close to my mouth so I can lick or suck it, then pulling away when I get too excited.

It seems like ages before he takes off the blindfold and the cuffs. And being able to hold him now, touch him and see his handsome face has never felt any better. Making love to him, I just feel so damn close. It's like the binding and giving up control has only enhanced our closeness.

As I lay in his arms afterwards, he kisses me on my nose and says: "You know, it's funny. In this short time you have done more for me than my therapist in this whole year. I've been in therapy for a year now, but only now do I feel strong and manly again."

"True," Amanda texts when I tell her. "That's one of the functions we have. Society might frown on us, but we are more important than most people realize. You can be proud of yourself."

I kind of react to the 'we'. *I'm NOT an escort. Where is the 'we' coming from?* But I also know that the two are dangerously close… And okay, so maybe I can be proud of myself. But somehow I don't feel proud. In a way I wish I could be so much more to him…

Thing is, I'm starting to fall for this guy. I'm really looking forward to his messages, to his visits. We don't fuck, we make love. And another thing is, I think it's mutual. I'm even starting to look forward to the moment he will leave his wife.

When Rudolph tells me that he is not looking forward to his Christmas vacation, I totally understand. One year ago he discovered about his wife's affair, so Christmas must still be a painful time of the year for him. And now they are going on a ski vacation with the whole family. *It must be so hard…*

But Amanda starts bugging me. "You should get back on Seeking Arrangement," she writes. "Keep your options open. If Mr. Handsome is going on a vacation with his wife, there is a good chance that he will get back with her."

And maybe I should have listened to her. She's the expert after all. But I'm just too stubborn. Or maybe too romantic. Or whatever. Fact is, that I refuse to believe her…

CHAPTER FOURTEEN:
CHRISTMAS

By now Christmas is fast approaching. The days are a whirl of end-of-term plays, carol concerts and the special school Christmas dinner.

Eric and I have divided the Christmas holidays. The first week and on Christmas Eve the girls are with me. The second week they will be with their dad. But I force myself not to think about that ... I should focus on the good things, as Jamal has taught me. *And for one moment I wonder how he will be doing...*

Fact is that life *is* good. The girls are thrilled with the upcoming holidays and Rudolph stays in contact from his ski vacation. Not as much as usual, if I have to be honest, but let's not spoil any good vibes with honesty now shall we.

He does send a line or two and a very handsome picture that I forward to Amanda. "See?" I write. "See he is still there for me?" "Nice picture," she replies. "Who is he smiling to so sweetly? His wife?" And I ignore her for the rest of the day.

I try not to think about him too much. Thanks to our arrangement, I don't have to worry about money. So I focus on what feels like my first real Christmas with the girls. I just want it to be magical. And it helps that London puts on a fabulous show when it comes to Christmas spirit. *For a second I remember how one year ago I was lingering in front of the windows, wishing for my girls to be there.*

So the first day of their holidays, we decide to visit London especially to see the decorations. We start at the Selfridge's department store, where my girls make a beeline for the toy shop. Next we wander along Oxford and Regent Streets, enjoying the Christmas ornaments. Then we head for Trafalgar Square to see the big tree and the street performers.

The next day we go for a real Christmas tree. We've never had a real one before, but I'm sure you agree that in our new hygge house our tree has to be real. The girls cheer when I tell them so, and they pick a really big one. Thanks to Rudolph's help I'm not worrying about the cost. I just let them choose the one they love most.

Now dragging the thing back home is a challenge, but the girls do their best to help me and we manage to drag the whole damn thing back home. Next we go and buy Christmas decorations, because I left our old ones with The Ex. Except for the ones the girls made themselves, that is. The Ex wouldn't care much for those anyway.

The girls cheer as they choose real glass decorations, not the plastic ones we left behind. They choose ones that are shiny and glittery, which embody all that children can wish for decorations.

Back home we put on our Christmas CD, the one we listen to every year. And singing loudly with their little voices, the girls spend the whole day decorating our tree, ending with a fairy on top.

Since the girls will be with their father on Christmas day, I decide to have our dinner on Christmas Eve. Because one thing I have decided, nothing will stop us from having a lovely Christmas dinner together.

Before we couldn't afford a turkey for Christmas. All I could buy was a chicken. But this year is different. I take the girls to the butcher and let them choose a big juicy turkey.

Next we prepare the Christmas pudding. The girls help me with it, giggling in their pink princess aprons. They make sure our cake contains just about every dried fruit they can think of and include blanched almonds, glace cherries and candied peel.

Soon the whole kitchen is covered with dough, raisins and almonds. And even the girls look like Christmas puddings themselves. Sophie's face is covered with white flour, while she has raisins and peel sticking in her wild ginger hair and even Lisa has a white smudge on her cheek.

Not long after we have put the cake into the oven, the house is smelling like a dream. And after it's finished, the girls are thrilled with how rich and dark the cake looks. Lisa covers it with a layer of almond paste and then both girls cover it with thick white icing, which we have made with icing sugar and egg whites.

Once our Christmas pudding is finished, we make the Mince Pies with a mixture of dried fruit, raisins, sultanas and candied peel. And the girls include apples, spices and sugar. I moisten it with brandy, before we bake it in small pastry cases. And soon the whole house is filled with even more sweet smells. The pies come out sweet, rich and fruity.

Now I did think of inviting my parents and other family members for our unusual Christmas Eve dinner, but I haven't. This is our first Christmas dinner together and I want it to be with just the three of us.

Mr. Viking keeps writing me about the Danish miracle of Christmas. And I have to say it sounds lovely. Danish Christmas is full of family and traditions. Therefore it's no surprise that he totally disagrees with me. But this is our Christmas. And I'm choosing for the three of us. Well, and Fuzzy of course. He purrs away in all the cosiness.

When it's dinner time, the girls sit expectantly at the table. As a starter we have smoked salmon, but the main course is what makes them cheer. It's the turkey, with roasted potatoes, vegetables, roasted parsnips and stuffing with gravy and bread sauce. They are quite stuffed after that, but both of them still manage to get some Christmas pudding in as well.

In the meantime I simply relish our first Christmas dinner together. And watching their happy faces round the dinner table, I know one thing for sure. Leaving The Ex, and the constant tension he carried around with him, was the best thing I could have done. I did damn well. And I'm still doing damn well. The girls are happy little beings.

After dinner we take out our family board games and play games until it's time to go to bed. It's Christmas Eve of course, and little Sophie is all excited. Lisa gives me a knowing look. She knows the truth about Father Christmas, but she plays her role well as they hang up their stockings, leave mince pies and milk for Santa, carrots for his reindeer and go to bed.

Before I tuck them in, the girls jump in my bed and I read them the last chapter of Richard Scarry's 'The animal's Merry Christmas.' It's one of our Christmas traditions. We read the book every year, just like my grandmother did with me. And I love the warm cosy feeling this tradition gives me.

After their story, I tuck each of them in, cuddling and kissing. In bed is one of the few places where I am still allowed to kiss and cuddle Lisa. When I check on them before going to bed, Lisa is sleeping neatly, but Sophie is tossing around in her little bed. I straighten her hair and kiss her.

She opens her eyes and hugs me. "Mummy, Santa must be really busy, making all these toys for Christmas," she says. I nod. "Do you think he has piled all his toys onto his sleigh now? Do you think he is riding across the sky now?"

I hug her. "I'm sure he is my love. I'm sure he is riding across the sky now. But you go to sleep now. Remember, the sooner you sleep, the sooner there is a tomorrow." Sophie smiles and kisses me on my cheek. "Night mummy. Love you to the moon and back…" And she snuggles up with Big Bear before falling asleep.

The next morning the girls are up real early of course. And I have to force myself out of my warm bed as well. Fuzzy is already circling around them meowing for breakfast. I make myself some strong coffee. And when the girls open their stockings from Santa, I just sit back and take in their happy faces.

They manage to go through all in twenty minutes, tearing off all wrapping paper. And not much later we sit down for breakfast. But I feel sad. Because I know that after breakfast my short Christmas with them is over.

It hurts when I deliver the girls with The Ex and his Girlfriend, packed in their warm winter coats. I sit down in the car for a second, fighting back tears. Then, before I start the engine again, I see Lisa's face appear in front of the window. She waves at me until the Girlfriend closes the curtain. And I can't fight the tears back any longer.

Soon I'm back in my Christmas house. Alone. The tree is shining in front of the open fire. Traces of the girls are everywhere. But without them the house is just so damn empty. Fuzzy seems to understand. He meows and sits in my lap when I sit with a steaming mug of tea on the sofa. I scratch him behind his ears. And that moment I'm just so damn happy we have Fuzzy, because I have never felt this miserable on Christmas day.

It's times like these that I check Seeking Arrangement. When I need a quick-fix kick. When I feel alone. Fact is that Rudolph has been awfully quiet these last days. And in my mind's eye I can see him and his family celebrating together. *Why does it hurt to think of that? All I have with him is an arrangement…*

Then there is Farshad. He seems to have vanished again. Apparently disappearing is something he is really good at. And then there is Sam … We have been emailing off and on since I visited Singapore. And whenever I contact him, he wants to meet me. But since the sex kind of sucked, I normally turn him down kindly. Telling him I can't because of the kids.

Well, now I can … I have a whole freaking week by myself. And though the sex might suck, I'm definitely in for some adventure. Something to keep my mind off my girls. So I send him a mail, I drink way too much wine and go to bed way too late.

The next morning I have mail. It's a message from Sam. He is in Hong Kong now, he tells me. In his Hong Kong apartment. Would I like to come visit him? Now I didn't even know he also had an apartment in Hong Kong, but I don't need much time to answer. I give Fuzzy a last crawl under her chin before I contact the cat sitter.

CHAPTER FIFTEEN:
THE FRAGRANT HARBOUR

So here I am, flying to Hong Kong. Another place I have never visited. And I can only muse about how different my life has become. Now I was hoping for a view of the city during descent, but when I look out of the window I sigh. There's nothing but clouds. It isn't until we are just about to touch down on the tarmac that we finally break through the foggy-haze clouds.

The airport is really hot. It smells of exhaust, food and recycled air with the faint scent of sweat and humidity. Though the air conditioner is blasting, there is a familiar clammy feeling that clings to my arms and hands. This feels like... Singapore. Just like in Singapore, the air feels thicker here than in the UK.

Now I had expected to get away from the Christmas spirit here, but as soon as I get through the superefficient and que-less airport, I walk into a leaping reindeer showered in glitter that is towering over me. And it's not the only one, there are decorations *everywhere:* oversized trees, plastic deer, angels, just anything I can possibly imagine.

Sam is waiting for me at the airport, with his black hair streaked with grey, his Asian eyes behind his gold-rimmed glasses. He seems sad and lost between all the Christmas decorations. And at that moment I realize why he has made me come. *Joshua...* This must be the time of year which he dreads most.

I can see the sadness in his eyes, but he hides it fast enough. "Welcome in Hong Kong," he says and leads me to the cabs.

In the cab, after some polite chit-chat about flights and the weather, he seems to be lost in his own thoughts and I stare out of the window. Now the taxi driver is driving warp speed. It feels like we are going faster than a bullet train, and when we hit a long stretch of freeway the driver takes over all the other cars. In a way I wonder why Sam doesn't get scared, since he has already been in a car crash and all. And for a moment I wonder: *was it here?* But when I look at him I realize that this is a man who has lost all that was precious to him. He has nothing to be afraid of anymore.

Even with the speed, it takes about forty-five minutes, through two tolls and many bridges before we finally arrive in the city area. And here the cab is thankfully slowed down due to traffic congestion.

Hong Kong is modern, with sky scrapers all around, but this is not a place where I could live. In Singapore I could, or at least I think I can. But one thing I learned in Venice: you never know how living in a place really is, until you do so.

Sam turns towards me and asks: "Did you know that Hong Kong means 'fragrant harbour' in Cantonese?" I shake my head as the taxi stops. But we're not in front of a beautiful Singapore shop house. We're in front of a Hong Kong skyscraper.

Sam's apartment is on the sixteenth flour and it's rather small. It has a bedroom, a tiny kitchen, a view on other apartments and – as he happily informs me – an indoor swimming pool on the first floor. But I have to get accustomed to the various city noises: the cars, horns, garbage trucks, loud water pipes, shouting, loud cell phone callers and construction that is going on somewhere.

Sam follows my eyes as I look around. "It's not like my Singapore home, right?" he asks and smiles. "I lived here right after graduation, when I was hired by an architecture firm based in Hong Kong. I moved back to Singapore years ago, but I'm keeping this on and rent it out through Airbnb." And he goes to the kitchen to make me some tea.

In a way Sam seems different here. He seems lighter. And there is no room with his son's name on it. I wonder if this is where he lived before his marriage. Whether here he is reminded of his earlier years.

"I know this place isn't big," he says when he hands me a cup of green tea. "But this is Hong Kong. Here you get an apartment about the size of a Manhattan apartment, if not smaller." And he laughs as he puts a strand of hair behind my ear. *I had forgotten this habit of his…*

"You know," he says, "if everyone on the planet lived as close together as in Hong Kong, all of humanity would be able to fit in Egypt." Sam looks around. "But I like this place. It's downtown, and I live far south enough to be considered Soho."

When we have finished our tea and he takes me out to explore, Soho turns out to be a fun neighbourhood. It has lots of cafes, restaurants, boutiques, art galleries, bars and parks. And there are a few streets that look like they could be taken right out of the UK, but then I turn a corner and I'm clearly in Asia. With Cantonese signs, Asian food stalls and tiny shops lining the streets.

Both Sam and I seem to avoid noticing all the Christmas decorations. They feel out of place to me anyway, since I'm dying from the heat. And it reminds both of us of loved ones we don't want to think of.

Christmas seems different here. There is no mention of Christmas dinners, which to me is the most important feature of it. And Sam explains that it is rare to give presents, which is the most important feature for the girls. Here it mostly seems to be a festive period, to enjoy the decorations and a week off work.

"Seeing all the decorations makes me sad," I tell him. "It makes me miss my girls." Sam grabs my hand and holds me tight. "Me too," he says. "Joshua loved to watch all the decorations with me."

And for a moment there, the two of us holding on to each other in the middle of all the Christmas-spirits, I feel so connected to him. No one else has ever understood. And when I look in his eyes it seems he feels the same.

Sam takes me down to Central, which is filled with shopping centres connected through bridges. And I notice a strange pattern of people on the bridges. Everywhere are women, sitting on flattened cardboard boxes, chit-chatting and unpacking food. It actually looks like they are having a picnic.

As we pass more and more of them, I ask Sam: "Who are these cardboard ladies?" Sam laughs. "Many are from the Philippines. They work as live-in help. On Sundays, they have a day off. So they meet in the city and have picnic lunches there." Now personally I can image loads of other interesting places to have picnics, but the women seem to be having a ball.

"You know why there are so many skyscrapers?" he asks me. I shake my head. "Hong Kong is the world's most densely populated area. To compensate, they build upwards. Therefore all these buildings are incredibly tall." And so are the trams and busses I notice. They are all double decked and make me almost feel like I'm home.

I also notice that because of the British history, there is a level of comfort to the city. Everywhere around me there is the English language and familiar food. But I do also feel out of place, because almost everyone here is Asian. I feel like a tall white girl in a sea of Asians hurrying around.

Now Hong Kong has a scent of its own. There is an essential base scent of the salty ocean, like in Barcelona. But here is also an exotic scent. The air can be thick with the strong scent of incense. Or with the fragrant sweet smell from the steam of bamboo steamer caskets. Or the vile odour of spiky durians. There is the smell of ginger and also of many unknown spices. Of scents I cannot describe.

As dusk is falling, we take a cab to Kowloon. It's another area of Hong Kong, just over the water from Central. "Do you know what the name means?" Sam asks in the taxi, kissing me on my cheek. I shake my head. "No I don't." "Kowloon comes from 'Gou Lung' which means 'Nine Dragons' in the local language. The Song Dynasty's Emperor Bing named the area for its eight tallest mountains." He chuckles before he continues. "The ninth dragon was the emperor himself of course."

After we cross the bridge and are riding through the streets it feels different. The streets are wider here and busier. And in a way it feels a bit like Manhattan. Not that I have ever been to Manhattan, but the Manhattan I know from the movies. But then a Manhattan full of Asians and Asian restaurants

"This is the darker and the more fascinating side of Hong Kong," Sam tells me. "It managed to escape some of your British colonial influences." And he gives me a stern look. "Prices tend to be cheaper, but it is also less tourist-friendly and English proficiency is not as strong as on the Hong Kong side."

The taxi stops in front of a hotel and with an elevator we whizz up to the restaurant on the 28th floor. The restaurant is elegant and welcoming, with muted colours, wooden floors and round tables facing floor to ceiling windows which show the city's amazing skyline.

When we are handed the menu, it has traditional Cantonese cuisine with a modern twist. But as is usual nowadays, I take one look at the prices and let Sam choose. He chooses a menu which starts with a bouncy textured Kung Pao Lobster with a spicy kick and a matching wine with a touch of acidity to counterbalance the spice.

Next we have wok-fried giant Garoupa fillet – a meaty fish – with black truffle, paired with a red Pinot Noir with earthy flavours. And we are served wok-fried beautifully tender wagyu beef cubes with crunchy green apple, mustard and a subtle hint of wasabi paired with sake. To finish we get a crumbly almond cookie with sweet chilled mango sago cream with chunks of pomelo, paired with a glass of sweet Japanese plum wine.

When we are finished with our dinner, we take a cab back to Sam's apartment. There won't be any Dettol baths, I'm happy to realize. He has no bath in his small Hong Kong apartment. Instead we both take a shower. Sam washes himself with his Dettol, I use my own lavender body wash which I took from the hotel in Barcelona.

When I come out and into his small bedroom, Sam starts kissing me. His gold-rimmed glasses are on the night stand and his Asian eyes are mesmerizing. They give him this beautiful exotic look. Though the Dettol scent which is still lingering on his skin is not a big turn on, I try to focus on the positive.

Sam pulls me on the bed. And this time he has a condom ready. *Apparently the guy is not only into wanking.* He rolls it on and then pulls me on top of him. I love the feeling of his Asian skin. It's soft but firm and feels lovely.

His curtains are still open and his bed is next to the window. Outside are the many lights of Hong Kong. This city never seems to sleep. And as I ride on top of him, I'm mesmerized by his Asian eyes. It's like I'm in another world. An exotic world. And for a moment I forget all about my normal life.

But then he pulls himself out of me and starts wanking again, telling me: "Please help yourself." After he comes he tells me: "That was marvellous." Then he turns around and falls asleep. But I can't sleep. I toss and turn in his bed until I must have finally drifted off.

***

When I wake up, Sam is already out of bed, wearing only jeans and showing off his nice torso. He is making me scrambled eggs on toast. "You know, things were so exciting when I just moved here," he tells me as he pours me a cup of hot coffee. And by the tone of his voice, I know he is talking about a different life. A life before his losses.

"I had just finished university in the US and then I got this exciting new job. We were re-inventing the villages in the mainland." He puts our plates on the table. "It was amazing. We would wipe away whole traditional hutong neighbourhoods and rebuild the cities. We were like Gods. WE would decide where the centre was going to be, where the shops."

Sam notices when I shuffle. "You like the hutongs, right?" he asks me. "Aren't those the traditional Chinese neighbourhoods?" I ask him. Sam nods and I answer: "Yes, I do actually." I have seen pictures of them and I just love the traditional Chinese houses.

Sam stares into space for a while before he continues: "I know. Most Westerners do. But they are awful to live in, you know. Most don't even have their own bathroom ..."

Romantic Westerner as I may be, I'm not totally convinced so I don't answer. And Sam doesn't talk to me for a while after that. For the first time I notice that he can be rather stubborn when someone doesn't accept his ideas. But he loosens up once we are outside.

He takes me on a train to the end of one of the MTR lines and from there we clamber onto a large cable car. "We are going to Lantau Island," Sam tells me. "Up the mountain to see the Big Buddha. Let me show you some traditional Chinese culture" and he laughs. *Apparently he is not pissed anymore,* I think with a sigh of relief. Or maybe he never was, I realize. It's hard to read him.

The ride up is spectacular. Sam has booked us the Crystal Cabin which has a glass floor and gives amazing views over the mountains. I can even look out to the airport, where I see planes taking off.

In the meantime Sam fills me in with information. Lantau Island is the largest island in Hong Kong, he tells me. It was originally the site of fishing villages and situated at the mouth of the Pearl River.

We first walk to the remote Po Lin Monastery, hidden away by lush mountains. It's colourful, with red outer walls, yellow roof tiles, the floor in the main hall is adorned with lotus flower patterns and three Buddha's sit on the flowers.

Next we climb up to the Big Buddha and the stairs are an impressive flight. When we are around halfway I ask Sam panting: "How many steps are there?" "Two hundred and fifty," Sam says and he doesn't pant at all.

God do I feel out of shape... "Don't worry," he tells me. "You can take some rest on your way up." I kindly decline, wipe the sweat off my forehead and feel a little embarrassed when a whole family of worshippers – including young children – passes without any sweat or panting, bending down to the stones on each step.

But finally we are at the top. And the Buddha truly *is* huge. "It's 34-meters," Sam tells me. "It's the world's largest, seated, outdoor Bronze Buddha. Built to symbolize the stability of Hong Kong," He gestures towards it. "See, each feature of it is symbolic and means something deep, virtuous and spiritual."

He points out the different elements as he explains them to me. "The pearl and conch hair represent wisdom, the right hand is in the gesture of compassion from sufferings, the left hand is fulfilling wishes and granting blessings to all, the cross-legged lotus-seat represents purity."

He smiles at me and says: "So what are you waiting for? Make a wish!" So as I take in the beautiful view, I do. I make one wish. I wish that I will be able to live well off my writing. Sure I have a book published now, but it barely sells. It's hard to live off just writing. But hey, I can wish for anything right? So that's what I wish for.

When we are back down, Sam takes me into the dining hall of the monastery for an authentic vegetarian Buddhist lunch. In the hall, the food typically eaten by the monks is served with a set menu. But Sam takes me into the VIP room for a deluxe version – it's the same food but served privately on our own table rather than sharing a table with others.

We get a very nice pumpkin soup, vegetarian lemon chicken with vegetables, tofu and oyster sauce, all served with rice in the traditional Cantonese style. And as desert we have mango filled rice dumplings and a freshly made bean curd dessert which we both share.

When we are finished, he looks at me with a twinkle in his eye. "Are you up for another traditional experience?" I nod. *Sure. I'm all in for traditional experiences.* "I'll take you to Tai O," Sam says. "It will be really traditional." And he chuckles.

The moment we get out of the monastery, he halts a cab and we drive down the mountain. "Tai O is home to the Tanka people, a community of fisher folk," Sam tells me. "They built their houses on stilts above the tidal flats of Lantau Island."

And it's beautiful. The houses are all interconnected, forming a tightly knit community that lives on the water. "Stilted houses were once common across Hong Kong," Sam tells me, "but Tai O is the last remaining stilted fishing village."

Now it's all very charming, if it weren't for the stench. It's very obvious that fish remain a central part of Tai O life. Salted fish and scallops are drying on verandas and the scent of the village's shrimp paste lingers in the air. The odour simply makes me feel sick. So I'm quite happy when Sam doesn't seem to be keen on staying too long.

And I *have* to go back, I realize when I check my watch. I have a plane to catch. We have a quick stop at his house so I can collect my things and at the airport we politely say goodbye to each other.

"Thank you," he says, "you made me forget … for the first time ever …" We hug, but then I have to go. And just before I turn the corner, I can see sadness is already filling his eyes again …

Back in my empty home Fuzzy is waiting for me. I sigh. Hong Kong was lovely, but I still have many days without the girls. And to make things even more splendid, I then get a message from Rudolph. And the moment I get it, I realize that he has been very quiet these days …

Amanda was right. Of course. First of all he wishes me a happy New Year. Next he would like to inform me that he wants to end our arrangement. His vacation has made him realize that he wants to fight for his marriage. They will go into marriage counselling …

And of course I *knew* it was just an arrangement. Whatever I had with Rudolph wasn't a real relationship. In fact, it wasn't much more than sex. We only had dinner once. Still, it felt like more. So much more. Still, *I* felt more. And I can't help it. I just feel totally utterly miserable …

But it's a waste of good drinking time to stay miserable for too long. And New Year's Eve the girls spend with me, filling the house with their voices. So I focus on them. I wake them just before countdown and look at their cold, rosy faces illuminated by the fireworks. On moments like that, my heart just swells from love for them.

When they are back in bed, I contemplate on my past year. Sure, it hurts that Rudolph is gone. But when I look back on it, 2016 has been quite an incredible year. I met four lovely men – Mr. Viking, Farshad, Sam and Rudolph. I've travelled to Barcelona, Paris, Berlin, Singapore and Hong Kong. I have my own hygge house. And the girls are happy and doing well. *What else could I wish for?*

Next I open my diary and read last year's New Year's resolutions. And it makes me smile. It's amazing how many of them really happened. I can't even imagine how much my life has changed this past year. It has been one hell of a year. So I think for some time before I write down my resolutions for 2017:

- Make more money
- Find inner peace: start yoga and meditate
- Face my fears and insecurities
- Get rid of negative people
- Have a year of firsts – do things I have never done before

It's 2017, a brand new year full of possibilities. And I'm sure it's going to be swell.

CHAPTER SIXTEEN: KICKED OUT

It's a cold Saturday in February. Snow has fallen and the girls are running around in the garden, wearing their snow boots, pink woollen hats and gloves. They are having a snowball fight together.

I'm at the kitchen table writing Amanda's story on my laptop, watching them from time to time through the window. A mug of hot coffee is next to me, Fuzzy is purring beside me. And whenever I look at the girls I smile. *Life is good. I can't even imagine how different it was one year ago.*

But I'm not as relaxed as I may seem. Because in the back of my head is this nagging worry. *Money.* Now I saved enough money to survive for two months after Rudolph. But the second month is now coming to a close way too fast. And fact is that I'm running out of money.

With a sigh I get on the internet. I guess it's time to re-activate my account on Seeking Arrangement. Now it's easy to get back on, because if you choose so, your profile is never really deleted. So I'm back in no time.

And one thing I notice. I get way more messages once I'm 'new'. It's like most daddies are searching for the new girls. So I decide to keep this in mind, for it might be wise to unsubscribe and subscribe again once in a while…

Now the moment I log in again, I get a whole load of 'Time Wasters' – as Amanda likes to call them. Guys that just want to chat or get naked pictures without any intention to meet. It's something I don't do. I never send naked pictures. But I'm just about to log off, when I get a message that sounds promising:

> "You are a rare find indeed. I am in search of a real lady for fun and adventure. Kindly check me out. With kindest regards."

I check out his profile. He is an American, divorced, mid-fifties and living in Paris. His profile reads:

> "Free thinker, Idea man, Mentor, World Traveller, Entrepreneur. Traveling and living abroad has given me a world view and a broad and deep knowledge to draw my inspiration from."

I thank him for his message and his reply comes quickly:

> "Thank you for the kind words and exciting news you are interested in learning more. We could have a lot "no fuss" "life is too short" FUN. And the fun could turn into an adventure ..."

But when the girls get back in – their cheeks, noses and foreheads red from the cold – I tell The American that I will contact him that evening. I unpack the girls and make them two mugs of steaming hot chocolate, settle them at the kitchen table and get a board game.

That evening The American and I chat quite nicely. He tells about his life in Paris, how he is interested in art and museums and that he wants to come to London to meet me. "I can come any weekend," he writes, "You pick one." So I pick the coming weekend when the girls are gone.

That night when I snuggle down under the duvet and close my eyes, it doesn't take long before I drift off to sleep. *Finally I'm not worrying about money...* But I did forget one thing though. I told him that I am looking for someone who can help me, but I forgot to arrange our agreement any further...

So that weekend I go to Heathrow to pick him up. But the moment I see The American swishing out of the doors my stomach turns. Now of course I already know he is bald. I have seen his pictures. And though I'm not particularly into bald guys, dating Farshad has kind of changed my mind. But the guy looks way older than his pictures, he is short, fat and is wearing pants that keep slipping down his ass.

For one split second I can see Rudolph in my mind. And I sigh, because thinking about him hurts. Even if I don't want to admit it. *How the hell am I going to stay in a hotel with this American?* And I am tempted to leave, since the guy hasn't spotted me yet.

But my conscience doesn't let me. This guy has come all the way from Paris especially to meet me, I need to show him some courtesies. So I swallow hard and introduce myself.

The American is friendly enough. He smiles, is kind and has brought me macarons. So I smile and guide him to the taxi stand, where he chooses a Tesla to drive us to the Hilton. He is friendly enough to the driver. They chat about Tesla's and what makes it so nice to drive them. So I try to relax. I straighten my skirt, sit back and listen.

But when we check in, I feel highly uncomfortable. I'm so obviously British. I'm so obviously normally *not* dating a guy like this. And I feel like 'HOOKER' is written all over me... So when he tries to kiss me in the elevator, I turn away and keep my distance.

In the room I still keep my distance. I keep my coat on, sit down on a chair and just keep my space, while The American unpacks his suitcase. When he is finished he tries to get close to me again, but I ask whether he wants to see a museum. He nods, so I jump out of the chair, practically run out of the hotel and call for a cab to take us to the British Museum.

I know it is not fair. He is doing everything he can to be kind to me. But I'm feeling so self-conscious about being with this very fat American that I make sure to keep my distance from him while racing through the museum.

Luckily the British Museum is big. You can run around for a couple of hours before people start thinking about their hotel again. But it's sad that you can't keep running through the British Museum for days.

So next I propose to drink something in the museum cafe. The American chooses a nice window seat as he gets us two cappuccinos and muffins. Outside I can see people struggling to get through the cold snow. And just by seeing their faces I know how bloody cold it is. So it's nice to sit inside and warm my hands on my mug.

But I can't relax. I know there is something I still need to do. For we haven't agreed on an arrangement... But I also feel very uncomfortable talking about it, because I actually don't want to sleep with him. And once we've set a price, it feels like I'll have to...

"You're a single mother, right?" The American asks, sipping his coffee. I nod. "Yes I am. I have two girls." "So where is their father, does he still play a role in their lives?" I shrug. "Not really," I admit. "Not as much as I'd hope for them. He's is mostly busy with work, church and the New Girlfriend. Having them every other weekend is like this obligation, not something he really seems to love or enjoy doing. It doesn't seem to come from his heart, you know."

I look outside for a while, at a kid throwing snowballs, before I continue. "It's not really his fault though," I say. "He has some personality issues, you know. I honestly don't think he is able to have any deep personal relationships."

The American looks serious. "I'm so sorry," he says. "I'm so sorry to hear that. See I always tried to be a real good father for my daughters. I tried to be in their lives, to be involved. It's so much fun to be."

Now he is the one looking outside before he continues. "But I wasn't raised like that. My own father was a tyrant. If I did anything he didn't like, he'd beat the living daylight out of me." He looks down on his hands. I put my hand over his and say: "I'm so sorry" but he quickly pulls his hands back. Pity is obviously not something he wants. He gets up and says: "Let's go."

Now while we are waiting for our coats, I just *know* he is all ready to propose going to the hotel again, so I check the time. *It's early, but not too early...* So I tell him: "Would you be interested in an early dinner? I am actually quite hungry." The American is eager to please. He nods, takes my arm the moment we are outside and asks me to take us to a nice restaurant.

We find a lovely place close to the museum. I order a salmon steak with mustard sauce and asparagus, The American orders a flank steak with baked potatoes and we share a bottle of Chablis.

"So why are you on Seeking Arrangement?" I ask him, to start conversation. It's one of the questions I ask a lot. The American smiles as he pushes his glasses up his nose with his middle finger.

"Well I divorced a year ago," he says. "See, I was married for twenty years, but I was never faithful. I was always traveling for work, so I was alone a lot of the time. And there were always temptations. So I cheated. A lot. Then since my divorce I have promised myself to be honest. To myself and to the ladies."

The American studies me for a moment before he asks me: "I don't believe in monogamy... Do you?" I think about that for a moment. "Well, I used to ... I always thought I was monogamous. But lately I'm not so sure ..."

"I'm not into escorts," The American continues. "I tried that. A lot. But I simply miss the connection most of the time. Though nothing is black and white of course. I also had escorts with whom there was a true connection ..." And he stares into the distance for some time.

"So that's what I want," he then says as he pushes his glasses back up his nose with his middle finger. "I want a relationship, but not monogamous. And I want to be open and honest to each other."

Now that he is talking about escorts and honesty, I *know* this is the perfect time to talk about the financial side of our arrangement, but I'm just too shy. And I'm still not convinced I want to fuck this guy. By now, I have finished most of the Chablis by myself. But even with the alcohol in my body, I don't feel like sleeping with him.

After dinner he helps me into my coat and I just *know* he is thinking about the hotel again. So I decide to keep him busy. "Would you like to see a show?" I ask him. He nods, though not very convincingly. "Shall we go and see 'Cats' at the London Palladium? I think you could still get tickets online ..." He nods, though still not very induced, while he checks his phone and I stop a cab.

Now it has been years since I have seen Cats. I was still a little girl. And I have to say I truly enjoy the show. I simply love the grand old building, the fabulous costumes and we have a front circle seat with an amazing view of the stage.

This new version seems to have a lot more dancing and less singing, but it is still amazing. The cast combines athleticism with stunning ballet as well as darned good singing, some of which is just spellbinding, especially the final rendition of 'Memories'.

On the other hand a musical might not have been the best choice. Because sitting next to me, The American is only getting hotter. And god am I feeling self-conscious with this fat guy next to me.

When he tries to put his arm around me, I feel like freaking SCREAMING. I manage to fake a sneeze to get rid of it. And one thing I decide right there and then. I am NOT going to sleep with this guy. But I still have no idea how to let him know politely. I do feel bad for him, coming all the way to see me.

After the show I can't come up with any more excuses, so we head towards the hotel. *With lead in my shoes.* "How did you like 'Cats'?" I ask him in the cab, to keep up conversation. "Well, it doesn't really have a very strong narrative, does it?" he says. I nod and say: "True, it's based on poems by T.S. Eliot and is more about the dancing and the portrayal of the different cats." He doesn't reply to that, but watches quietly as we speed through the London night streets.

Back in the hotel I put on my sexy nightgown in the bathroom *and regret I didn't bring anything less sexy.* When I come out – covering my breasts with my arms – he is already in bed. And not wearing much, by the looks of it. I run around to my side, jump in under the duvet and say: "Let's watch a movie on TV!"

The American sighs, puts on the TV and we watch some movie. It's an awful movie, but who cares. I act like I am really interested and do my best to remain on my edge of the bed. When the movie is over The American bends over to kiss me. But I turn my head and tell him I am sleepy. I say goodnight to him and turn around.

I don't sleep much that night, lying next to this naked guy. Yes, he is naked. I know, because I saw it when he got up to get his mobile, in the light coming in from the streetlamp. And the shrivelled worm I saw is *not* going to make me change my mind.

* * *

Luckily, when morning comes the guy is still asleep. So I jump under the shower and get dressed. When I come out of the bathroom, he is dressed as well and asks me whether we shall go for breakfast. I sprint in front of him – doing anything to look like I have nothing to do with this guy – and splurge on the huge breakfast buffet.

When we come back to the room, I ask The American: "So what museum are we going to today?" But he looks at me tiredly. Then he takes out his wallet and hands me a bunch of bills – five hundred pounds in total.

"You know, Monique I really like you," he says. "But I don't think you like me. I don't think we are going to do much more than this. So we better not waste each other's time. I still have some work to do." And with that he literally shoves me out of the room and closes the door in my face.

So what do I do? I take the elevator back down and walk a couple of blocks through the snow-lined streets. I'm not up for public transportation yet. In a way I feel like I am in a trance.

I wrap my arms around me, because it's icy cold outside. The sound of my heels echoes softly of the pavement, dimmed by the thick white snow. The wind carries the scent of wet snow as it blows through my hair. And inside my feelings are blowing like the wind.

On the one hand I feel bad for being kicked out of the room. For living a lifestyle that makes me even consider having sex with men like this. But on the other hand I feel this great relief that nothing happened. For a moment I focus my thoughts on Rudolph. And thinking of him makes me smile.

When I am finally up for the tube I text Amanda. She reacts surprised. I don't think she understands my problems with sleeping with this guy. "He gave you 500 for nothing?" she asks in disbelief. "Monique, this was a good one! If he gives you 500 for nothing, can you imagine how he can help you when you start an arrangement with him?" But all I do is shrug. At that moment, I honestly don't care.

Later on I will wonder of course. *If The American had made me a nice offer, would I have slept with him?* In my former life – before becoming a Sugar Baby – the answer would have been easy: hell no.

But as this year progresses and I have been a Sugar Babe for longer, gaining more experience, I will know that probably I would have. See, when money becomes an issue, and you want to protect your kids, there are a lot of things you are willing to do. And there are a lot of things that I am going to do that I would never have believed before…

But for now I am home and happy I didn't do anything. I take a shower to feel clean, because for some reason even wondering whether I was going to sleep with the guy makes me feel dirty. Then I slip into something comfortable, make myself a cup of tea and watch the snow outside with Fuzzy purring in my lap.

Tomorrow I will pick up the girls. Eventually I will forget all about this. But one thing I know. I do need to get an arrangement. Otherwise I am definitely going to be in trouble. But I ignore that for the moment. For now, I'm just happy that I didn't do anything with The American…

CHAPTER SEVENTEEN: HITTING ROCK BOTTOM

Time flies. It's March now, and I have been divorced for exactly a year. It's also one year ago that I signed up with Seeking Arrangement. And almost a year ago that I met Farshad. Now as I already realized with New Year, my last year with SA was fun and prosperous. I have met four lovely men and I have been fond of all four of them in a different way.

But so far, this year seems less prosperous. It has been three months and I still don't have a new arrangement. And fact is I need one now more than ever. I'm battling to make ends meet. Because since January The Ex has started to fail paying alimony for the girls, I still haven't been able to find a job and without the help of Farshad and Rudolph, money is scarce.

I do the best I can with the money I have, paying the most essential bills first. But I do realize that if I don't find a solution fast, I'll get into trouble. I hate opening the mail again and I hate the feeling that I am sliding back to the life I had with The Ex…

This afternoon, coming home from picking up the girls at school, I can see at least two red bills amongst the post lying on the doormat. I don't open them. I shove them unopened in a kitchen drawer, because I know that I have no money to pay them right now.

Yes, I'm still on SA. And by now I have chatted with a whole range of new men whom I haven't gotten into an arrangement with. There was Mr. Dance. He was end-forties, married with three kids and obviously in some sort of midlife crisis. He had never really lived, he said. He had never connected to his true feelings.

But now he had discovered Biodanza – a way of dancing to get into contact with your true self again. And he wanted to find women to experience new forms of intimacy with. I met him once, we had dinner and kissed on a bridge, but I wasn't really into him. And neither was he, apparently. We never met again.

Next there was a guy who said he was a writer, and I was really excited about that. But, as usual, reality wasn't so exciting. We set up a meeting and he showed up an hour too late on a really cold windy winter evening. Thinking of it now, I don't understand why I waited that long for him. Outside. With an icy wind blowing through the streets. Now I wouldn't have. But I did. I was desperate, I guess.

When we had dinner, it turned out that the guy had never published anything. In fact, I was more of a writer than he was! Then he told me that he just had lunch with another Sugar Babe before our dinner – which explained why he was so late. And she turned out to be the love of his life. So I decided to at least enjoy our nice Italian dinner, then wished him all the best with his love and never met him again.

Then I had lunch with a muscly kind of guy whose vibe I really didn't like. He seemed to love himself, but he wasn't really polite to the people around him. He had a lousy attitude. So I was actually rather happy when he offered a crappy allowance, this way I wasn't even tempted ...

Next I met a really nice British guy, twice. First we had lunch in London. And he may not have been the handsomest guy, but there was something about him ... He had lived in Brazil for twenty years, had a Brazilian wife, two sons and had just moved back to the UK with his family to rebuild his life here. AND he was okay with an arrangement of a thousand a month.

I liked him. I liked his worldliness. And he drove me all the way home in his big black Porsche. *This guy I might even receive home again*, I thought. Now Amanda thought that was a lot of fun. "Make sure he parks his Porsche around the corner," she wrote. "I can already see your neighbours thinking…"

The next time I met him was in Brighton. We had a nice hot chocolate and walked on the cold beach together. He was really nice. He put his arm around my shoulders, kissed me, brought me back to my car and paid my parking- and gas money. And before I left he looked at me and said: "Maybe next time we should book a hotel…" I smiled. "That would be lovely."

But after that he disappeared and I never heard from him again. I don't know what happened. We really did have a connection. But maybe he got cold feet. He had never cheated on his wife, he said. He had no escort past. Or maybe he found a girl who offered a cheaper arrangement. Whatever happened, the guy disappeared into thin air.

Next I chatted with this guy who turned out to be into BDSM. I'm not sure I am, so when he offered me a lousy allowance I wasn't disappointed. And then there was a Spanish guy who told me he wanted to be dominant and only wanted anal sex for a hundred pounds PPM. I guess I don't need to tell you that I never met him. There was this married French guy who wanted me to have sex with both him and his wife, but I wasn't really into the wife.

I'm learning though. By now I'm filtering them out. I make sure I talk about arrangements before we meet. There are just too many Salty Daddies out there. And too many men who don't know the meaning of Sugar. But fact is that lately this is all turning into a disaster…

So one night when I have tucked girls in bed, I make a cup of hot tea and think about my choices. Best would be someone locally, whom I can see during daytime. Just like Rudolph. And that makes me wonder... *Maybe Seeking Arrangement is too international? Maybe I need to check the local sites...*

So I open my laptop and google British sugar sites. There turn out to be a couple of them, but I do have to pay for them and in a way that doesn't feel good. I'm used to Seeking Arrangement now. I'm used to the Sugar Life. I'm used to the men paying. It just doesn't feel right to be paying for a Sugar Site as a woman.

This makes me laugh about myself though. Because one year ago I wouldn't have thought like this. And I can see that the Sugar World is changing me. Though in a way I don't really think it's changing me in a bad way.

I'm becoming much more business orientated. And maybe that's a good thing. Before SA I have always given myself away too easily. Maybe I should have wondered 'what am I getting out of this' with The Ex. Especially when you get children, it's nice to have a man who can take care of you. Yes, I know a lot of women would disagree with me, but at least for me it is.

Now the moment I sign up with a British site, messages start coming in. *Apparently this is a busy site!* But I do have to say that I'm not thrilled by the men who contact me. There is nothing Sugar about this. These are just men looking for cheap fucks.

Men keep sending me messages like: "Are you as horny as I am? I can come over to your place for a couple of hours. Will help you with a 100 pounds." Other ones look decent, but they aren't willing to give financial help, they seem to be looking for dates through this site. It seems to me that both kind of men are on a wrong site. Or maybe I am.

But one man who contacts me catches my interests. He is British and into finances. He looks classy enough on his picture.

And when I do reverse picture search on google I find him right away. He has his own financial advice firm.

So I do two things. First I save his contact information, then I delete my account. I have decided I'm staying with Seeking Arrangement. If it's cheap escort work I want, there are lots of agencies I can register with.

Mr. Finance and I set up a meeting for lunch. We will meet in Marks and Spencer, at the escalators. And I spot him before he sees me. He looks all right, with red hair, glasses, thin lips and a tweed jacket, but he has a nervousness about him. He keeps looking around him. And when he sees me, the nervousness doesn't go.

I know a couple of things about him from chatting. He is in his fifties, married with two teenage daughters. And I notice that he seems to be really uncomfortable with me in public. We have a hasty cup of coffee in the coffee shop, then we go out to look for a place to have lunch.

Suddenly he hisses: "There's someone I know. Keep walking. I'll meet you around the corner." So I walk on, pretend I don't know the guy and stop in front of a window to admire the window display. I'm too far to hear him, but from the corner of my eyes I can see him chatting with a middle aged woman holding loads of shopping bags from design stores. Then I turn the corner and wait for him.

He is all flustered when he comes to me, saying: "See, I just *knew* I was going to meet someone!" He looks around him. "Can we get into my car?" he asks. "I'll take you somewhere. I just don't feel comfortable here."

Now I think about that for a second. I don't know this guy and I'm not sure whether it is wise to be alone with him in his car just yet. But then I nod. *Sure. Why not. I need an arrangement.* So he leads me to his MINI Cooper and starts the engine.

But we don't go for lunch, which kind of turns me off. I was looking forward to a nice lunch. It's all the extra's I like about

Sugar Life. But I don't complain. I need this arrangement. So as Amanda has taught me, I keep my eyes on the money.

"Have you had arrangements for long?" Mr. Finance asks, when he has parked his car in a quiet parking lot near a park. Now Amanda has taught me one thing, men like exclusivity. Always make them feel like they are the only one. Or one of a select few. "I had one," I say. "From Iran. We have had an arrangement for a year, but now he is back to his wife." And I smile.

Mr. Finance nods. "Good. Good. So you're dependable. Before I had many escorts. Many of them. I don't really have sex with my wife, you see. She is just not that … sexual. So I've been looking for it elsewhere." His eyes follow a woman in a red coat who passes by.

"Then I fell in love with one of them," he continues. "We fell in love with each other. She was an airhostess, but she was escorting on the side." He sighs when he remembers her. "I would drive her to her meetings and wait for her to finish." He plucks something from his trousers.

"But then I asked her to quit," he continues. "And she did. Just for me." He looks at a cat running by. "We had an affair for two years. We were so much in love …" "So where is she now?" I ask him. He shrugs. "She got an offer to be an airhostess in Dubai. That's where she is now."

I frown. Amanda has told me a lot about Dubai. In fact, I am just writing one of her chapters about it. And one thing I know. There are lots of wonderful arrangements there. So I don't believe that an ex-escort who was in an arrangement will be an airhostess in Dubai. I think there will be more splendid ways for her to make money over there.

But Mr. Finance doesn't give me a lot of time to think. He suddenly starts kissing me. And I have to say that I'm not really into the kissing. We have no arrangement yet and this is our first meeting. I'm used to meet, eat and get to know each other. Not to be kissing in a car on a parking lot.

Also he is a rather sleazy kisser. There is no sexual spark whatsoever, he doesn't turn me on and his breath smells. And I know Amanda will scold me for letting myself be kissed in a car without an arrangement. *This is just not classy.* But I push that feeling away.

When he drives me back home, he asks me whether I can receive him at home. Now thinking of having sex with this guy in my home makes me feel like screaming. "I can't," I tell him. "Not in my neighbourhood …"

Talking about this, I finally ask about the arrangement. I know I should have done that way before, but for some reason I always feel awkward talking about it in person. And I forgot to arrange it before meeting him.

"With how much will you be able to help?" I ask him. He looks at me and asks: "With how much did the Iranian help you?" "With a thousand pounds," I tell him honestly. And Mr. Finance is quiet for some time.

When he drops me off he says: "I can help you with seven hundred and fifty" and he tries to kiss me again. "I can't here," I tell him. "This is my neighbourhood." It isn't totally, I never let a new guy bring me too close to my home. But I just don't feel like kissing him.

"How often would you like us to meet?" he asks me. I try to give him my most charming smile. "As often as possible, of course," I tell him. But in truth I'm not convinced. *I don't feel that great about the 750.* So I pick up the girls with this heavy feeling inside of me, but I manage to push it away and enjoy our dinner and bedside story before I tuck them in. Then I contact Amanda.

"Way too little!" she says. "And never let a man treat you like that! Next time don't get into his car. Meeting in public is better. He shouldn't be kissing you like that already."

I feel miserable. So I send Mr. Finance a message. I'm still in love with the Iranian, I tell him. So I'm afraid I can't get into an arrangement with him. I don't want to tell him it's the money that I don't like. Now the guy acts rather disappointed. "I really like you," he writes. "Take your time. When you're ready I'd love to hear from you."

When another unexpected bill rolls in the next day, I reconsider my options and text Amanda. "I think of contacting Mr. Finance," I tell her. "I can make sure I meet him only three times a month. Then it's the same as Rudolph helped me with!"

Now I know Amanda thinks Rudolph wasn't helping me with enough either. She used to be a top-end escort. She is used to way different amounts of money. She would get two thousand for an evening. But she does react supportive.

Mr. Finance is all excited when I contact him and we meet the next week in Brighton. There is no lunch this time either, just a cup of coffee. And he doesn't offer to help with the parking money, nor with the gas. We have one cup of coffee then he takes me to the beach for more of his favourite kissing. And fondling too, this time.

When he leaves, he asks me: "Next time a hotel?" So I nod. "Sure darling, that would be lovely." "Send me an invoice for your allowance," he tells me before he drives off. So when I drive back to pick up my kids from school, I do feel a bit better this time. *At least I will be making money.*

I meet him the next week during school time in the lobby of a hotel. And I feel rather awkward. *It just seems so obvious.* And I realize that I have no idea whether what I'm doing is legal. Most probably it's not. I'm having sex with men who are helping me out financially. That would be for most people only one clear thing…

We take the elevator up like polite strangers. And in the room he starts undressing immediately. So I follow suit. Now I have never had this before, but his body kind of repulses me. He is flabby and has big orange moles all over his chest. And his dick is the tiniest thing ever. *Well, whatever. I'm here now. I should focus on the money.*

So I start kissing him and slowly go down on him. He moans and pants: "You know, my wife has never given me a blowjob." Well, I have to say that surprises me. *Are there seriously still women in the UK who don't give blowjobs?*

Next he flips me over and starts licking me, while he says: "My wife doesn't let me do this to her either. Never." I smile politely. I'm not sure I need to know all these details about his wife, but whatever. I try to moan a little, but good god does he suck at giving oral. He has really no idea what to do with a woman. If this is how he does oral, I start to sympathise with the wife.

I hope that at least the fucking will be better, because it has been ages since I had a good fuck. I *need* something good. Some doggy at least. But it's all over before it has even started. He takes me missionary and is finished in five minutes. Five. Fucking. Minutes!!

After sex he crawls into my arm. Now I don't feel that close to him, so I'm not sure that's where I want him to be. But since I don't really feel like doing anything more with him, I'm happy when I feel his body getting heavy. I decide to let him sleep for the two hours we still have in the hotel.

So I'm just waiting. I don't want to move, because I don't want to wake him. But after half an hour, I slip my arm from underneath his head. I take a nice hot bath. Then I collect all the bath amenities in my bag. And I chat with Amanda on my phone.

After one and a half hours I wake him. "I need to go," I tell him. "I have to pick up my girls." He nods and dresses. And in the lobby he tells me to wait outside while he checks out. But I do notice the sour look on his face. It looks like he detests paying for a hotel.

That evening, when the girls are tucked in bed, I take a long shower. For some reason I don't feel good. I have been a Sugar Baby for a year now, but I have never felt like this before. I feel dirty. It just doesn't feel right. It feels like I have hit rock bottom. And I know that I just can't do this.

So after my long hot shower, I send Mr. Finance a message. "You were lovely honey. But it just feels like I am not the right arrangement for you. You need someone who can receive you at home. Not like this." And I'm hoping I'm right about his feelings about paying for the hotel.

Well, I've struck the right chord. He reacts immediately and agrees. I sigh. And when I let Amanda know she cheers. "He gave you 750 for one time then," she cheers. "Good job!" And with that I can finally smile again. *I should feel good. I can survive another month. So why do I have this bad feeling in the pit of my stomach?*

That night, snuggling up under my duvet, I just can't sleep. Because I know one thing. I *need* another arrangement. But I also know that I never want to go for one like this again. I should only go for one that feels good. From now on I should trust my gut feeling.

And just before I drift off to sleep, I think: *So maybe I've hit rock bottom. It feels like I have really hit rock bottom now. But being here, there is only one way left to go, and that's up. From now on things can only get better…*

CHAPTER EIGHTEEN: NEW BEGINNINGS

It's a rainy afternoon in the beginning of April, the girls are at school and I'm just back from my weekly grocery shopping. I should actually be writing, but I'm chatting a little with Sarah and Barbara when I get a message from Seeking Arrangement.

Now I have had a lot of those, and I rejected most. Since Mr. Hideous I've become quite critical. I haven't met any new man since. But fact is that my money is running out. I *need* a new SD to survive. So I open the new message. It reads: "Hi. You look and sound nice :)"

Well, that's short. But it's a friendly message, so I check out his profile. There is no picture, but his profile tells me that he is a married businessman from India, looking for a discreet girl for partying when he is in Europe for work.

India... *The cute father at school is from India.* And in my mind I can picture me dating him... So I reply back immediately: "Thank you, so do you! Or at least you sound nice... What you look like still remains a mystery... ;-)"

His reply comes fast: "Hey, thanks :) If you've read my profile you'd know what I am looking for. Are you game? Cheers."

I picture the cute father before me as I type my answer: "I guess so. I'm looking for one preferably long term SD. I'm discreet – here in the UK I have my own life with my two daughters and I'm happy with it, and you can trust me to respect yours. But since it can be hard as a single mother, I am looking for a SD who can help me out with a monthly allowance. Are *you* game? ;-)"

This time his answer comes a bit later: "Well, actually that's why I'm here. You sound like fun. My preference is for ladies who want a good time, good hotels, enjoy, party. I am open to discussing a MA. Is there an amount you have in mind? Cheers"

I write back: "Fun is good … my normal life is so … normal LOL I'm in for fun and new experiences … I had one SD from Iran before, he helped me with a 1000 pounds."

I leave Mr. Handsome out of it, no need to mention him. And let's not even start about Mr. Hideous … But after my message Mr. India doesn't reply. *My god, this guy has gone fast …* So I wait for some more time before I type: "Did you run away now?"

But it remains silent. *Maybe I should make it clear that a Monthly Allowance is negotiable?* So after some time I write back to him: "Of course you are not Mr. Iran and I don't know how often you would like to meet. What would you suggest?"

It remains silent for a bit longer until he replies: "Sorry. Did not run away. Also need to work once in a while :) How does 800 sound? I come to Europe 8–10 times a year. Of course, the chemistry is also important. I like having fun, party, stay at good places. You ok for that?"

In a way, bargaining doesn't feel that great. Thanks to Farshad, I now prefer to get my 1000 pounds. So I text Amanda for advice. "Well, it depends on how long you will see him," she writes back. "Actually you were cheap for Mr. Iran. You saw the guy two whole days for a 1000."

Now I might be naïve, but to me it doesn't feel like that. I wasn't with Farshad for the money. I enjoyed every second with him. The money was extra, to help me, but not a compensation for how often we had sex or whatever we did.

"If you can see this guy less for 800," Amanda writes, "you might have a better deal. At least it's more than Mr. Hideous. And you don't have to see this Indian guy too much." Not seeing much of him is also not really something that crosses my mind. The men I've been spending my time with, I truly enjoyed being with. *And I don't even know how that will change this coming year.*

But now that she brings up Mr Hideous, I guess she is right. So I reply back to Mr. India: "800 sounds good. So do fun, parties and good places, those definitely sound good too :-)" He replies back immediately: "Super. You wanna come on hangouts or Skype text? By the way, do you like your drinks? What do you prefer? Champagne, wine, spirits?" And one second later: "Going for a meeting. Not running away :)" I reply: "LOL. I like champagne, white wine and cocktails"

He replies back when the girls are in bed. And we move to Skype from there. He sends me two quite good looking pictures of himself and writes that he will in Europe next week. Would I want to meet him in Barcelona for a day and one night? I smile. *Sure.* Amanda cheers when I text her. "You might have just found yourself a good one."

Now Mr. India tells me he will get his secretary to arrange my ticket, I just need to send him a copy of my passport. And at that moment I'm happy I have put down my true age on SA.

"There are two flights back," he writes next. "One earlier than mine, one later, which one do you prefer?" "The later one," I reply. "That way we still have some quality time together." And he sends me a kiss back. ' '

He keeps chatting that night – it must be early morning in faraway India – while he is drunk and at a party. Now that he is drunk, he is quite open about the things he likes. We both like to have sex in kinky places and he tells me that he loves giving oral sex. Now I'm a little nervous about that one. As you might know by now, I normally feel very uncomfortable about receiving oral.

Farshad and Sam never did, Rudolph I kind of told not to, and Mr. Hideous … well let's not get into him shall we.

But the week finishes fast and that Friday I bring the girls to their father. Driving past the parking lot I once had car-sex on with Rudolph, I smile as I remember him. Still it always leaves me with an empty feeling in the pit of my stomach when I bring the girls away. But I push the feeling away. I should focus on my trip.

I spend the whole evening preparing. I take a hot bath, paint my nails, have a mask, I go for all of it. Next I chat with Amanda, checking out the 'W hotel' that I will be staying in. You know, checking out the hotel is part of the fun. It's so exciting to see the beautiful place you are going to stay …

Of course Amanda is not easily charmed – she has stayed in places way more posh and decadent. To her what I'm doing is child's play. But with the life I'm coming from, I'm thoroughly enjoying it.

So the next day I leave a note for the cat-sitter, pat Fuzzy goodbye, take the train with one small suitcase and board an airplane for Barcelona. Again. *It feels like ages since I left for Barcelona with Farshad…* The flight is short, but I do decide to splurge. This time I buy a drink and snack for myself. And in my mind I say cheers to Farshad.

It doesn't take long before I have arrived. And being at Barcelona airport feels so strange … It's just so familiar, it's like I walked here with Farshad yesterday. But now I am alone. Heading towards another man.

So after customs, I don't go to the rental cars. I go straight towards the cabs. And once I'm inside a cab, I text Mr. India to let him know that I'm on my way. I'm off to the W hotel. And I text Amanda the name of the guy. Sanjay Gupta. Now I only need to let her know the room number. And send her a message after the sex at night to tell her I'm okay.

Then I sit back and try to stay calm. In a way this is crazy. I'm off again to meet a stranger in a foreign country, knowing I am most probably going to sex with him. But you know what? In a way, that's also exciting…

And driving into beautiful Barcelona I'm starting to get even more excited. *Now this is life!* This is what I love most about the Sugar Life. The travelling, the great hotels, the good restaurants. I missed this with Rudolph…

But when I see the palm trees, the squares I walked with Farshad, I realize with a pang that I miss him. I quickly push that feeling aside. I'm not even hearing from the guy. I should be enjoying this new adventure. I'm here in this beautiful city. And lately my life has been nothing but one big adventure. *Life is good…*

Hotel W rises up at the end of the beach like a tall, shimmering sail with the sea lapping at its feet. And Mr. India is waiting in front of it. He is my height, has a kind face and is slim. He's wearing a nice shirt and jeans, has full lips and a warm voice.

He's a real gentleman. He takes my suitcase, avoids reception – I have one quick glance at the stylish lobby with a water feature and a floating fireplace – and takes me into the elevator with a smile. "Nice to meet you, sweetheart," he says in the elevator. "You look even better than on your pictures."

In his suite he keeps his distance as I unpack my suitcase. The room is bright, airy and pristine with an all-glass front which gives a spectacular view of the sea. It's decorated in shades that reflect the sea and the sand and it smells of fresh linen.

When I'm ready, Mr. India gives me two presents from his country. A beautiful silk shawl and an exclusive perfume made from the essential oils of cold-crushed jasmine flowers. And I give him a peck on his cheek to thank him.

Next he takes me out. The sea is right in front and we walk past it along the boulevard. But suddenly his phone rings and he puts his finger in front of his lips to hush me. *It must be Mrs. India.* They chat for some time – apparently she thinks he is in Munich – while I silently walk next to him until he has finished his call.

"Are you ready for lunch?" he then asks me and leads me to a restaurant right on the boulevard. We have a lovely chicken and chorizo paella and Mr. India orders a litre of Sangria – and after that another one. I make sure he drinks most, still I get rather tipsy.

While we eat, Mr. India tells me about his marriage. He has an arranged marriage and is married for twenty-five years now. "If I could divorce her, I would," he says. "If there are two people who are completely different, it's us. But you just don't divorce in India…"

Just like many SD's, Mr. India confesses he has had his share of escorts. And he also doesn't seem to feel any shame about it. "But I don't do escorts anymore," he tells me. "It's too impersonal. Believe it or not, I'm actually doing this for the romance…"

After lunch he leads me into a maze of streets with Catalonian flags hanging out of the windows. "The love of my life are my three daughters," Mr. India continues. "I don't think I ever knew love until they were born." And a soft look comes over his face.

"I'm not so sure they love me though," he continues. "See, I'm too busy. I'm away too much…" He stops when we pass a beggar, searches his pockets and throws some coins in her tin can. *And it makes my heart smile.*

"What do you do?" I ask him. "I'm working for my family's enterprise," he says. He is silent for a while before he continues. "But what I would really like to do, is to be a yoga teacher." This surprises me. But I do feel a depth in this guy. And an unhappiness. He might be rich, but I can feel he is not happy with the life he is leading.

"When my daughters grow up," he continues, "I want them to live abroad." "Would you mind if they marry foreigners?" I ask him. He shrugs. "If it's a good man, why not?" Then he frowns. "Though I'm not sure a foreigner can handle them…"

He seems to be buried in thoughts for some time before he continues. "See, they have grown up very privileged. I live in this very big house – my wife, daughters, me and my parents. That's seven people. To keep our household running we have twenty-five servants and two guards."

Mr. India – or maybe I should call him Mr. Yoga – is silent again for some time, while I make an image in my head of his huge family estate. "But India is changing…." he continues. "See, I have a personal servant who has been working for me his whole life. He packs my bag every trip I take and makes sure I have enough money, while my wife supervises."

Mr. Yoga pauses for a second, while he swallows hard. "Then one day my safe was locked and my wife couldn't remember the code. My servant spent hours on YouTube searching and then he opened it for me." By now Mr. Yoga is getting emotional. I can see tears welling up in his eyes. He averts them for a moment before he continues.

"Now this guy has no education whatsoever. Can you imagine how his life could be, if he had gotten any proper education?" He wipes a tear off his cheek. "Imagine what the two of us have spent so far. On the hotel, our lunch, our drinks. I'm here in Barcelona spending this fortune just to have fun. And it's more than my servant makes in a year."

He shakes his head in disbelief. "It can't go on like this in my country. Things will change. When my daughters are grown-up, I'm sure they won't be able to live the life they are living now. So I hope they will find their future elsewhere." And he stares into the distance for some time.

"You know, they have no idea how privileged they are," he then says. "When I buy them something special, or organize a luxurious party for their birthdays, they aren't even that happy. For them it's just normal."

I'm silent, while I think of my own girls. And I realize that I'm happy with the way they are growing up. They are happy with anything, really. After I do the groceries, they thank me for buying their favourite peanut butter. If it's one thing that I can say about them, it's that they are definitely not spoiled.

If I could say something else about them, it's that they are really happy little girls. They can be happy with anything. A trip to the woods. Jumping in rain puddles. Our movie night on Saturday. I smile. *Things are turning out well.*

It's like Mr. Yoga has read my mind. "You know, you are doing a good job," he says. "You are spending your time with your girls. Make sure you enjoy it. Their youth only lasts for such a short time ..."

I kiss him on his cheek. "It's your help which allows me to do so ..." And he beams, grabbing my hand and murmuring: "You are brilliant. Don't let me fall in love with you."

After that we remain silent for quite some time. We both seem to be lost in our own thoughts. But eventually I do start feeling uncomfortable. *I do need to come up with something to talk about!*

So I point at the flags hanging out of the windows, fluttering in the small spring breeze. "What is this about Catalonia?" I ask him. "Do you know more about it?" He nods. "The Catalan identity has been around since the 8th century A.D." he says. "It was an independent region of the Iberian Peninsula with its own language, laws and customs."

"The Iberian Peninsula?" I ask him. "Yeah, that's modern day Spain and Portugal. See, with a distinct history stretching back to the early middle ages, many Catalans think of themselves as a separate nation from the rest of Spain."

For a moment he seems to think before he continues. "I also think there something during the Franco dictatorship. They attempted to suppress Catalan identity I guess."

We are heading back towards the boulevard and Mr. India gestures towards the busy restaurants. "Because of the economic crisis in Spain, calls for Catalan independence have only increased. They see the wealthy Barcelona region as propping up the poorer rest of Spain."

He kisses me lightly on my lips and then asks: "Do you know Gaudí was a born and bred Catalonian?" And with that name my thoughts are back with Farshad...

Back in the hotel he keeps his polite distance while I tell him I will change for dinner. Now I have several evening dresses with me, so I declare I will put on a fashion show. Mr. Yoga sits back and smiles as I show.

The bathroom door is made of almost see-through glass, and in a way it feels strange – stripping down and knowing he can see my contours. He's a stranger. But he's a stranger I know I'm going to be intimate with. And in a way that's strangely exciting.

Mr. Yoga choses the same tight black dress that I wore with my sexy dinner with Rudolph. Next he spends quite some time in front of the mirror himself. He is inspecting a shirt he has just put on before turning to me asking: "I just bought this shirt in Munich. Do you like it? Does it look good on me?" Now it's just a regular navy blue polo. And in a way his insecurity surprises me. But I tell him: "Love, you look so handsome." And he smiles as we leave the room.

The W hotel is high-end, but also young and sexy, I realize when we take the elevator and whizz up to the Eclipse bar on the 26th floor. All tables are taken, so we are shown to the bar, where

Mr. Yoga orders a Japanese Hakushu whiskey for himself and a Passion Fruit Martini cocktail for me.

Sipping my cocktail and looking around I realize that the crowd is a pretty one. But what is most spectacular is the night view over Barcelona. Mr. India lightly takes my hand, while his other hand is drumming the rhythm of the music on the counter. "This place is brilliant," he says. "Simply brilliant." Then he looks at me. "I'm so happy you came sweetheart. I'm having a brilliant time with you." And we have another cocktail.

When a waiter comes to tell us that our table is ready, we follow him to a bench with a low table close to the huge window. Mr. Yoga smiles happily. He asks for the menu and orders us sushi, tamaki, tempura grilled monkfish and shrimp skewers, Gallegan spicy beef tenderloin and grilled octopus. And a bottle of Chablis to go with it.

It doesn't take long for the food to arrive. Still Mr. Yoga has managed to pour us three glasses of wine. And I'm starting to get drunk. Now while we are drinking I realize two things.

First, this guy really likes to drink. He drinks a lot. And in a way I wonder whether that combines well with his dreams of being a yoga teacher. But when I ask him, he ensures me that he only drinks when he is abroad.

I also realize that we probably have different ideas of parties. For me a party is going somewhere dancing. For him *this* is the party. He tells me: "I love parties like this. You know, drinking, eating good food in a brilliant place with great company."

Mr. Yoga is real open now. He tells me that instead of escorts, he is having girlfriends now. And apparently I am one of them. There are many more, he makes no secret about that. And truth is that since Rudolph, I actually prefer it this way.

I now prefer someone who is married and wants to stay like that. Someone who is open and honest about other women. It just makes things clear and draws boundaries. I lost myself too much with Rudolph, wishing for a future that was never mine to have.

Mr. Yoga and I don't kid each other on having sexual exclusivity. Nor about emotional exclusivity for that matter. But we do have enough respect and genuine interest in each other to feel a unique connection.

But I do get a feeling that he is living a life of dualities. In India he doesn't eat meat, doesn't have alcohol, and is loyal to his wife. In Europe he goes wild. He parties and does all the things that are normally forbidden.

It might be fun, but in a way it also seems to be nagging him. In a way he seems to be yearning for a different life. A spiritual life. With no obligations, just the chance to grow the spiritual spark shining within him.

Suddenly Mr. Yoga beams, breaking my reveries. "Hey, I'm having a bachelor's party in Dubai with some friends next month," he says. "Would you like to join me?" "A bachelor's party?" I ask him. "But you're married...."

Mr. Yoga shrugs. "I have two each year. With two different sets of friends. We choose a city and have fun. Some of my friends bring a girlfriend, others will pick up the girls right there..." And from the tone of his voice I understand that those are women they pay for. *But in a way, isn't he actually paying for me too?*

He gives me a scrutinizing look. "That is if you don't mind *that* of course." I shrug. "No problem," I tell him. "As long as *you* are not picking up girls when I'm there." Mr. Yoga laughs loud. "When *you* are with me? No way!" I smile. "Well, sure. I'd *love* to come to Dubai with you." Though in a way I'm not convinced his offer is true. Since Farshad I'm used to take all these offers a bit lightly. *We'll see*, I think.

Eventually Mr. Yoga proposes to go to our room. We have finished our bottle and he has had two more whiskey's so we're both quite drunk. I know what is coming next, but I'm not really nervous about it. I've started to like him.

The moment we enter the room, he starts kissing me passionately. And this guy is a great kisser. Really. I can't help thinking that he knows how to arouse a woman with just his mouth. *And soon I will find out how true that is.* Then he takes my hand, leads me to the bed and strips off my dress.

I'm wearing my sexy outfit that I wore with Rudolph. A suspender belt with real suspenders and high heels. Mr. Yoga slowly slips my bra strap of my shoulder and starts kissing the Happy Boobs. I lean my head back as he starts to suck my nipples. And he sucks so hard that they become real sensitive. They stand erect like little soldiers.

Next he pushes me on the bed, while he stands between my legs, taking off my knickers. He makes sure I'm keeping my high heels and my suspender belt with stockings on. I naturally try to close my legs with him standing there, feeling a bit shy, but he opens my legs again and then goes down on me.

Now as I said, I have always felt self-conscious about receiving oral sex and therefore never truly enjoyed it. But this time I am prepared. I already knew the guy was going to do this. So I decide right there and then that I am going to enjoy.

And Mr. Yoga is amazing. He is as good in giving oral as he is in kissing. He has a sucking power that amazes me, while his tongue is so soft and he knows exactly where to use it. Maybe I never appreciated receiving oral, but this is simply one word. Amazing. This guy knows how to please a woman.

Only when I start pleasing him, I start to feel a bit uncomfortable. Now I *know* how to please a man. I know men like my blowjobs. I'm used to enthusiastic Farshad. To Rudolph wiggling underneath me. But when I suck his cock, Mr. Yoga is just so quiet that I'm not sure he likes what I am doing. I'm not sure I'm pleasing him and I start to feel insecure. He does come eventually. In a totally quiet way. Then he puts in his earplugs, turns around and goes to sleep.

I hardly sleep that night. I send a message to Amanda telling her all is okay, then toss around in bed with this heavy feeling in the pit of my stomach.

In the morning we wake like polite strangers, which makes me feel a bit uncomfortable as well. The only Sugar Daddy I ever woke up with is Farshad. And I'm used to him hugging and kissing me like a long lost lover.

But between Mr. Yoga and me there is a polite distance now. He is chatting with his wife on his phone and there is no physical contact between us. I stay in bed a little longer, *maybe he wants to make love again. Maybe this time I can please him.* But eventually I get up and start preparing.

When I look in the mirror I notice that I have two love bites. One in my neck and one on my nipple. *Bloody hell. I'll have to wear scarves the coming week.* I put on a nice dress and ask him: "Would you like to go for breakfast?" But he looks up disturbed. "I don't do breakfast with girlfriends," he says. "I'll order something in the room. I need to do my yoga and some business, just be back in an hour or so."

So I go down by myself. *Damn, I miss Farshad now.* Checking in for breakfast all by myself feels rather awkward. I get a table right in the middle, surrounded by families and couples. When the waitress tells me that breakfast is not included in the room and my favourite breakfast buffet is rather expensive, I order a yoghurt with muesli.

And for a moment I feel miserable. I miss my girls. I miss Farshad. I just feel awkward. I take out my phone and text Amanda to tell her I'm having breakfast by myself. "Oh but that's nice!" she replies. "I always liked to do my own things. No need to be seen too much with these men." And with that answer I put my phone back on the table. *Sometimes we are quite different…*

Yes, I do need the money. With Farshad it was just a bonus, but now I'm living off this. But if it would be just the money that I was going for, I could just as well be an escort. What I like about the Sugar World, are all the things around it. The interesting men, the hotels, the food, the gifts, the way it is a relationship in a totally different and undefinable way.

And then I realize something. *Maybe I'm doing it for the romance too! Just like Mr. Yoga.* Though just like with parties, it turns out that Mr. Yoga and I have a different idea about romance too … Or maybe he is feeling guilty once the alcohol is out of his system … who knows …

After breakfast, the hour isn't finished yet and I don't feel like disturbing Mr. Yoga, so I lie down on the sun deck. It's already nice and hot in Barcelona. Spring has most definitely started here. So I let the sun caress my face, relaxing me, making me feel warm and loving inside.

When I go back up, Mr. Yoga is ready. And it's time to head for the airport. *At least I took the later flight back,* I think. *Now we still have some time together…*

We take the cab like two polite strangers, and then the moment we have entered the airport Mr. Yoga says: "Darling, I want to check the news and all. Do you mind if I say goodbye to you here?"

So we give a polite peck on the cheeks and he leaves to one side as I leave to the other. And one thing I decide right there and then. Next time I'll meet him, I'll take the early flight. Well, if there ever will be a next time, that is …

Fact is, I'm feeling awful while I wait all that time at the airport. It feels like I couldn't please him in the bed last night and since then he has been nothing but polite. *What happened?*

I really thought we had a connection yesterday. I really liked the guy. *Did I do something wrong? Didn't he like the sex?*

I text Amanda, but she doesn't understand. "Did he come?" she asks. "Yes," I answer. "Then he is satisfied," is her reply. "But I just don't know whether he really liked it," I write back. "And he leaves me alone all the time." "If he came, he liked it."

I also don't really understand why I am feeling bad. Maybe it's because for the first time this doesn't feel like a relationship. It feels like what it is. An arrangement. And for some reason I'm having a tough time with that.

When I'm finally in the airplane back, I try to push the bad feelings away. I picture my girls. Both of them. Serious Lisa, with a small frown on her face as she carefully explores life. Vibrant Sophie, a broad smile on her face as she bursts through life. I'm doing this for them. And in my handback I'm carrying 800 pounds, tucked away safely. *Life is good, actually…*

CHAPTER NINETEEN: FLYING HIGH

So Mr. Yoga had invited me for his 'bachelor's party' in Dubai. Now with Farshad I have become accustomed to promises that aren't kept. Farshad was always promising to meet again next month, but that wouldn't happen. So since I am in the Sugar World I don't believe anything until I have an e-ticket in my inbox.

But Mr. Yoga turns out to be different. He is a Man-Who-Keeps-His-Words. So only a few weeks after our first meeting, I have an e-ticket for Dubai in my inbox. *Can you believe that?* I can't. I'm going to Dubai! And I feel a surge of happiness rush through my body.

But the girls won't be with their father. So just like I did with Barcelona, I take the kids and visit my Ex-In-Laws again. Fred is shoving the garden. The moment he sees the girls he gets on his knees and gives them a big hug, giving me a warm hug afterwards.

Wilma is inside working on her stamp collection. She pats the girls on their heads and gives me a polite nod. "Some tea, dear?" she asks as she gets up. "Don't bother Wilma, I will make some," I tell her. She settles down again, looking at me critically from over her reading glasses. No doubt she is wondering whether making a decent cup of tea is something I will be able to perform.

When we are all having our tea and polite questions are being asked about how we are all doing, I manage to get the conversation to work. "You remember my last job in Italy?" I ask them. Fred nods enthusiastically. He loved having the girls those two days. But Wilma just tilts her head and looks at me, suspecting what is to come … "They have offered me another project!" I say, beaming. *And for a moment I muse about how good I have become in lying. For when I am lying it actually feels like it's real. I'm almost believing my lies myself…*

Fred pats me on my back. "Good job! Go for it! We'll take the girls!" And he drops on his fours and crawls around with Sophie on his back. Wilma gives me a long look, sighs and then nods. I give them both a hug to thank them and Wilma gives a wooden hug back.

So one week later, I leave the kids with my Ex-Parents-In-Law and off I go. In a way I feel bad to leave the girls behind, but I try to focus on what lies ahead. I'm flying to another country. Another one which I've never been to before. Isn't life great?

The flight is quite long, so I watch some nice movies. Then Dubai airport is crazily busy and it takes me more than an hour to get through customs. I have never seen a crowd like this. It's just crazy. So I just look around, at the Arab men, wearing long white robes with a headscarf. And I realize that it feels like I am in a movie …

Mr. Yoga keeps texting, asking me where I am. He is with his friends at some 'Brilliant Party'. *No surprise there of course.* And he keeps me updated. First they are at the Chin Chin bar. Then at Cavalli in the Fairmont. Now I have never been to Dubai and I have no image of these places, but knowing Mr. Yoga they will splendid.

When I finally get through customs, Mr. Yoga texts me again. There is no need to change money, he tells me. He will wait for the cab and pay. So for the first time ever I am in a foreign country with no currencies on me whatsoever.

Mr. Yoga is waiting in front of the Fairmont hotel chewing gum. And it's actually really nice to see him again. He rushes out, holds my door, pays the driver and takes my suitcase. And I realize that Dubai is HOT, even at night.

Inside the hotel one of the friends is waiting for us, introducing himself as Raja. And all three of us take a cab to the hotel. In the cab Mr. Yoga tells Raja: "This is my girlfriend." Making it very clear that he wants Raja to know some distinction. Raja moves his head a little without looking too convinced.

Mr. Yoga has booked a large suite in the JW Marriott Marquis Hotel Dubai. Now of course I have already checked out the hotel when texting with Amanda. And though it isn't as top notch as she is used to, for me it is pure luxe. It has a scenic view of the Dubai skyline, a living room, a bedroom and a luxurious marble bathroom with a rain shower and an oversized tub.

But we don't stay there for long. After dropping off my suitcase, we go to Raja's suite. Two other friends – with bored looking girls – have joined Raja. The friends introduce themselves as Kabir and Surya.

Kabir is tall, cheerful, quite fair and wears glasses. Surya is short with greasy long hair. The girls both give me a weak hand before they turn their interest back to their phones. "Raja was too picky, he hasn't been able to pick up any girl," Mr. Yoga says. "These guys had already taken the two good ones."

I have another look at the totally uninterested girls in cheap latex clothes chewing gum and playing games on their phone. *THOSE were the good ones? Jeez…* "Since Raja is the youngest of us, he could only pick last," Mr. Yoga continues.

I check out Raja. He is the youngest and the handsomest guy in the room. He is tall, with a mahogany skin, nice features and waving hair. In a way he reminds me of Jamal the

Pakistani. Only his voice is a little too high to be very manly. See, that's something I love about Mr. Yoga. I love his deep warm voice.

I look some more at the girls. This is actually the first time that I am close to prostitutes. Both are Russian. They have dark hair, tons of make-up on their face, wear tight latex suits and give no hint to be enjoying what they are doing.

Mr. Yoga takes my hand and presses a light kiss on it. And at that moment I understand what Sugar Daddies say. That with escorts it's just not personal. But these are cheap ones. I'm about to meet two who are very close to what I am providing. But more about that later ...

Holding Mr. Yoga's hand, I look around me. It is a nice suite, just like ours, with a bar with vodka, champagne and an open package of condoms – apparently there to pick for anyone who needs them.

Mr. Yoga pours me a glass of champagne and some vodka for himself, then he sits down again and we join their drinking. Though I make sure I don't drink too much.

As Mr. Yoga sits next to me and caresses my leg, I realize for the first time how absolutely huge his hands are. In Barcelona I apparently never had a good look at them. And since he has taken off his shoes I get a good look at his feet, which are just as enormous. I do realize why I like his fingers inside my pussy so much ...

"Sweetheart, would you like to go Skydiving?" he then asks me, taking me by surprise. "These guys said that you would never agree, but I told him that *my girlfriend* is different." And he smiles at me proudly.

Now that flatters me. And looking at the two other girls, I really do want to be different. So to my surprise I am saying "Sure, why not?" Mr. Yoga claps his hands. "Good! Raja here is chickening out. You can take his place." Now I am never good with withstanding challenges. No one is going to say I am chickening out! "Sure!" I say, feeling brave.

That night we don't drink for long. First Surya leaves with a girl, and the door slowly closes behind them, so I can see them walking away into the hallway. The girl swaying her hips in her cheap heels, no physical contact whatsoever. I can't imagine their sex to be anything passionate. Then the other couple leave in the same manner. And next Mr. Yoga tells me we are leaving as well.

Mr. Yoga is quite drunk, but he starts kissing me the moment we are close to the bed. And he still knows how to kiss. He is quite dominant and I love that. He first kisses my lips while his hands unbutton my shirt.

He lets it slide off onto the ground, while he zips open my tight white trousers. His kisses go down, to the Happy Boobs, and down, down on my belly while he peels my trousers off. Coming back up to my lips, he kisses me while he guides me firmly to the bed, taking off his own trousers and shirt on the way.

Throwing me on the bed, he soon continues his kissing, on my lips, trailing towards my breast and sucking my erect nipples. He still knows how to suck as well … He sucks my nipples until they are so sensitive, that I know they are going to have love bites again.

Next he trails down to my belly, kissing my belly button and going down, pushing my legs apart and kissing my pussy. His kissing, sucking and licking make me so sensitive that I come. And I normally *never* come through oral.

Mr. Yoga looks up at me, smiling a mischievous smile. Then he goes off to the living room. He returns with a bottle of champagne. "This is one of my fetishes, sweetheart," he says, opening the bottle and pouring a bit in my mouth. Next he is pouring a trail down on my belly, which he licks all off, opening my legs and pouring champagne into my pussy.

Licking and sucking he finishes it all, then pours in some more. "I just love this," he says in between his sucking, champagne (or is it my juice?) still dripping from his chin. "Normally I never drink champagne, but when it's drunk from a pussy it has such an exquisite taste…"

And that is the last thing he says. He truly enjoys himself down there with his champagne bottle and he makes me come twice more before I lean up, put the champagne bottle on the floor, flip him over and slowly go down on him.

Again I'm amazed how little sound and movement he makes, though I do believe is enjoying himself now. Still it makes me insecure in a way. I'm used to Rudolph, who makes blowjobs such a joy to give. Mr. Yoga comes in utter silence. Then he kisses me, puts in his earplugs, turns around and goes to sleep.

I am tossing and turning, but I just can't sleep. But it's not because of any Sugar Arrangements. It's because of the skydiving. *Because what the hell have I gotten myself into? What the hell am I going to do? Skydiving?? Why did I have to act so brave?* I hardly sleep that night. I keep waking up imagining jumping out of that airplane and I just can't figure out why I would do that.

The next morning I have a mini-crisis with clothes. I didn't pack for jumping out of planes and Mr. Yoga insists that for the sky diving I need long sleeves, so I decide to wear the same clothes as I was wearing upon arriving. White pants and a nice night blue blouse. It's the only thing with long sleeves I have taken with me to hot Dubai.

As usual I have breakfast by myself, while Mr. Yoga does his yoga. But I don't eat much. My stomach is terrible. Next we all meet in the hotel lounge. Well except for the two girls – they must have left after their business was finished.

Raja is there to wave us off, Kabir and Surya are all excited and two other guys have also appeared. One is an older man with glasses and a receding chin introducing himself as Sanjeev, the other is a rather shy young guy with stubbles who tells me he is called Amir.

"So are you ready for skydiving?" Kabir asks me. "Are you?" I ask. "Yeah sure." And Kabir claps his hands a few times to show his excitement. "You're brave, you know," Amir tells me shyly. But I have no time to react. Because then to my surprise Mr. Yoga says: "Well, have fun. I'm not going. I still need to work." And off he goes.

So there I am, with four men that I didn't come for. And for a moment I hesitate. But then I think: *What the hell. How often in your life do you get a chance like this?* So I join them in one of the two cabs. In the cab I am still thinking that maybe I shouldn't go, but I'm too proud to say so. I don't want to be the only one who isn't going to jump out of this airplane.

At the Sky Diving place I fill in all these forms which I don't want to read, informing me about all the bad stuff that can happen and how the sky diving place isn't to be held responsible. *Should I be doing this? What about my girls? What if something DOES happen to me?*

They also want me to leave a contact's phone number. Now that is a problem. I'm not going to leave my parent's number. They don't even know I am here, let alone that I am jumping out of airplanes. I'm supposed to be in Italy working. But Kabir saves me and fills in Mr. Yoga's number.

When I return the forms, the woman asks me, "So how will you pay?" And I must look shocked. "Pay?" I ask. The woman is getting cranky. "Yes, you know, pay for the skydiving? Its 2000 dollars you know?" Well I have no answer for that.

But Kabir quickly jumps in for me and asks Amir: "Can you take care of this? We'll arrange it together later." And Amir pays with his credit card. You know, these guys are all really nice to me and it is starting to feel like I am actually dating all four of them.

Next we all get an instructor – mine is Russian and called Sasha. He tells me what to do (head up and legs in the air) while we all get roped into some harness and get our own cameraman to make a movie and take pictures of the flight.

So there we go. Off to the airplane. *DAMN* I think. *Am I really going to do this?* And I even have to go in first, then the other four friends follow.

So up we go. The engine of the little plane roaring like a lion. Below me the Palm of Dubai gets smaller and smaller until it looks like some of the pictures I have seen on the internet.

And then, when we are up to 14,000 feet, the first instructor opens the door and jumps out. And at that moment I realize that I have never been in an airplane with the door open.

Luckily I have gotten in first, so I am the last one getting out. One by one I see the friends drop down. Surya is just before me, but he gets second thoughts and tries to grab onto the plane before his instructor pushes him out.

And then there I am. Standing with my toes on the edge. Sasha says "We'll jump on three! One, two" and then he pushes me, because people tend to grab on three.

It's crazy. First there is a free fall of almost sixty seconds, and I can tell you one thing. Free fall is freaking wild. I think my eyes are going to pop out and it feels like my nose is going to explode with all the air in it.

Now the cameraman is flying close by and I really do try to smile and make nice gestures, but I am also freaking scared. Adrenaline rushes through my body, my nose is hurting and I am just falling, falling, falling.

Then suddenly – after the longest sixty seconds of my life – Sasha pulls the parachute and we are soaring. We are like an eagle flying over Dubai. Right over the Palm, which is the most beautiful sight ever.

Sasha straightens my hair, loosens my harness and says: "Now just enjoy." And at that moment I just simply want to marry the guy. I have never felt so close to a complete stranger.

This guy has jumped out of an airplane with me and we survived. I could have married the guy at the spot, seriously. It seems to last for ages, soaring over Dubai. And it is the most blissful experience ever. It feels like a pity when we have to land.

The moment we land and are taken out of our harnesses, Kabir is jumping up and down all excitedly and makes sure all five of us do a group hug. Though Surya – who was trying to grab the plane not to jump – is still totally shocked and not happy with his experience.

Those four guys feel so close to me now. We have all jumped together – that creates a bond, you know. Next my four dates take me to a bar close to the Skydiving place, where we all have a shot of tequila. Amir – who is quietly sitting next to me – and I have a cocktail next, while the rest has vodka. I feel so strong. So alive.

Back in the hotel Mr. Yoga is calling with his wife, so he puts his finger in front of his lips to make sure I will stay quiet. He kisses me softly so she won't hear. *God, this guy has no idea what I have just done!*

I take a shower, change into a nice dress and put on makeup. Then we take two cabs to the Four Seasons at Jumeirah Beach to have dinner, where another Indian guy called Vijay is waiting for us. Vijay is a friend of either one, or all of them, I'm not quite sure. He is a well-groomed guy, tall, with eyes like fire.

But I'm too busy to really notice him. I am admiring the Four Seasons. From the outside the hotel looks like an Arabian palace, all lit up and beautiful. Vijay takes us to Coya – a Peruvian restaurant in the Four Seasons. And I've never had Peruvian food before, so I am quite excited.

When we enter, two girls are already waiting for us at the bar. Apparently some of the five friends have met them before. Now these girls I like. One is from Israel, the other one from Russia. They are just like me, nobody would even think they were doing this kind of work.

Victoria, the Russian girl, is the experienced one. She immediately choses Sanjeev, the oldest guy, and he is a wise choice. He will stay with her for two nights. Rachel from Israel goes for Raja – the youngest and handsomest guy – and seems to have a lot of trouble arranging a price.

I look around me. The bar area is buzzing. There's a DJ, great music, some tables and high chairs. And once our table is ready, we are taken inside the restaurant dining room area which is like stepping into a different place altogether. The décor is classy, the music softer and the set up beautiful.

We have a Menu De La Casa to share, with dishes like sea bream with crispy corn and coriander, salmon with celery juice, ginger, daikon and wasabi, yellowfin tuna with stem ginger, maracuya, hazelnut and radish. And it is simply 'brilliant', as Mr. Yoga agrees. All three of us girls share a bottle of Chablis.

I am sitting between Mr. Yoga and Victoria and have a great time chatting with her – though we make sure we give enough attention to our guys. Victoria is living in Dubai, she has a regular who pays an apartment for her and she has her private yoga teacher here. I can't even envision the kind of life she is living.

After dinner – which Vijay insists on paying for us all – he takes us to the terrace of the Four Seasons where we get our own private area with water pipes and drinks. I sit with Victoria smoking my water pipe with apple tobacco.

Victoria is lightly holding the hand of her beau, sometimes pouring him drinks and chatting with him, but also laughing with me. Rachel is still having trouble choosing between Raja and Surya – no idea why. It would be obvious to me. Raja! The handsome one! To me Surya looks quite sleazy, but I guess he offers more.

Mr. Yoga is with his other friends, his arms loosely around their shoulders, sometimes winking at me. Out of the Arabian window I see the moon. And life is good. Life is just damn good.

It is quite late when we go back to our suite and Mr. Yoga is rather drunk, but that doesn't stop him from throwing off my clothes and pulling me on the bed. We're doing the usual. He kisses me and licks me. And since we didn't make it to intercourse last night, this time we make sure we do. I sit on top of him while he holds the happy boobs, moving slowly.

When I squat for deeper penetration, he stops me. "You're too tight," he moans. I laugh. "Now that's a compliment," I say. "I had two kids!" He nods "I know. I know. But you're just too tight…" So I go back to riding on him, letting him slide in and out until he quietly reaches his nirvana. Then he puts in his ear plugs, turns around and falls asleep.

But I can't fall asleep. I still can't believe what I have done. *I have jumped from a plane! My god!* And also I wonder why I had been so scared, the night before. *What did I need that fear for? For what?* I hadn't even been near that plane yet!

Everything before the actual moment of jumping had been without reason. It had just ruined my sleep. And right then I realize that maybe the best things in life are at the other side of terror. Maybe all the best things of life are on the other side of your maximum fear…

The next day I have breakfast by myself, while Mr. Yoga does his yoga. And when he leaves to do some business with his friends in Raja's suite, I check out the hotel. It has a nice pool, so I go for a cooling swim. "Book some treatments!" Amanda texts me. But compared to her, I'm cheap. I do check out the spa, but Mr. Yoga has never told me that I can book any treatments. I did kind of hint that I wanted to go, but he didn't make any offer and when I see the rates I decide not to go for it. I don't have any money anyway, whatever the currency is in this country.

Now Mr. Yoga has said there is a very nice and famous shopping mall in Dubai and he has put my envelope with pounds on the desk so I can go shopping, but I don't want to use my own money to go shopping. This is money I need for my life with the girls.

Something I *do* need to do, is work on Amanda's story. And there are several chapters about Dubai to write. So that's exactly what I decide to do. I sit at the nice oak desk and write. I order lunch in the room, a nice big Caesar's Salad with a glass of Chablis, and take a hot bath afterwards. And as the evening is falling I'm getting excited. Yesterday was awesome. I'm looking forward to another Dubai night.

But whenever you have expectations, things always turn out differently. When Mr. Yoga shows up again, I am dressed in a classy dress. But he looks me over and says: "Better change sweetheart. Vijay has invited us to his home to have drinks before dinner and meet his wife. Better wear something more casual."

My excitement drops. *Going to a home? Meet a wife? With my six dates?* "But who am I then?" I ask him. "I mean, why do you guys have a British girl with you?" He shrugs. "We better make up some good story."

Well, my only 'decent' clothes are the ones I was wearing upon arriving. And when I was jumping out of the plane. So there I go again. I am spending three days in Dubai wearing the same clothes.

Mr. Yoga is still lingering in front of the mirror. "Sweetheart, you like this shirt on me? I bought it new in New York." I check him out. It's just a regular polo again. "Sure," I say, hugging him from behind and giving him a kiss in his neck. "You are so handsome." And he smiles happily.

So off I go. With my six dates. In a private car, through a guarded gate, to some Dubai living quarters. The Indian Wife is waiting for us at the gate, smiling kindly. But my uncomfortableness only grows.

Mr. Yoga vaguely introduces me as some friend from London. Vijay – his eyes still shooting fire whenever I cross his gaze – starts mixing drinks, while The Wife takes my arm and proudly shows me around her house, the garden, the pool.

I decide to talk about all kind of homely matters. How I am studying yoga (that is how I know Mr. Yoga, we have decided), about my girls – talking about my children might make me sound more innocent I think– though I suspect she most definitely knows...

After a few drinks, Mr. Yoga falls asleep in one of the chairs and his friends give me some sideways looks as if it's because of me that the guy is so tired. Amir shyly sits almost next to me. I like him and I would love to talk to him. But I decide to focus my attention on none of my six dates, but on my hosts.

Vijay and his Wife are very energetic. They talk about all kinds of things in Dubai, while their staff brings in food. So I try to make the best of this. I try to make sure I stay away from Mr. Yoga. He's sleeping anyway. And all five of his friends do their best to take good care of me.

Drinks soon turn into dinner. *My god. This is NOT what I had in mind with partying in Dubai.* And The Wife sends out her staff to get some 'excellent Lebanese food'. The dinner is really nice, with fresh humus and juicy meat, but I just don't feel comfortable in this homely atmosphere. I was actually looking forward to another awesome Dubai restaurant.

Finally we are off. We have spent hours in the home. Vijay and his Wife wave us off, she gives me a strong hug just before I get into the car, and off we go to our hotel.

To my surprise Victoria and Rachel are waiting for us in front of our hotel. Apparently they have been called for. So the elevator whisks us all to the 71st floor – to the bar of our hotel called The Vault. Now the place does have breath-taking views over Dubai, but I prefer the terrace of the Four Seasons with the water pipes which made me feel like I had just arrived in 1001 nights.

The Vault is literally filled with hookers trying to get customers. And I am still wearing my 'decent' clothes, I look totally out of place. It's nice to look different from the hookers of course, but I would have liked to be wearing a nice dress like Victoria and Rachel.

Mr. Yoga chats with his friends, Victoria with her Sanjeev and I can't help but feeling a little lost. Then Amir quietly sits down next to me and starts asking me questions. About my life. About me. He tells me his wife just had a baby, their first, and proudly shows a picture of their daughter. And I have to say that I like him. I like his shyness. His genuine interest in me. And for a moment I wish that *he* is my arrangement.

But I have no choice here. Mr. Yoga has flown me in and paid for everything. And the moment he notices something blooming between Amir and me, he calls him over, throws his arm over Amir's shoulder and takes him on a walk, no doubt pointing out all the hookers that are available.

When Amir is back, he is even more silent. He makes sure he sits quite a distance away from me and he never talks to me again. And watching all the hookers in the place, I am starting to wonder. *Is what I am doing really so different? AM I having a choice?* But on the other hand, if Mr. Yoga was my boyfriend, I wouldn't so easily run off with one of his friends the moment I liked him either …

After an hour Mr. Yoga takes me to his suite. We are both drunk and I'm not feeling that great, but I manage to step over my feelings. It's time to perform. We make love. Our usual love-making. Kissing, oral and he quietly comes while wanking off.

The next day we take two taxi's to the airport, to the Business Departures. I kiss Mr. Yoga goodbye and hug his friends. I love them. They are great guys. Then I take my suitcase and roll it to my section of the airport: Economy.

Somehow I feel bad. And I can't put my finger on why. Mr. Yoga has been nothing but nice to me. He is predictable, does what he says. And I have been to great places, done sky diving, all paid for.

It might be because this really feels like an Arrangement. When we talk it feels like we have a connection, but this time we almost had no talks together. And he doesn't even pretend that he cares for me.

At least with Farshad and Rudolph it felt like they really cared (though did they really? Rudolph dropped me as easily as it started and Farshad I only hear from when it suits him). In a way it felt like they were in love with me.

With Mr. Yoga there is no illusion about that. He treats me well, we do have some kind of relationship talking about each other's lives. But in the end he doesn't really care. I'm something disposable.

I text Amanda. Her answer comes quick. "This is a good guy. Predictable. Honest. Keep your focus on the money."

When I arrive at Heathrow airport, I get the shock of my life. Because The Ex-In-Laws are there with my girls. "We came to pick you up!" the girls shout, handing me a bunch of flowers. And I try so hard to let go of the bad feelings, because I don't want anyone to notice.

For a moment I remember I haven't made up any work stories – I was going to make those in the train back home. But I don't even need them. As Mr. Viking has once said, most people are only interested in themselves. And that's especially true for Wilma.

She gives me all gory details about every second of these last days. How they made new dishes which the girls liked, the chores they gave my girls, how they taught them to behave, the way their dresses are now ironed.

She has no interest in what I did at all. I don't even need to make up stories. So on our way back home, I let the talks run over me like a tidal wave. I don't really listen anyway. I nod absently, hugging my girls.

Because I'm just so happy to be holding them again. I do my best to push away the bad feelings. I focus on the money and all the things I can do with it. And I focus on the nice things I experienced – because, seriously, what single mother goes sky diving in Dubai?

CHAPTER TWENTY:
THE PRETTY WOMAN DREAM

It's a beautiful morning in the end of May. The girls are at school and I should be writing and working on some new copywriting projects, but I'm chatting with Paul. Lately he keeps sending me nice messages asking me how I'm doing. He also keeps trying to have another dinner together, but I always make up excuses. For some reason I don't want him too close. I'm living off Sugar Dating. I can't afford to fall in love.

See, life is good as it is. There is no need to make things more complicated. Mr. Yoga has invited me to come to Frankfurt for two days in the beginning of June. And to make things even better, a new message now pops up: "I like your profile. Please reply if mine interests you."

I check out this new guy's profile. He is also from India, fifty-two years old and his profile is headed with: Passion/Romance/Fun. In the 'About Me' section it reads:

"I am a mature person who is young at heart. Born in a respected entrepreneurial family and have been bought up with the right values. Believe in YOLO (You only live once). Work Hard and Party Harder is my motto. Well-travelled all over the world. I travel to Europe two to three times a year and can meet then only."

The 'What I'm Looking For' section reads:

> "I would like to meet for having fun, romance and pas-
> sion together, enjoying each moment we spend together.
> Also like nice meals, romance, love to give and receive
> massages, intimacy etc. I understand why we are here
> and want a mutually beneficial, NSA relationship.
> Respect and Privacy is of utmost importance."

Well that sounds good, I have to say. The nice meals, massages,
NSA and especially the mutually beneficial part sound good to
me. And I have good experiences with Mr. Yoga. He keeps his
word and does what he says he will. So India is good. I reply back
and tell him that I'd love to hear more about him.

His reply comes fast: "Thank you for your kind reply. I travel
to Europe about twice a year and am interested in meeting then.
Does this suit you?" I answer that it would be lovely to meet.
He replies: "Great that we can meet. I should be visiting London
around the last week of June. May I ask what arrangements you
are looking for?"

Well, by now I am used to being open and honest about this.
So I reply: "I am a single mom of two girls and it can be hard to
make ends meet, so any help would be most welcome :-) though
I do have to feel a connection ..."

Mr. India2 replies: "I appreciate your straight forwardness
and respect you for that. For me too a connection is a must, without which there is no point. Ideally if we connect would love to
spend time together where we enjoy with no boundaries. Do as
we please and have a good time together."

Hmmm ... this might turn into something kinky ... No
boundaries ... Though I do have to say that since Mr. Yoga I
realize that cultural differences might lead to different inter-
pretations. I answer: "Sounds lovely :-) My 'normal' life is very

normal. It will be nice to have someone special to have a good time together with :-)"

Mr. India2 replies: "Great. It would be really nice to meet someone like you. I feel we will have a connection. Let's not plan anything as of now and take it as it comes when we meet. I should be there for a day or two. Most probably I should be coming in on 24th June morning. Do you have WA?"

So that evening we chat on WhatsApp. It turns out Mr.India2 is rather kinky. He's into sex clubs and wants to take me to an exclusive swingers club called Killing Kittens. Now I'm not sure India2 is someone I want to be seen in sex clubs with. He has sent me a hazy picture and I know he's shorter than me, but on the other hand, why not. I've never been to a club like that and the idea is rather appealing…

India2 agrees on my arrangement. He will help me with a 1000 pounds for our little adventure. So I agree upon meeting him. This means I will make 1800 pounds in June. This is turning out well…

But then I receive a new message which will totally mess things up. It reads: "Hello, Great profile and picture, love to meet you. Hope for a response." I check out this new guy's profile. He's a forty-seven years old widower living in London. He doesn't chat on SA for long, we immediately move to WhatsApp. And one hour later he is already calling me…

And I have to say that I'm a little taken aback by him. He doesn't talk about arrangements, he's saying he wants to help me. He tells me he has been struggling as a widower to raise two boys. That he knows how hard it is to raise children by yourself.

"You can be proud of yourself," he tells me. "You're doing a great job. I am proud of you!" He can't call long, he has business to attend to, but at the end of our talk he says: "I have found you. I'll delete my account. There is no reason to stay on SA anymore." And he really does seem to delete it. Though later on I will wonder. *Did he really, or did he just block me?* I guess I will never know.

His name is Jermaine and he starts calling me every day. And though the pictures he sends me aren't that great – he's rather fat, reminds me of a toad and is not a guy I would normally fall head over heels for – I do love his calls. His voice is warm. He seems to listen well and he asks lots of questions.

He asks simple, meaningful things. About being a single mom. Raising kids on my own. He tells me what a great job I am doing. Things that feel so good to hear. I've been struggling by myself for so long now. I've had to deal with so much criticism from Wilma. And each time I answer, I feel he really listens and registers. Everything he says makes sense. And I feel like everything I say is understood.

Now The Widower promises to help me out with money. No arrangement. Help. And for the first time in more than a year, I feel like I can breathe again. It feels like this big burden is taken off my shoulders. For the first time I realize how hard I've been swimming against the current. How close I have felt to drowning. *This is him*, I think. *The One.*

When I tell Amanda, she is happy for me. "This might be the one you were looking for," she writes. "Go for it. Good luck. I hope you can finally get a real good one." And Paul seems happy for me too. "Good for you baby!" he writes. "You might have hit the jackpot!"

But before I get all excited, I do want to meet him. So we set up a meeting for lunch. He chooses a place in my neighbourhood and is sitting at the bar when I enter. It has been a while since I was nervous meeting someone. But this time I am. Adrenaline is rushing through me.

When I see him at the bar, the excitement drops. I wasn't that enthusiastic about the pictures, but I'm even less in real life. He's looking way older than on his pictures, he's way fatter and he is wearing obnoxious shoes. But then I think: *Well, who cares.* So I politely introduce myself.

When we sit down opposite of each other, he talks nicely. But there is something about him. I can't put my finger on it. There is something in his eyes… They have a calculating look. I miss the warmth and caring that's in his voice when he is calling me. It's like his voice on the telephone and his body belong to two different persons. But I push my feelings aside.

When we leave, he pays for my parking ticket, gives me a hard kiss in front of my car and then leaves, his jacket blowing in the wind – showing its trendy red inside. I wait for him to turn so I can give him a blow kiss, but he never turns. He's already occupied with the other deals in his life.

That evening when he calls, I do feel a bit different. I don't feel that warmly towards him. I'm starting to have my doubts… But somehow his voice on the phone manages to change my feelings. He is kind. Caring. Telling how much he loves to take care of a woman.

"How much do you need to survive?" he asks me. "A thousand pounds a month." "Okay, okay," The Widower answers. "But that is just to survive. You are such a precious woman. You shouldn't be surviving. You should be enjoying life. So we should talk about more…" And he tells me that next time we meet we should talk about this. "See," he tells me, "You should spoil yourself. Are you spoiling yourself enough? You should!"

Then he asks me: "So where will you take your girls this summer?" I sigh and answer: "I don't have any money, love. I can't take them anywhere." "You should," he says. "That would be such a great experience for them. Memories are priceless. Don't worry, I'll help you with the money."

I try to picture myself with my girls on vacation and it feels great. But it also freaks me out. So I tell him: "Darling, I'm not sure I'll be able to travel with two small children all by myself."

Jermaine almost sounds angry. "Of course you can! You are so strong. Look at everything you have done by yourself. Believe in yourself. Go for it."

Then when we talk about relationships we both want to same thing. He also doesn't want a regular relationship anymore. He prefers a LAT relationship, having fun together but keeping the kids out of it. Which is exactly the way I feel about relationships now. So with his warm voice on the phone I melt again. He has a gift of knowing how to say all the right words...

We have dinner two weeks later. He comes to pick me up, and to my surprise he is holding a bicycle when I open the door. It used to belong to his oldest son, he says, but he wants to give it to Lisa. He has one for Sophie as well, he tells me. He will bring it real soon.

In his sports car we drive to London where he takes me to a Japanese restaurant. Not as fashionable as Sushisamba, but I push that thought away. The food is really nice and he is kind to me. We have a miso soup as a starter followed by a great selection of Sashimi and Sushi which just melt in my mouth. All washed down by a nice Viognier.

In the meantime The Widower talks nicely and I start to believe in the dream. The one Amanda talks about. She calls it: 'The Pretty Woman Dream'. You know the movie right? Where rich Richard Gere saves Julia Roberts out of prostitution?

Well there is one more thing Amanda says: "Never believe that a man will get you out of trouble." But I decide to ignore that one for now. Because I really believe that this guy is the one who is going to get me out. He is going to take care of me. He is going to save me.

But The Widower doesn't talk about money during dinner, though he had said he would. And I feel awkward to start talking about it. So we talk about raising kids on your own. We talk about relationships. And I'm starting to fall for him, even though I'm still not really physically attracted to him and there still is something in his eyes ... Something I do my best to ignore. *Because isn't this what I have been looking for?*

After dinner, when he brings me back home, I invite him in. Even though I'm not in an arrangement with him and we haven't talked about money. I only have his vague promise that he is going to 'help' me. But I believe him.

He starts kissing the moment he enters. And I'm happy to notice that the guy has passion. He kisses me all the way up to my bedroom, where he takes off his clothes including his hideous shoes.

Now that he is naked, I'm even less attracted to him. But I had my alcohol so I can dismiss that fact. There is also something not intimate about getting intimate with him, but I can't really put my finger on it. Somehow it doesn't feel personal.

The Widower is in action. But it feels like he could be in action with anyone, as he opens my legs and starts licking me without much preparation. He licks for some time, then he comes up and kisses me on my lips. I don't really like to be kissed immediately after a guy has been at my pussy, but I ignore it. He is already trying to enter me.

"Do you have something with you?" I ask politely. *I have a family package downstairs, but The Widower doesn't need to know that...* He looks up. "No. Should we? Can't we do without? I'm clean ..." *Yeah. Well, aren't they all? It's surprising how many men are clean. And how many want to skip the condom.*

"I'm not sure I am ..." I lie. "I once had a condom that broke ... I want to be sure before we ... But I think I might have one downstairs, shall I look for it?" *I will definitely find it, I have hundreds downstairs in all different sizes ...*

But The Widower shakes his head. "No, it's okay. Just give me a blow job." And he is already pushing my head down. He is a quiet guy, like Mr. Yoga. And he comes in utter silence. Then he puts his clothes back on, pushes his tongue down my throat one time more and leaves.

Should I have known better? I guess I should have looked at his deeds, right? But I'm still dazzled by his words. I know it's ridiculous. Here I am. Forty years old. A single mother with a failed marriage behind me, with an almost-escort Sugar Babe career and still believing in fairy tales...

But with The Widower I realize something. I realize that in fact all I long for is a man to put his arms around me and say he'll look after me and my girls. A man to take care of me. To take some of the weight off my shoulders. And The Widower promises to do all that...

Not long after he has left, Amanda sends me a message. "Did he help you?" And I don't want to tell her that he didn't. All he brought was a second-hand bicycle for Sophie. So I lie to her. I tell her he gave me 500. I feel embarrassed that he didn't, but I still want to believe so much that this is *The* One.

"This is him!" I tell her. "This is really him! I'm going to get off Seeking Arrangement. And I'm going to cancel the two India's." Amanda is not so easily convinced though. She isn't dazzled by his words. "Don't," she tells me. "Don't cancel them until you are sure about this guy. Until you have a monthly arrangement. You need the money."

I reply annoyed: "But he is calling me every day. And he just seems to know things. He knows exactly when I'm feeling blue. I'm sure he'll know I'm lying by the tone of my voice. He found me on SA. Then he will know what I am doing..."

But Amanda persists. Until this guy has actually paid me for a couple of months, she says, I should keep the others. "Mr. Yoga is your best one," she tells me. And that pisses me off too. I don't want Mr. Yoga to be my best one. I would prefer Farshad to be my best one. Not polite distant Mr. Yoga. But fact is that Farshad is as unpredictable as the British weather...

Paul also gets involved. He sends me a message asking how things with The Widower are going. And when I tell him I want to cancel my other appointments he tells me: "Don't. This Widow Guy sounds too good to be true. I think he is bull shit."

But I don't listen to any of them. I send two messages. I send an honest message to Mr. Yoga, telling him that I met someone, a widower, who might be the one and that I am so sorry but I won't be able to meet him anymore.

He reacts back immediately and is very kind. He is sorry for himself, he says, but he is truly happy for me. I'm a great person and deserve all the best. He will find another solution for Frankfurt. And I smile reading 'Another solution.' That's how disposable a Sugar Baby is ...

The second email I find harder to write. I send an email to my second Mr. India, who is especially coming to London to meet me tomorrow. And I feel that I can't be honest with him, so I send him a nasty lie. "I'm so sorry," I write to him. "I'm sick. I can't meet you tomorrow." He reacts back immediately. "My sweetheart, what is the problem? I can nurse you!"

Oh my god. My disease should be something serious. I can't let him nurse me. "I'm in hospital," I write back. "I need urgent surgery." And I truly feel horrible lying like that. Especially since he reacts so nicely. "I am so sorry to hear that sweetheart. Don't be sorry, just take care of yourself. I'm in a city with plenty of options so I'm sure I will find some substitution ...."

Amanda is laughing her ass off when I tell her. "Substitution! 😅" But for the rest she is not agreeing. "I really hope you know what you are doing," she says. "I guess you're sometimes too naïve for this world. These men promise heaven on earth. I don't want you to be disappointed ... You need the money for your girls ..."

Then I send one more message. To Jermaine. Letting him know that I will be free tomorrow evening ... He reacts fast. "I will arrange something. I will come to you. Will let you know the exact time. Get back to you ASAP." And little do I know the trouble I'm getting myself into …

That whole evening I wait by the phone, dressed in a nice dress so I can leave last-minute. But The Widower never sends a message back. So in the end I change into my pyjamas and go to bed.

When I switch off the light, I feel something in the pit of my stomach. It's a sad feeling. A deep sad feeling. The feeling when all your hopes come crashing down on you … For the first time since my divorce I feel truly and utterly hurt …

CHAPTER TWENTY-ONE: FROM SHATTERED DREAMS TO THE CITY OF DREAMS

In the end, words are all The Widower has got. He has promised me heaven on earth, but I never even get to see a glimpse of it. The day after he hasn't shown up I send him a text and ask him what's up. He does reply then. Apologizing. Saying some of his work projects are not going well. Telling me he is just too busy.

Our next appointment he cancels last minute saying he is a little sick. Another time he says he is in hospital. And truth is I'm hearing less and less of him. Of all his promises, the only one I see is a second-hand bicycle for Lisa. All others disappear in thin air.

So does it affect me? I would love to tell you that it doesn't. I'm not even in love with this guy. And whenever I met him I wasn't really attracted to him. So why does it hurt?

Was it just the dream of someone who was going to take care of me that made me so happy? Someone who would take some of the load of my shoulders? Some shining knight who would come and save me?

Well, one thing I know now. No one is going to save me. There are no knights on white horses galloping around saving damsels in distress. I'm the only one in this world who can save myself. And my girls. Amanda is right, of course. Never believe a man will get you out of trouble.

For one night I feel miserable. Truly and utterly miserable. For some reason this guy managed to touch all my hopes. My heart. But there's one thing about me. Whenever I hit rock bottom, I never stay there for long. I'm like a cat I guess. I always end up on my paws.

So after a good night of sleep, I lick my wounds and go on. I pull my chin up, straighten my back and decide that this is one lesson taken. Amanda was right, of course. Never cancel your SD's until you are sure about the guy.

Fact is that I have more serious worries. I have no time to whine about my shattered dreams. Since I cancelled my two appointments for The Widower, I haven't had any money coming in. And with The Ex not paying any alimony, I'm quickly running out again. Before long all I have left is enough to buy for food for just one more week. And I realize I need to make money. Fast.

Something has definitely changed inside of me with The Widower Experience. I realize that Amanda is right. I can see clearly now how I've been doing this all wrong. I'm making it all way too personal. So I decide that from now on I will keep my personal feelings out of this. From now on I will focus on the money. Also I need to start saving money, so I will never be in a situation like this again.

Now, I'm desperate for money, so I contact all my men. I send an email to Farshad, but he doesn't reply. *No surprise there of course.* I send a message to Rudolph. He mails back saying he misses me, but obviously he is not interested to refresh our arrangement.

I even contact Sam, even though he has never helped me with any money. Sam is all happy and cheerful when he replies. He seems like a changed man. He has found a girl, he tells me. Which means that – so sorry – he won't be able to see me anymore.

And in this ocean of cheating men, it's nice to find at least someone honest. Someone who is staying loyal. I am almost tempted to reconsider my conviction that 'all men cheat,' which I've held since Giovanni. Almost. So I smile, wish him all the best and move on.

In the end, it's Mr. Yoga who comes to the rescue. When I send him a message that I miss him, he reacts fast: "How are you doing sweetheart? Hope you are happy…" So I tell him that I'm not seeing The Widower anymore.

"Really?" he reacts. "Well, I would love to see you again. I'm just not bothering you, because I don't want to stand in the way of your happiness. How would you feel about coming to Vienna for one night next weekend?" And I cheer. *I would love to!*

With Mr. Yoga being a Man-Who-Keeps-His-Words, I have a ticket in my inbox that afternoon. And with that ticket I can feel this heavy burden lift a bit from my shoulders. I sigh. For now I'm saved. *I'm going to survive another month…*

Since I now know I'm going to make money next week, I can finally spend my last cash on grocery shopping. Though I do hope that he will wait for me in front of the hotel. Otherwise I will need to use Lisa's pocket money to pay for the cab. She will never know of course, but just the thought already feels miserable. It makes me feel like a complete failure…

Outside the store I just sit in the car for a while, watching the people go in and out. The weather is lovely and the summer holidays are coming up. I smile. All this is so normal. Who of these people would guess that I'm in a plush hotel the next weekend? And I feel happy. *I'm back in the saddle again.*

So the next weekend I bring my girls to The Ex-In-Laws. And I can't afford to feel bad about leaving them there. I can't afford to let Wilma get under my skin. I need the money.

Soon I'm in a plane again, smiling in my heart. The flight is short and before long I'm in a cab driving towards Vienna. It takes a while before the road becomes pretty, but the moment we enter Vienna I'm surrounded by beautiful stately buildings.

Now I was hoping that Mr. Yoga would be out waiting for me so he could pay my cab, but he texts me that he is taking a shower. So with a heavy heart I use Lisa's pocket money to pay for the cab. And that feels like a real low. One thing I promise myself, right there and then. I'm never going to let it get this low again…

The hotel is on a great location right in the city centre, but away from the bustle and opposite a beautiful park. I wait in the big lobby for Mr. Yoga to finish his shower and come down to pick me up.

When he does, he takes my suitcase and leads me to his room, as always skilfully avoiding reception. In the elevator he smiles and says: "Nice to meet you again, sweetheart." And I smile back. *It's so nice to see him again.*

Mr. Yoga's suite is beautiful, as always. It has a lovely park view, a neutral décor with a polished oak desk and a bulging fruit hamper. And as usual, he is the real gentleman. He keeps his distance as I unpack my suitcase. When I'm ready, he hands me two pretty paper bags with presents he has brought me from China. One has Chinese tea in it, the other one pineapple cookies for the girls.

To thank him, I kiss him lightly on his lips, but Mr. Yoga reacts quite eagerly. And he still knows how to kiss… Now I thought the guy was only able to have sex drunk, but he is already leading me to the bed…

He kisses my lips while his hands reach behind me and unzip my skirt, letting it fall to the floor. Next he pulls my top over my head. His kisses go down, to the Happy Boobs, and down on my belly. Taking off his trousers and shirt, the throws me on the bed where he continues his kissing, on my lips, trailing towards my breast and sucking my erect nipples.

Jeez, he is still such a good sucker. He sucks my nipples until they are ultra-sensitive. Next he trails down to my belly, kissing my belly button and going down, pushing my legs apart and kissing my pussy. He licks me for some time, till I flip him over. I go down to give him a long unresponsive blow job.

Then I climb on top of him, moving slowly while he holds the Happy Boobs. When I try to squat for deeper penetration, he stops me again, moaning: "You're still too tight…" I laugh and go back to riding on him until he quietly reaches his nirvana.

We don't stay in the bed for long. We're soon up again, getting dressed. Outside Mr. Yoga takes my hand and says: "Let's go to Stephansplatz, in the centre." And I'm happy to walk with him through this beautiful city.

Vienna is really beautiful. It has baroque streetscapes and imperial palaces alongside coffee-houses and design shops. And the scent of this city seems to be a mixture of warm plums and the acrid smell of the carriage horses.

"Did you know Vienna is called the City of Music?" Mr. Yoga asks me. I didn't, but if I remember it correctly Haydn, Mozart, Schubert and Beethoven all had something to do with this city, so I can see why it's called like that.

Mr. Yoga continues: "Another name for Vienna is less known though. It is also known as the 'City of Dreams'." And he smiles. "You know why?" I shake my head. "No, no idea…" "Because it was home to Sigmund Freud, the world's first psycho-analyst." I look around and murmur: "City of Dreams. I like that…"

For some time we walk in silence. But when the silence seems to be getting to long, I search my mind for a subject and ask him: "How are your daughters?" A soft look comes over his face. "They are fine," he says. "I just registered the oldest one for university in the US." But then a cloud passes over his face. "You know, it's one of the best," he says. "It's real expensive, but I don't even think she even appreciates ... She just thinks it's normal that I do that for her."

And in a way I feel sorry for him. His daughters are the love of his life. The ones whom he tries so hard to please, though they will probably never realize or appreciate it. *How sad.* On the other hand, maybe expensive things is not what they long for. Isn't in the end what we all want just attention, to be seen and heard? No money on earth can buy that ...

We remain silent for quite some time. We both seem to be lost in our own thoughts. Suddenly his phone rings and he puts his finger in front of his mouth to hush me. *It must be Mrs. Yoga.*

They chat for some time – apparently she thinks he is in Frankfurt this time – while I silently walk next to him. And in a way I feel bad for his wife, as I'm walking next to him. *I was a wife once. I wouldn't have wanted this.* But I can't afford those thoughts right now, so I push them aside ...

When we pass the Ritz-Carlton hotel, Mr. Yoga takes me by my elbow. "Come," he says. "Let's go for a drink." And he takes me to the rooftop cocktail bar, where we get a snug corner. The place has beautiful views over the skyline of Vienna and a creative drink menu. Even the mix masters at the bar seem well skilled. This is going to be good ...

Mr. Yoga orders me a refreshing Summer Mule with gin and lemon, garnished with a slice of cucumber and a sprig of mint. For himself he asks one of the mix masters to prepare a special cocktail. It's beautiful when it arrives. It has vodka with a slice of cucumber and a spicy Spanish pepper, giving it a slight spicy bite I notice after he gives me a sip.

It's a beautiful summer evening, so sipping my cocktail I sit back and enjoy the view over Vienna. Mr. India lightly takes my hand, while his other hand is drumming the rhythm of the music on the counter. "This place is brilliant," he says. And we have another cocktail.

After dusk has fallen, Mr. Yoga takes me to an elegant Japanese restaurant, close to the opera and right in the heart of Vienna. We are lead inside and the interior looks grand, but Mr. Yoga has one look on the menu and says: "I can't eat this, I'm sorry." So the waiter takes us to sit outside, where we can order a la carte.

We start with a shrimp tempura for Mr. Yoga and a spicy salmon sashimi for me. The sashimi simply melts in my mouth. Next Mr. Yoga has the Sukiyaki Omaha beef while I have the sushi. It's a nice mixture of contemporary sushi with vegan futomaki, maki with eel and avocado and flamed scallop sushi. Yes, flamed. And it is amazing. By now we have finished a whole bottle of wine and Mr. Yoga orders some sake. As always with Mr. Yoga, I'm starting to get drunk. I always get drunk with this guy. I should learn how to drink less…

Then suddenly a thought comes up. Mr. Yoga knows what it is like to love children. And now that The Widower has put this dream in my head, there is one thing I would really love to do. I've been googling for trips since The Widower said he'd pay and I found a real nice cheap trip to Greece.

Now that I have the dream, I would love to take the girls on vacation. But obviously The Widower is not paying. And the money Mr. Yoga is giving me now I will need for our daily life. *But,* I think, *maybe he could pay our next meeting ahead?*

So I ask him. "You know darling, I would love to take the girls on a summer holiday. I never have. It would be our first vacation together. And I found this cheap vacation, but I still can't afford it. Would it be possible if you give me an advance payment?" Mr. Yoga smiles. "Sure sweetheart. No problem. You give your girls a nice vacation." And right there and then I could have kissed him. I feel just so damn happy.

After dinner Mr. Yoga proposes to go back to our hotel. We have finished our bottle, our sake and he has had two more whiskey's. So we're both quite drunk. And in a way I wonder. *Will he remember his promise to help?*

We walk back to the hotel, lightly holding hands. It's dark and everywhere around us people are enjoying themselves. People are laughing, smiling, kissing. I just love it.

The moment we enter the room, Mr. Yoga starts kissing me passionately, leading me to the bed. And we do our usual love-making. Kissing, oral and he quietly comes while I ride on top of him. Then he puts in his earplugs, turns around and goes to sleep. I send a message to Amanda telling her all is okay, then turn around and fall asleep.

As always we wake as polite strangers. But I'm used to it now and it doesn't make me feel uncomfortable. We keep our polite distance while he is chatting with one of his daughters. And I know there won't be any more lovemaking, so I get up and start preparing while Mr. Yoga starts his yoga routine. I smile. He has never done his yoga in front of me. There is a difference this time. There is some kind of intimacy. It's like we are getting used to each other. There is a familiarity that I like.

When I'm ready to go for breakfast, he tells me to wait and says: "I'll come for breakfast with you." *Now that's surprising, I've never had breakfast with him before.* "I thought you didn't do breakfasts with girlfriends?" I ask him. He shrugs. "I didn't. But I changed. Now I do."

Well, of course I will wait for him. So I watch him as he goes through his yoga routine. He does the same as I do, I notice. It's the Sun Salutation. For some reason, with him wanting to be a teacher and all, I had expected him to do something more unique. "You're welcome to join me," he says looking up to me from the cobra. I smile. "Maybe some other time." Truth is I'm shy. I'm scared my yoga will suck next to his.

When he is finished, showered and dressed, we go to the club lounge where as a Gold Member Mr. Yoga has his breakfasts. It's a nice, relaxing, open plan restaurant with a lovely buffet. I choose a fresh orange juice, some yoghurt with fruits and some fried eggs from the friendly girl at the egg station. And having breakfast together feels nice. In a way it feels intimate to swirl around each other choosing our dishes.

But suddenly he is frowning, when he comes back from a second round of scrambled eggs. "I just met a friend," he says as he drops in his chair. "A very close friend from India. He is here with his wife. I truly hope he hasn't seen me with you..." And that's the end of the lovely breakfast.

We quickly go back to our room where Mr. Yoga says: "I have some work to do," sitting down behind his silver laptop on the polished oak desk. "But you are welcome to explore the city by yourself. Go ahead and enjoy Vienna. But take your suitcase with you, I will check out later."

So this was it. And I wonder. *Has he remembered his promise? Should I say something about it?* But I'm too shy to ask. So I pack my bag and kiss him goodbye.

But I'm lucky. Before he lets me go, he gets an envelope out of his bag and gives me a thousand euros. "Take your girls on vacation," he tells me. "Enjoy your time with them. And send me the pictures afterwards." And I thank him from the depth of my heart. I kiss him goodbye – not knowing it's the last time I will ever see him – roll my suitcase to reception, leave it there and head into Vienna to explore.

Once I'm walking through Vienna by myself, I realize something. *I'm not feeling bad.* This is the first time that I've been with Mr. Yoga and not feeling bad. I'm actually feeling rather good. I feel like singing. Or dancing. Or bursting out with laughter. He has really helped me. And here I am. In Vienna. With all the time in the world to enjoy.

First I go to the elegant Schönbrunn Palace. And the moment I step in, I feel like I'm being transported to the old times. I take the Grand Tour with an audio guide. It takes forty minutes and takes me through forty of the exquisite palace's 1441 rooms. *And I can't help thinking that this place would be perfect for hide and seek with my girls.*

I wander through the apartments of Emperor Franz Joseph and his wife Elisabeth, through the magnificent Hall of Ceremonies, the imposing Gobelin Salon with exquisite Brussels tapestries and the impressive mirror hall – where a six-year old Mozart gave his very first concert.

I walk around the enormous ballroom, watching the huge paintings on the walls and am at awe by the gorgeously painted ceilings. And I sit for some time on a bench in the perfumed Rose Garden, watching the locals that are out for morning jogs and enjoy the sunshine on my face. And that moment I realize that it's the first time I enjoy being alone.

Next I just follow the crowd and wander around Vienna aimlessly. I tail in after people who file into grand buildings. I follow the crowd into churches where I listen to classical music. And though I sometimes lose my way, the chimes of the St Stephen's Cathedral always situate me.

But eventually it's time to go. I have a plane to catch. So I go to the hotel reception where they arrange a car for me. The driver is a handsome dark guy wearing sunglasses. "I'm Aleksandar," he says. "Nice to meet you."

While we are driving through the beautiful streets, he says: "I'm from Macedonia. Where are you from?" "I'm Monique. I'm from the UK." He is quiet for some time, then he says: "Listen. I am never going to meet you. So let's do something special. Let's be completely open and honest with each other."

Well, why not. And before I know it, I blurt out: "I'm a Sugar Babe." I'm surprised how easily I've said it. But it's refreshing to be open and honest about it. My life has become such a bunch of lies that it feels special to be open about it, even if it's with a complete stranger.

Aleksandar takes off his sunglasses and looks at me through the rear mirror. "What does that mean?" he asks me. "Well I date rich men who help me out. See, I'm a single mother with two kids to take care of … I just was with one of them. A married Indian businessman."

"Good for you," Aleksandar says and he smiles at me. "You're a great mother, taking care of your children." I smile and he is silent for some time. But then he continues. "If you're honest though, is that going to save you in the long run?" *Now that's not what I wanted to hear…* Reluctantly I shake my head. "No it won't …"

"I'm not judging you, just asking. See, I used to be a gangster," he says and checks my reaction. "As I said, I'll be completely honest with you. I used to make money the fast way. Then I ended up in prison. But when I had lost everything and I had nothing left to fear, I decided to finally go for my dreams. So I saved money and came here. Now I'm living my dream. I have my own car, my freedom."

He looks at me. "What would your dream life look like?" I close my eyes and picture my ideal life. And I realize that I'm actually pretty close to it. My ideal life would be in my house, with the girls and Fuzzy.

But some things would be different. I would be making enough money through writing, so we can live a nice and comfortable life. So that I can take the girls on vacation and have no more worries about finances. And to my surprise I even see some hazy guy dooming on the horizon … *Imagining this life feels really good.*

"So why aren't you living this dreamlife?" Aleksandar asks me. I ponder on that one, but Aleksandar already answers:

"Because of your limiting beliefs." I frown. "My what?" "The beliefs which limit you in some way. Just by believing them, you do not think, do, or say the things they constrain." He looks at me in the rear mirror again.

"Often it's all about fear. The fear of rejection, failure, success, something new. But you know what? Most of the time, fear is just an illusion." I nod. *I experienced that with skydiving…*

"So what do you do with fear?" I ask him. He smiles. "Whenever you have a fear coming up, realize that it's just a thought, that's all. It's just a belief that you can get out of. Believes are something you can change. It may make a hell of a scene, but it cannot stop you. You stop you."

We are at the airport now and Aleksandar is steering the car towards the Departures hall. "Fear of failure is a huge limiting belief," he says. "It's one I have struggled with for years. But then I discovered that if something didn't work out, nothing bad happened to me."

Aleksandar has stopped the car, but he continues talking. "So I changed my mind-set. I would remember something which I've once read somewhere: 'There's no failure, only feedback.' So I would find the good in it, or turn it into something good. I would look at it in a positive way. I would think: how can I use this? What did work? What can I do with it?"

Aleksandar takes my suitcase out of the trunk and says: "Have faith in yourself Monique. You can solve any problem you'll encounter. If we can get rid of our limiting beliefs, the sky is the limit!" He gives me a kiss on my cheek and says: "Goodbye Monique. Enjoy your life. Make it a great one!"

And you know what? That's exactly what I'm planning to do…

CHAPTER TWENTY-TWO: TANTRA

The beep of my phone wakes me up. *Jeez… I should remember to put the sound off at night.* Still drowsy from sleep I peek through my eyelids. Apparently Sophie has had nightmares again. She is lying next to me hugging Big Bear and has taken most of my blanket. I try to pull some back. She moans, turns and cuddles me, making the sucking sound for comfort she has made since I stopped breast feeding her.

Careful not to wake her I get my phone. To my surprise I have received a message from Mr. India2. After cancelling last time with some lame excuse, I thought I would never hear from him again. I still feel a bit guilty, since the guy had come all the way to London to meet me. But his app sounds happy enough.

"I'll be in Europe again! 😄 Are you free on Saturday the 15th?" I check my schedule on my phone. There's nothing on the 15th. The girls will be with their father. So I reply: "Sure! I look forward to finally meeting you. 🐱"

Shiva's reply comes fast. "We can meet for the night. Say from 10 pm till 9 am. I am sure we should hit it well. You are a beautiful lady. Coming to London again just to meet you. 😊 We must both enjoy and look forward to meet each other. Be like lovers. Looking forward to giving you a sensual massage. And making passionate love to you. Get some sexy lingerie please. 🐾"

And he keeps sending short messages before our meeting. On the 11th of July: "Hi, I am in London. See you soon. 😊" On the 13th of July: "Hi, just three days to go before we meet. Looking forward to it! 🐵" On the 14th of July: "We're staying at the Hyatt Place. So looking forward sweetheart. 😊"

On date day, with the girls at their fathers place, I have oceans of time before meeting. I chat for some time with Mr. Viking, Sophie, Barbara and Paul. I take a long hot bath, spend a nice amount of time on choosing clothes and applying make-up. You would think I am used to this now, but truth is I'm a bit nervous. This is the first time I'm meeting a guy in this way.

Of course Mr. Yoga and Sam were a bit like this, but at least I had time to get to know them, have dinner and some – very much needed – drinks before the lovemaking started. Meeting this guy at 10 means no dinner, no drinks…

That evening I'm waiting for him in front of reception in a nice classy black dress, and I discover that the place is flooded with Indians. Truth is I have no idea who the guy is. Sure, I got his picture, but I don't really remember what he looks like…So I look kindly at a couple of the Indians, but they either ignore me or give me a puzzled look so I decide they can't be him.

Finally a guy walks out of the elevator and straight up to me. Though to be honest I'm not totally pleased. He is a short middle-aged man with a protruding belly and a moustache. His clothes don't even look real expensive. Mr. Yoga is always wearing nice designer clothes and flashy shoes. This guy looks humble. And he has a red sacred Hindu thread tied around his wrist.

But this definitely is the guy. He introduces himself as Shiva, moving his head from left to right. So keeping the money for vacation in mind, I follow Shiva into the elevator, where two other men are chatting.

They look a couple of times at us from the corners of their eyes. *Yes, it's very obvious what our relationship is. I'm not with this Indian guy for love.* But the guys get out soon enough and we go on to the top floor, to the executive suites.

Shiva very politely invites me into his room and to sit down on a soft camel sofa. Then he leaves the room to get some ice. *God do I feel uncomfortable. I'm still not sure I'm going to do this. Am I seriously going to sleep with this guy?? I'm not really sure I'll be able to ...*

In a way I feel like I did with the American. But I've changed since then. And I do want to take the girls to Greece. With Mr. Yoga's extra money I could pay the tickets and the hotel. But this date will mean we have cash for on our vacation and after it.

Shiva is back soon enough. He has brought a big bottle of Moet & Chandon Rose Imperial Champagne for me from the airport and for himself some Chivas Regal.

There are no glasses in the room – the Hyatt Place is pretty crappy compared to the hotels I normally stay in. Even the mini bar is empty. So we drink from coffee cups. He first joins me with a little champagne, then pours himself some whiskey.

Now Shiva is very polite. I do have to say that. He chats away about India. About his marriage. He has a love marriage and he and his wife still love each other a lot. They have two kids together who are now teens. He doesn't travel for his work like Mr. Yoga, but twice a year he comes to Europe to party.

"But if you love your wife," I can't help asking, "Then why are you on Seeking Arrangement?" The guy shrugs. "The body also has his needs sweetheart." And he pours me some more champagne.

"I've had many escorts before," he says, holding his head sideways. And there is not even a hint of shame on his face. *Jeez, haven't they all?* "But I quit them," he says. "I need something more personal. I need a connection. I cannot do it without a connection."

So are WE having a connection, I wonder. But I try to keep the conversation going, because the moment we stop talking something else will start. And the sex-part is not something I really want to think about...

I do have to say that there is something about him. It's his eyes I guess. He has this really intense look that seems to look right into my soul.

He smiles at me. "You are a mother," he says. "It's important that you take good care of yourself. That you enjoy life enough. Your own happiness will pour over into your girls." Then he puts his coffee cup with whiskey down and says "Sweetheart, it's time for your Tantra massage."

And I almost choke on my champagne. *It's time for my WHAT?* Tantra...Of course I've heard about it...I know it's something sexual. I know the Tantric Yab Yum images from India and Tibet. But I have no idea what Tantric massage is.

"Tantra is derived from 'tan', meaning to expand and 'tra', meaning instrument." Shiva explains. "It is a spiritual practice. We use a form of sexual ritual as a way of entering an intensified and expanded state of awareness while dissolving mind-creating boundaries."

Well, whatever I am up for, Shiva says he is first going to take a shower. So I down most of the bottle in that time, and then notice his laptop screensaver. It's made up by this one sentence. '*This is the laptop of Shiva Mitra.*' So I finally know his real name. I always like to know their real names.

I take out my phone and app Amanda: "In room 2120. Everything ok. Name is Shiva Mitra." And she gives me a thumbs up. " Let me know when you are finished. Want to know you're ok."

Shiva calls me from under the shower and asks me to get some matches for his candles at reception. *Candles? We aren't going to do wax play right?* But I decide to do as asked and go down to reception.

Getting back into the elevator with the matches, this handsome guy gets in, looks me over and asks: "Are you going to a gala?" I giggle and say no. When he sees I press the button of the top floor he says "Ah, you're exclusive!" I nod. "Yes, I'm very exclusive."

Back in the room Shiva is out of the shower and wearing just a sarong. From his laptop comes enticing tabla music. He takes the matches, hands me a similar sarong and says: "Please wear this with nothing underneath," while he starts lighting candles all over the room.

So what am I to do? I go to the bathroom, take off everything except my slip and put on the silky soft sarong. *What has happened to the 'bring some sexy lingerie please'?* Sometimes I seriously don't know why I bother choosing nice lingerie for my Sugar Daddies.

In the room Shiva has turned off all the lights. Only the scented candles give a faint shimmer. They give off an exquisite oriental scent. On the night stand he has put a bottle of Johnson's baby oil. He catches my glance. "So sorry, sweetheart. I brought really nice essential oil for us from India," he says, "But they took it in Heathrow at customs."

He hands me my coffee cup with more champagne and dances with me while I drink. His hands slowly caress me, but he stops dead track the moment he feels my knickers underneath the sarong. "Remove all" he says sternly. So I go back to the bathroom to remove it.

It's stupid, I know. I'm going to have sex with this guy so why am I going to the bathroom to take it off? But I just don't feel that comfortable with him yet.

When I get back, he stands in front of me, kisses me on my forehead – he has to stand on his toes to reach – and says: "I hope you are going to enjoy this as much as I will. Please trust me completely. If there is anything I do that you don't like, please feel free to let me know. Now please close your eyes." And he gets back on his toes to kiss me once more on my forehead.

I close my eyes. He comes behind me and tells me to take some deep breaths together with him and keep breathing like that during the massage. Then he comes in front of me, kisses my feet and puts his head between my feet.

Now I know for a Hindu touching feet is not really considered appropriate, but there he is. With his head between my feet. Worshipping me like a Goddess. And he keeps treating me like a Goddess for the whole two hours that he massages me.

I don't recall everything he does. He kind of puts me in a trance. First he worships me while I am standing, then he pulls me to the bed and asks me politely to lay down on a massage space he has prepared on the bed.

He first puts me on my back. Keeping my sarong on, he is massaging me from head to toe, very respectfully, in a very loving manner. It's actually very exciting, lying there with a complete stranger, naked, with just a sarong on and waiting for him to take it off. It greatly arouses me and I can feel I'm getting wet. I know he is getting glimpses of my naked body underneath, but he takes his time.

Finally he takes off my sarong and asks me to turn around. He massages my back, my legs and then my ass. First he is just caressing, drawing slow circles. But the circles become faster until he enters his thumb inside my back door.

Until then the massage has been very relaxing, but now I get excited. It seems like with every thrust he drives energy inside of me. I can feel I am getting soaking wet. I don't know for how long he goes on, till he turns me around and starts caressing my 'yoni' as he calls it.

First he just massages the outside. I am already highly stimulated so I want him to be inside, but he takes his time before he puts his finger inside of me.

Now most men have no idea how a woman works. But not this man. This little Indian guy – whom I had not been so excited about, with his moustache and his protruding belly – none of which I am seeing since he still orders me to close my eyes – knows more about a woman's body then most women probably do themselves. It is amazing. And he isn't even entering me yet. He makes me come real close to orgasm four times.

Then I can't stand it anymore. I get up, slipping my legs over his, and start kissing him, while he whispers "You're beautiful. You're so beautiful," still looking at me like I am a Goddess. *We're really looking like a yab-yum sculpture now*, I can't help thinking.

He slips on a condom and we make love like that. With him sitting and me sitting on top of him, kissing him passionately. My breasts are moving against his chest, sometimes I lean back on one hand for deeper penetration, until I can see his orgasm building up and he comes loudly.

Afterwards I am lying in his arms. He kisses my forehead and says: "Thank you, sweetheart." Though I feel like *I* should be the one thanking. I have gotten this magical massage AND get vacation money paid to receive it. *How strange the Sugar World can be.*

As I lay on his hairy chest he mumbles: "I didn't have such good lovemaking in a long time." Now I don't know how that could be, since he had mostly been pleasuring me. But I whisper back "I have NEVER made love like this before." He looks at me surprised. "Really?" I kiss him. "Really." And I seriously mean it. He smiles happily. "Well it won't be your last tantric massage."

He sleeps quite fast after that. I spend some time listening to the hotel sounds. Someone is flushing a toilet. A TV is on too loud. And I think about my girls – *they must be sleeping now* – as I look at the reflection of the car headlights from the highway on the ceiling. The same highway leading to my house. *How strange life can be.*

When Shiva wakes, we take turns in the shower and after we're dressed he gives me a 1000 pounds. "I'm sorry I don't have an envelope sweetheart," he says. "I should have prepared."

I arrive back home at 10. Fuzzy greets me a bit grumpy – I'm late for his breakfast. But apart from him, not a soul has noticed that I have been away. When I check my phone there is already a message from Shiva. "It was such a pleasure meeting you. Next time we should have more time. 🐾"

Of course I google him the moment I am home, after I have made myself a nice cup of hot tea. But when I find him, I'm shocked. He is from Calcutta – the same city as Mr. Yoga. But that's not all, their companies are working together and I find both their names on several committees. One thing is for sure. These guys know each other. So I can only wonder. Has Mr. Yoga recommended me? Or has he tested me? And if he tested me, have I thrown away my dependable eight-to-ten times a year Mr. Yoga for a one-to-two times a year Mr. Tantra?

Fact is, I will never meet Mr. Yoga again. After Mr. Tantra, he politely lets me know that he is not travelling to Europe anymore. And I can only wonder. Is he quitting our arrangement because of Mr. Tantra? Or did our Arrangement become too intimate? Is the intimacy which I liked our last meeting, exactly the thing he doesn't want?

Whatever it is, truth is that I don't regret it. I had a great experience with Mr. Tantra. I told him: "I NEVER have made love like this before." And you know what? I really meant it. I don't know exactly what Shiva did to me, but I had this energy vibrating through my body and this Goddess feeling that lasted for days. Next time Shiva calls for me, I'll be there. Definitely.

CHAPTER TWENTY-THREE: SUMMER TIME

Summer starts with a small drama. It all starts nice enough. Fred and Wilma invite us for Shrek's Adventure in London and dinner in a fancy restaurant. Which is nice, right?

The girls love it. They run around with Fred. But I'm left with Wilma, whose 'happy pills' apparently aren't working anymore. Fact is, she's finding fault in everything the girls do. In everything I do. The girls are not quiet enough. They don't give her enough attention. They should definitely be better brought up. See, Josephine...

So I'm doing my best to brush it off. To not listen to whatever she is saying. But then at dinner things don't get any better. And I admit that maybe I drink a bit too much wine in frustration. So when she has another remark ready, I talk back. For the first time ever.

I ask her: "Why do you always have to be so critical? Why can't we do anything right in your eyes? I'm a single mom, doing the best I can. I'd like some appreciation for that."

With her mouth still open, her ice-blue eyes lock on mine for a couple of minutes as total disbelief flushes over her face. But that doesn't take long. She gets her purse, jumps out of her chair and marches away. Shouting over her shoulder – in the middle of that damn full restaurant – : "I get why Eric wanted to divorce you. Don't even think we're ever going to look after your girls again. From now on, you're on your own."

Fred hugs me and apologizes profoundly, then pays the bill and hurries after her. Leaving the three of us at the big table, with the whole restaurant looking at us. The girls look at me with worried little faces.

Inside I'm fuming, but there is no use in upsetting the girls. So I smile and tell them: "Don't worry girls, it will be all right. Now let's finish our desert, shall we. It would be a waste to leave it behind. I guess our ride home just left, but no worries. We'll take the train."

In a way I'm already looking forward to tell Sarah. *At least, for the first time ever, I've stood up for myself.* But that's the end of any relationship there ever was between me and The Ex-In-Laws. I will never hear from them again.

I have no time to ponder over it for too long though. I have my life to live. And as any mother knows, life with children takes on a momentum all of its own. Also Amanda's book is finished. Finally. And I have prepared a whole list of agents to contact. But the endless summer holidays have started, so I will send proposals when the girls are back in school. Now it's time for us to go on our summer holiday …

Sophie is jumping in front of the door, Lisa is cuddling with Fuzzy, telling him goodbye. We are all packed. I don't have too much with me, and we won't be staying for long. Four days, if you extract the two days traveling.

But still, this is big. This will be our first vacation together. This is the first time I'm taking the girls somewhere. And I am doing it all by myself. This is BIG in a good way. It's a big step forward in my life as a single mother.

Now of course Amanda has strongly advised against it. She has reminded me how only a month ago I had to use Lisa's pocket money to pay for that Vienna taxi. But I'm stubborn I guess. I decide to go anyway. There is only one summer vacation a year, only one chance to give my girls an unforgettable experience. And it is possible thanks to my two India's: Mr. Yoga and Mr. Tantra. ☺

In the train to Heathrow the girls are all giggles and excited whispers. They don't travel much by train, for them this is all an exciting adventure. And at the airport they stay close to me.

Sophie is carrying Big Bear in her arms. She insisted on taking him with her, and she is in tears when he has to be x-rayed. Lisa has a tiny stuffed rabbit hidden in her backpack. So no one will see it, but she can still hug with it when needed.

After customs we have lunch, right there at the airport. I decided that since we will have to pay for food on the plane, why not enjoy something nice here instead. And thanks to The India's I can splurge a little. Both girls have a kid's meal with a tiny little burger and fries and I don't go for the cheapest but for what I like. I have a tuna steak. It's bedtime when we board, so the girls are rubbing their eyes already and boarding takes way too long to their taste. But once inside, the airplane from within is another big adventure.

Sophie is all excited about the little table, which she keeps opening and closing until I stop her. Lisa has gotten her tiny rabbit out and is cuddling him secretly – somehow she has decided she is too old to openly show affection to stuffed animals.

Finally it's taking off time and that's another thrill and joy. But when the plane is in the air, the girls are so exhausted by all their adventures that it doesn't take long before they are both asleep.

I'm sitting in the middle, with a heavy head on each shoulder, as I cover them with their airplane blankets, kiss the crown of their heads and smile. *This is going to be great…*

On arrival we are guided to a bus filled with other British tourists which is supposed to bring us to our hotel. But apparently we are staying in a hotel where most British don't stay, so after some heated discussion in Greek by our driver and another man we are taken out and get a limousine-like van for just the three of us. The girls cheer.

Outside it's pitch dark. It's after twelve and the city is deserted. All we see is the lights and the palm trees. But the palm trees are enough to make the girls cheer again. It takes some time before we arrive at the gate into the old town. That's where we are staying, in a boutique hotel. You need to go in through a special gate and normal cars are not allowed.

In the old town we drive through a maze of streets until the driver gets out, gets our suitcase and we walk the last mile to our hotel. It's nice and warm outside even though it's in the middle of the night. And the girls are tired, rubbing their eyes.

The hotel is pitch dark, but Lisa nudges Sophie and points at the dark swimming pool glimmering in the courtyard. They both smile. But we don't have much time to look at the pool. Soon the receptionist arrives. He is very friendly, tells us his name is Dimitris and says we should follow him to our room.

Our hotel turns out to be a maze of mansions, each with a couple of guestrooms, where the rooms have names rather than numbers. When Dimitris opens the big wooden door of the mansion, we walk into a lovely courtyard and we follow him up to our room.

Our room doesn't have a number, but a name. It's called Anna. Now it isn't very big, but for the three of us it's perfect. It has one big double bed, a small bed in the window sill and a small but functional bathroom.

Dimitris wishes us a good night and quietly closes the door, while Lisa is already busy arranging. "You sleep in the big bed with mommy tonight, Sophie," she says. "Then I will do so tomorrow. We will take turns."

After I put Sophie into her pyjamas, she drops down with Big Bear and falls asleep, all sprawled across the bed. Lisa is still busy for some time, unpacking her bag and making her bed comfy, before she takes her tiny little rabbit and tucks into her bed.

"Mommy," she whispers as I'm softly pushing Sophie to her side of her bed so I have some space myself. "Yes dear?" "Thank you for taking us here, mommy. It's so beautiful." And with that she closes her eyes and turns around. And all I can do is smile...

The next morning both girls are up early. No surprise there of course. They always are, no matter how late I put them in bed, much to Wilma's chagrin. *Wilma? Why am I thinking about Wilma here?*

I breathe in and out for some time to let the thoughts about her vanish. *This is not the time to think about her. This is* my *time. My* time with the girls. And they are already jumping around, all ready for adventure. So we take a shower and go down.

Breakfast is outside in the main mansion, around the small pool in the inner courtyard. Now the girls never had a breakfast buffet before, but it turns out they love it as much as I do. There are freshly baked eggs, pancakes, all kinds of cereals, tasty tomatoes, olives and oven-fresh bread.

And after breakfast we are all ready for the beach. We drop in at reception for advice and a new guy there tells us that there is a private beach close by. We only need to walk through the old town towards the harbour.

So that is where we go. But not without making a quick stop at a small grocery shop to buy some mineral water. We end up with three different bottles, so we can sample all.

As we walk, we get a better view of our neighbourhood and it's just one word: gorgeous. Now I already knew that our hotel was going to be in the old quarter. I did some google search before leaving. But little did I know what a picturesque cobbled old quarter it would be, with Greek and Roman ruins.

It has maze-like narrow streets lined with restored white-washed red-roofed mansions, most of which are now boutique hotels, souvenir shops, art galleries and restaurants. The streets seem quite easy to get lost in, but isn't that half the fun of exploring?

The private beach is at the end of the winding street, where the old city wraps around a pretty little harbour with gently bobbing yachts looking out over the shimmering Mediterranean. The beach is basically a small cove, surrounded by dramatic cliffs and luxurious vegetation.

To enter, we have to pay a small fee at a restaurant and then we go down a whole flight of stairs that are made of big uneven rocks. It's still early and there aren't many people, so we can choose which sunbed with parasol we like.

The girls choose one that is on top of a wooden stage, so they can just dip their toes into the sea and jump in. Luckily I have brought their water booties with me, because the beach isn't a sandy one, it's made up of small rocks.

Both girls jump in right away, Lisa with her snorkel and diving glasses, Sophie with her water gun. And as the splatter around in the water, I sigh as I look around me. It's just so lovely here. There are only a couple of other people, all local I guess. Mostly women with children or elderly couples, just wading or swimming out as far as they like.

But the girls don't let me sit and contemplate for long. Soon they want me in too. For one split second I hesitate. I'm never a big fan of being in bikini. I just don't like my belly. But right there and then I decide that it's pure nonsense.

What do I care about my belly? For whom? Will I ever see any of these people again? And anyway, is my belly any worse than theirs? I'm stripping naked for total strangers lately. So why am I bothering? I'm here to make memories with my girls. So I strip down to my blue bikini and jump in.

The water is delicious. It's warm, clean, clear and blue. And through the crystal clear water I can see the bottom of the sea.

There are large rocks to stand on and the bay is littered with nooks and crannies where tiny little fish swim around.

Both Sophie and Lisa jump on me. And we swim for quite some time together, splashing water on each other, pointing out fish while Sophie is hanging on my back, her plump little arms wrapped around me and Lisa is swimming like a mermaid.

When Sophie has had enough, she gets out of the water and starts searching pebbles. I also get out, to dry and do a little sun tanning, while I watch the water gently waving beneath the wooden stage and the boats drifting past. Lisa is still snorkelling, sometimes lurking her head out of the water to tell me what kind of fish she has seen.

By noon the girls get hungry, so we change in the dressing room, climb back up the stairs and return through the beautiful streets. Passing all the different ice cream vendors, with the girls watching but neither of them whining or asking, I tell them: "You know what? This is vacation time. You can try a different ice cream every evening we are here." And the girls cheer.

We have a nice lunch in the courtyard of our hotel, close to the swimming pool. Then I take the girls back to our room for a siesta. Tonight they can stay up, I promise. So they strip down to their underwear, not much else is needed in the hot weather – thank god for the air conditioning – and soon they drift off to sleep.

They wake two hours later and we head towards the little swimming pool of our hotel where they splatter around while I read my book on a sunbed in the shade. Then in the late afternoon the hotel undergoes a transformation – from sunbeds to dinner mode. All sunbeds are cleared to make room for dining tables.

Dimitris is back and tells us: "You are most welcome at the other swimming pool." The girls first look at each other, then at me before shouting: "OTHER swimming pool?" Dimitris nods, smiling. "Yes the big one, in the annex building. It's only a little down the road from the mansion you are staying in."

"BIG ONE??" The girls don't need any more explanation. They run off in their swimming suits, with their goggles still on. I collect our stuff and stow behind them. I don't need to wonder where they are. They leave a trail of laughing Greek men at the cafes behind him.

It's quite easy to find the other pool and the girls are already splattering in it when I arrive. Apparently I'm the only person in the boutique hotel with kids, but nobody seems to mind. So I settle down on a sunbed in the late sun and read some more while the girls play.

Sometimes I watch them and smile. Sophie is running with her chubby little legs along the side of the pool in her pink little swimming suit, wearing her purple goggles with glitters, even though she isn't in the water. She is busy throwing in plastic toys for Lisa to dive up.

Lisa is wearing her turquois bathing suit. She is growing thin and tall now, all baby fat is gone. Mostly she is trying so hard to be big, but not now. She is playing around, laughing out loud. And I smile. It's not often that I see her so happy and playful.

At seven the pool closes, so we go to our room to change. When the girls are wearing their pretty dresses for the evening and I have braided their hair, we go back to the courtyard for dinner. But the girls stop dead track after we enter, because the courtyard looks like a fairy tale.

The pool is lit up, there are small candles on the tables and there is live piano music, which makes the girls beam. Sophie tucks my dress. "Mommy, mommy," she says when I bent down. "I have never seen a real person play the piano!"

We get a table on the side, from which we can see the pool and the pianist. To our joy, dinner is also a buffet and we can choose between grilled fish, lamb or chicken with potatoes, vegetables and all kinds of Greek delights. And for desert there are no less than five different cakes. The girls cheerfully ponder around with their plates, choosing their dishes and taking one little piece from each cake for desert.

After dinner, the girls' eyes are shining. For it's not bed time, it's Mediterranean time. So we stroll with the locals down to the harbour to promenade, the girls licking their first Greek ice cream. Lisa is beaming. She finds a new cat in every corner to pat. Sophie doesn't notice any cat, she is too busy thoroughly enjoying the taste of her ice cream.

That night it's Lisa's turn to sleep in my bed. Sophie is already sleeping, sprayed out on her windowsill-bed and I put a chair in front of it so she won't fall out. But Lisa isn't sleeping yet. She is still talking about the day. Right before she finally turns to sleep, she gives me big hug and says: "Mommy I'm so happy we came here." And I can feel tears welling up. No tears of sadness. Tears of happiness. *This is life as it should be.*

In total we spend four days in Greece. We head out onto the Mediterranean on one of the many excursion boats from the cosy little harbour to swim at an empty beach. We have a tour and watch the ruins of an ancient Greek town. We go to an aqua park. Sophie charms everyone who works in the hotel and Lisa befriends every single cat in the neighbourhood.

Then the fifth day we're leaving and Lisa is saying goodbye to all the cats, while Sophie is playing chess with Dimitris. "Mommy I'm going to miss this," Lisa whispers when she comes back to me. She is standing close to me, almost ready to hug me, but holding back since we are not alone and she considers herself too big to hug now. But with sparkling eyes she asks me: "Can we go back next year?" And before even thinking about it, I tell her "Sure we will. I promise."

That evening we arrive back in our cosy hygge home, with Fuzzy swirling around our legs. And when I look at my girls, my heart swells. I see two relaxed, sun-tanned, happy little girls. Sophie is beaming. And it's like Lisa is finally carrying less burden on her thin little shoulders.

Fact is, they have built up memories to last a lifetime. For months to follow our vacation is something they will talk about. They keep saying things like: "Remember that time in Greece …" "Remember the cats." And I have made a promise … Next year we will go again.

But this means that I will need to start saving money. So after our vacation I realize three things. I realize that I need to start Sugar Dating on another level. If this is what I can give my girls, I'm prepared to do a lot.

But I also realize that Aleksandar was right. This is only thinking short-term. If writing is my dream, I have to make sure that I build up a writing career and that I can make money in a different way. The Sugar Dating is giving me a chance to do so.

And I realize that this is at least one good thing The Widower has left me. He has made me believe in my own strength to take the girls on a vacation. He has made me jump a big leap forward in my new life as a single mother …

CHAPTER TWENTY-FOUR: GEISHA FOR A DAY

It's the second half of the long summer holiday. The girls are with their father and, well, you know me by now. I am not enjoying the empty house. In a way I'm starting to get used to it. There are things that I do enjoy by now. I do enjoy having finally some time for myself. Not having to wake up early every morning. Deciding what and when I do it. Or just not having to do anything. But I still don't like the emptiness of the house. Thank god for Fuzzy. At least he brings some life to the house.

So I am thrilled when I get an email from Sam in my mailbox. He seems to be so much in love and I am happy for him. But he also comes with an interesting offer… A colleague who lives in Japan has seen my pictures, he says. And he would love to meet me in Tokyo. Three days, flight and all expenses covered, *and* he would love to help me out with 1500 pounds.

Jeez… Japan… I have never been to Japan. But with all the Japanese food I have been eating and the hospitality I have been seeing, it's one of the countries that's on my list of countries to visit. So why not? If Sam recommends the guy, he must be ok. So I accept the offer.

One week later I'm at Narita airport. A big black car with a driver wearing a cap and white gloves comes to pick me up and drive me to my hotel. I am staying in a luxurious hotel in the expensive Ginza area. Now Japan is not how I had expected it. At least Tokyo isn't.

It's ultra-modern, with tall skyscrapers, billboards with no Japanese but western models promoting brand clothes, and no sign of traditional Japan seems to be left. Or so I think.

Soon I will discover that isn't true. Traditional Japan is still there. Right underneath my nose. In the little alleys with mini gardens. In the interior design of seemingly normal restaurants. In the people, admiring their porcelain cup before sipping their green tea. But having just arrived, Japan is still a mystery to me.

I take a shower in the hotel and do my usual ritual with make-up and choosing clothes. Then the driver comes to pick me up to have dinner. I will meet Mr. Japan at a traditional restaurant.

Outside the restaurant a Japanese man is awaiting me, bowing and introducing himself as Mr. Yasashii, a colleague of Mr. Japan – or Ecchi-san as he calls him – who tells me that he is going to translate. I bow back.

Then he gives me a blue bag from Tiffany and Co. Now in my guidebook I have read a bit about Japanese culture and I know that I'm not supposed to open gifts in front of my host. So I say "thank you" a couple of times and bow, while Yasashii keeps bowing with me.

Inside, the restaurant looks all traditional. I love the design. It is all wood and there is a little garden with bamboo and a small pond with goldfish. The kimono-clad woman takes us to a separate room, where I have to leave my shoes outside.

Ecchi-san is already in the room waiting for me, facing the shoji door. Normally I'm not really into Asian men, but I have to say he is rather handsome. He is tall for a Japanese I notice when he gets up to bow, and he has wavy black hair that makes me think of Dr. Shepherd in Grey's anatomy.

But he also looks like a proud and stern man. He doesn't smile at all. He just gives me a bow and then sits down again. First I get some hot sake to warm up. Mr. Japan doesn't speak much English, but Mr. Yasashii tries his best to talk with me and translate for him.

He is very friendly and smiling and keeps filling my sake cup. I actually like him much better than Mr. Japan, but it doesn't feel like I have a real choice here. It's Mr. Japan who has flown me into Japan, so Mr. Japan is the one I have to charm.

Therefore I do my best not to seem too friendly to Yasashii and focus my interest on Mr. Japan. Not that he says much, so I decide to keep filling his cup. Maybe alcohol will make the guy nicer.

The woman keeps coming in and brings one dish after the other. Now most of these I have never seen before, and I'm not really keen on eating, but Yasashii translates for me that Mr. Japan insists I experience 'true Japanese culture'.

Apparently I am also supposed to learn the Japanese names, because Mr. Japan keeps repeating them sternly until I pronounce them correctly. One dish is 'Fugu' – the fish that is poisonous if not prepared in a correct way. Only chefs with three or more years of rigorous training are allowed to prepare the fish.

Another dish has orange fish eggs called 'Ikura' on top. They taste salty and pop in my mouth when I eat them. Then there is something white that looks weird. It looks like something brainy or like intestines, but Mr. Japan insists it is a fish dish called 'Shirako', so I try it. It has a very soft and creamy texture and melts like butter on my tongue.

Mr. Japan seems very interested in me eating it and looks at me intently. "You like?" he asks after I swallow. I nod. *It was ok.* Ecchi-san says something loudly in Japanese so I turn to Yasashii. He looks a bit embarrassed and refuses to translate.

Finally he says; "It's sperm." "Excuse me?" "It's fish sperm! What you call ... cod? It's cod sperm!" And Mr. Japan hits himself on his leg laughing. Then he puts his hand on my leg and squeezes it.

At the same time, Yasashii is trying to explain the meaning of the Japanese concept of 'Shoganai' to me. "It can be translated as 'it can't be helped'," he says. "See, shoganai is essentially a philosophy. It means that if something is out of your control it's better to quickly accept it and move on." *So I guess me eating fish sperm is shoganai...*

"The Danes have a similar concept," I say, *though I'm not sure all of them do. At least Mr. Viking does.* "They say that worrying about things you cannot change is a waste of good drinking time." Yasashii translates that and both men burst out laughing.

After dinner Yasashii informs me it is time for the 'Ni-jikai'. Our 'Second Party'. We take a cab to the Cerulean Tower Hotel in the Shibuya area. *God, Tokyo is a bustling city. People are everywhere.* We pass the Shibuya crossing, which I have only seen in movies. The crossing is crazy – it is just so busy with people.

In the hotel we take the elevator to the 40th floor and enter the Bello Vista Sky View Bar. I do have to say it is amazing. The super-polite Japanese staff takes us to a table in front of the window looking all over Tokyo.

In the centre of the bar a western pianist is playing and a black woman is singing soft jazzy songs. At the bar Japanese bartenders make a real nice show of shaking their cocktails. *Now this is life!*

Mr. Japan orders a bottle of champagne for us. So there I am, sipping from my champagne, looking over the night lights of Tokyo and I am actually getting quite drunk. Normally I take care not to get drunk, but the sake has been stronger than I had expected.

I excuse myself to go to the Ladies and I really do my best to walk straight. Now the toilet is a surprise. The seat has all different kind of buttons and since I am drunk anyway I try them all.

One makes the seat warm up, another makes the sound of flushing – probably to hide other, zestier sounds – and one button sprays water in different parts and almost makes me come. I dry my hands with a cotton towel, deposit it in a straw basket and look at my face.

God, I am getting drunk. I have to get a hold of myself. I need some water and something to eat. But back at our table, Yasashii exclaims that we are going for our 'sanjikai'. Our 'Third Party.' We are going for Karaoke.

Both Yasashii and Ecchi are worse drinkers then I am. Their faces are all red and they don't even pretend to walk straight – they are swaying all over the place. But the staff doesn't seem to mind, they are obviously used to drunk Japanese.

Ecchi-san throws his arm around my shoulder and is staggering next to me muttering things in Japanese. All I understand is the word 'Samurai.' Yasashii is tottering behind us, telling me: "Ecchi-san says he is a real Samurai. You have experienced Samurai?" But I ignore the question for now.

A cab takes us to the Karaoke place. It's a big tower with glass windows through which you can watch all the different Karaoke parties taking place. In some rooms girls are dancing, in some of them groups of boys or girls are singing together, and in some couples are sitting together on sofa's singing love songs.

We go to a room on the top floor. Ecchi-san and Yasashii keep taking turns singing Japanese songs. If they aren't singing they are drinking. And I learn a new word. 'Iki iki iki' which means you have to empty your glass in one shot. Luckily there are also snacks to sober up a bit, but it is not going well with me not getting drunk...

In fact, I don't remember much afterwards. I remember I sing some songs as well. I remember walking somewhere on the street with my two drunk Japanese hosts, no idea how we got there. I remember driving in a cab, with Ecchi-san sleeping in front. No idea how I got in there. I remember vaguely saying goodbye to Yasashii in front of my hotel, Ecchi-san still sleeping in the cab. And then all goes black.

The next day I have the worst headache ever. *Jeez.* I can't stand light, I can't stand sound and I have to throw up several times. I skip breakfast and just ask for sports drinks and aspirin – according to Amanda the fastest way to get over a hangover – then go back to sleep.

I promise myself that from now on I will drink one glass of water for every drink of alcohol to prevent a hangover, not to mix drinks anymore and to pace my drinking from now on. Let the men get drunk, I shouldn't lose myself. But I have to get my shit together. I have one more day and night with Ecchi-san…

The Japanese driver shows up in the afternoon. And luckily I am finally in a bit better state. I have slept most of the morning, taken a shower, and now I'm feeling a bit better, though I am still drinking sport drinks and wearing my sunglasses against the light.

Ecchi-san is waiting for me in the car, also wearing sunglasses. And to my surprise there is a ginger girl in the car as well. She introduces herself as Natasha and then giggles. I hesitate for one moment. I'm not sure what Ecchi-san is up to, and I have never had a girl experience… But then I get in. *Whatever… this may be interesting…*

The driver tells us that we are going to a traditional Japanese inn with its own onsen, a Japanese hot spring. And it is going to be a long drive. Now that is fine with me. Ecchi-san is sleeping in front, I sleep most of the ride in the back.

Dusk is falling when we arrive. I have slept most of the day and finally start to feel better. The hotel is very traditional, it looks like our restaurant from yesterday. I don't see any beds – they turn out to be rolled up in a closet – it is just a big room with a low table and no chairs.

Everything is done on the floor. We have a traditional dinner on the floor again. But only after we change into cotton kimonos, because Ecchi-san insists we wear kimono here. I drink less this dinner and even Ecchi-san seems a bit less eager to drink. Only Natasha is happily drinking. Ecchi and I also eat less. This time my stomach isn't so keen on all the special Japanese meals. Luckily Natasha finishes most meals.

I do notice two things. If I don't empty my glass, Ecchi-san doesn't refill it. Now that is a good thing to know, it makes it easier to stay sober. The same goes with my food. If I leave enough on my plate, he doesn't fill it with more.

So I sip politely from my drink and nibble politely from every dish, making sure to keep enough on, and in, both my plate and my glass. I can't really communicate with Ecchi-san. He speaks a little bit more English now that he has to, but he really doesn't say much. Natasha chats a lot though. And giggles in between. She is a model, living in Tokyo and has lots to tell about living in Japan.

"You know," she says, "We are geisha for the day." And we both laugh. "What are geisha exactly?" I ask her "Weren't they … ?" "Prostitutes?" Natasha fills in. "No way. Sex wasn't the most important part. They mostly entertained men with their wit."

She pulls her hand through her ginger hair. "They were not prostitutes. They were mistresses. In fact, they may have been the most powerful and influential women of Japan. The wealthy and busy Japanese businessmen visited them to get out of the stress of daily life and spend some time in a dream." And she giggles.

Dinner is finished and the hotel staff comes to tell something. "Onsen," Ecchi-san says and gestures us to follow him. Now, just for you to know, don't ever expect a Japanese man to show you courtesies like 'ladies first', you'd be disappointed.

So we follow him on a path of big stones through a Japanese garden to a gate which the staff opens for us. Inside is a big wooden tub filled with water and oranges floating in it, which evaporate an exquisite scent.

The tub is overlooking the ocean. It is mesmerizing. Sun has set. The ocean is black, but you can hear the rolling waves. The pitch-black sky above us is sprinkled with stars and a pale moon. It is beautiful. Simply beautiful.

Ecchi-san slips off his kimono, gets into the tub, lets himself slide into the water, closes his eyes and has a look of total bliss on his face. Natasha and I look at each other and then follow suit. We let the kimono slip off our bodies and enter naked into the hot water.

It might be because of the hangover, but that is the best bath I have ever had. The water is just the right temperature, the sweet scent of oranges is everywhere, and I see the moonlight glimmer on my skin. It is a moment of total bliss.

Now I expect Ecchi-san to make some move. To want some lovemaking in this tub. But he doesn't. He just sits there with his eyes closed, enjoying the bath with full ecstasy on his face. After a long time, we dry and get back into our kimono.

We follow Ecchi-san back to the room, where he opens his suitcase and gives us two schoolgirl uniforms. "Put on," he says and he sits down on the floor in front of the table. I feel a little uncomfortable putting it on with him watching me intently, but I obey and soon we are dressed in the uniform. The skirts are really short. And Natasha is giggling again.

Next he gets a paper from his bag and unfolds it. On it is a cartoon of two school girls in uniform showing their underwear. He points at the pigtails they are wearing and points at us.

Ok, so Ecchi-san wants us to wear pigtails. We help each other making pigtails with Ecchi-san watching intently. Then he gestures us to come, pulls up our skirts and checks our sexy underwear.

He shakes his head and gets two big white knickers from his bag that are similar to the one on the cartoon. We have to change into it right there, with him watching. Then he nods and gestures that we have to sit on our knees with our hands on our knees and bow our heads.

He sits at his table watching us for some time, getting up a couple of times to adjust one thing or the other. Our skirt has to be higher up. Our shirt has to be straight. Our pigtails have to be in a certain way.

Then he just watches us for some time, caressing his crotch. I can't see well, since we have to look down, but I think he is jerking off a bit.

First he chooses Natasha, while I have to stay there on my knees, looking down. My knees start to hurt, but I try to stay still. In the other room I can hear him with Natasha. I hear her giggle and say: "Yes Samurai" and then I hear her groan. *Is she acting? Is she really excited?* Fact is, I am actually getting excited myself.

In a way this all is very exciting. Waiting, not knowing what is going to come. Him being all in control. Just hearing them in the other room. I can feel I am getting really wet.

Then Natasha is sent back and he calls for me. "Come," he says. "Yes," I answer. "Yes SAMURAI," he grumbles. "Yes Samurai," I repeat. I do notice the lubricant and the 'ultra-strong' condom package on the floor, but naive as I still am, I figure Ecchi-san just wants some extra security...

He wants me to be on all fours, then he just walks around me and pulls up my skirt so my underwear is showing, hitting me softly on my ass. Next he slits my underwear to one side and puts his finger inside.

"You like?" "Yes," "Yes SAMURAI" "Yes Samurai" He keeps moving harder and harder. Then he suddenly pulls out and walks around me again. Kneeling down behind me, he slips off his kimono, slits my underwear to the side and puts his finger back inside of me.

I hear him tear open a condom package, slid it on, put lubricant on his condom and then I feel him pushing. But it is against another hole … Against one that I have never used before …

I move a little to make him understand that it is the wrong hole, but he is quite persistent. It obviously isn't the wrong one for him. It is the one he is aiming for. He has to put extra lubricant on to enter, it is damn tight.

At first it hurts a little and he is careful, but then it actually starts to feel good. Real good. He keeps moving his finger inside of me as well. I am totally filled. And soon he is holding my hips as he takes me from behind.

I am surprised with the force with which he takes me. The guy hadn't seemed very sexual until now. But he takes me damn hard from behind and it is just so good.

Being taken anal, I feel an extra sensitivity that I have never felt before.

I start to play with myself and it doesn't take long until I come hard. Real hard. The guy hasn't finished though, so I keep playing. The third time I come is just before he does, groaning real loud and deep.

He waits a few minutes after coming, holding my hips, catching his breath, then he slaps my ass, pulls out, puts on his kimono and gives me a sideway smile. *His first smile since I have met him.*

And for a moment, with that gorgeous hair all messed up, the golden glow of his skin, his toned body in that kimono and his total dominance, for a moment he looks damn handsome. "Good?" he asks. I am still panting. "Yes Samurai," I say. And in a strange way it has been. It has been damn good.

That is all the sex we have. I wouldn't have minded to be taken by him once more. And in a way I was excited to get my first girl experience, but I feel too shy to start it myself. So that's it. Ecchi-san sleeps in between us that night, not touching us. He makes us wear the big white underwear that whole night.

The next day he folds them carefully and puts them in a pretty Japanese pouch. "Souvenir," he says, bringing the pouch to his nose and smelling it with a total look of delight.

It isn't until I am at the airport that I remember my present. The blue Tiffany & Co bag is crammed in my suitcase somewhere below my clothes and it takes a while before I get it out. In it is a sterling silver key-ring in the shape of a heart. And I can't help but laugh as I put my keys to my new key-ring. A heart from a guy I will never meet again. But it is a nice gesture.

I still have the key-ring and though most of the time I don't even think of it, sometimes it makes me remember my strange Japanese encounter with a secret smile…

CHAPTER TWENTY-FIVE: THE DREAM

The autumn term has started again and weeks full of school, play dates and sports are looming up again. It's September 4th and I've just brought the girls to their first day of school. *Now it's going to be exciting. It's time for Amanda's book...* The moment I'm back, I make myself a strong coffee and settle behind my computer. I'm all set to go.

Before the summer vacation I have already plucked a whole list of UK agents from the internet, in alphabetical order. And I have deleted all the ones that are not into memoirs. I have also prepared a book proposal, synopsis and three sample chapters. I'm all ready to go. All I need to do now, is check with each agent before submitting. For each agent requires something different. And of course all my inquiries should be personal.

I have also prepared a special email address from Protonmail to keep Amanda's identity hidden. Because she is freaking out, now that the publication of her book could come close. She is scared to death that her real identity will be discovered. She is married now. She has a kid. And she has no idea what her husband will do if he finds out about her past.

So on this nice Monday morning, I take a deep breath and send my first book submission. Preparing takes longer than I expected and afterwards I let go of a deep sigh. *The first one is out. Thank god.* Now this first day I discover that I can send ten book proposal to ten different agents before I have to pick up the kids from school again. Tuesday is another day. And I send ten more. But on Wednesday I only have the morning. And still thirty-one agents to go. So I prepare to send five this day.

One of these agents is big. He is the biggest agent in the UK dealing with memoirs, and in a way he feels too big. But I think of Aleksandar, my Vienna driver. *This is only my fear speaking. If I don't try I never win right?* So on this crisp Wednesday autumn morning, he is the first one I send Amanda's book to.

To my surprise, he reacts back within an hour, while I'm still working on book submission number three of the day. And it's The Agent. The Big One! I take a deep breath before I open his mail. He writes:

"Dear M,

Thanks for this. It is well written and has potential but I'll need a full proposal for a book of 90,000 words. You write well and explain how Amanda was drawn into escorting. It does sound glamorous, which is the market but it will need a distinct hook as market is crowded.

It could also be a bit more sexually explicit. We need a stronger sense of what Amanda looks like, what she enjoys in terms of sex, is she big-breasted, shaved etc. We also need some hints of real identities of her customers otherwise it's just a series of anonymous encounters. I think it's important it isn't too heavily fictionalised as authenticity is key.

It will be difficult to promote the book without some publicity involvement of your client – even if her identity is disguised. Would it be possible to meet the two of you in confidence? It would be great to talk with Amanda on

Skype. Why has she now decided to write the book? How do you know her?

Who else in publishing have you approached and what was the reaction? Who else is considering the book? Hold fire from submitting to any more agents and publishers as I'm taking this seriously and am spending time & money on assessing the book. Out of interest, how did you learn about me?

Best wishes, The Agent."

Jeez… This is BIG! And 'well written' is something that makes me sing! Writing has been my dream and my fear. I've always been afraid to really get into writing, thinking that maybe I'm just not good enough.

But here I am. With an email of this Big Agent, telling me my book is well written! I could dance all day! Would I have had the guts to send it to this agent without Aleksandar? I guess I will never know for sure. But he definitely kicked me in the right direction. So I reply back:

"Thank you for your quick reply. Let me think about the 'hook'. The story can become more sexually explicit, no problem. And I can give a better description with some hints about customers and about Amanda – she becomes big breasted in book two- after a customer pays for her boob job.

Amanda and I went to primary school together – we know each other since we were five years old. We kind of lost touch when she became a model in Paris and I had no idea what she was going through. We did write emails from time to time, but not much. It was not until much later that she told me what she had been doing and that she wanted to write a book about it. She has decided to share her story because she wants her story out there – she believes there are still many misconceptions about the business – and also because she hopes she will make money with it.

Thing is at the moment I am not totally 'clean' myself. As a single mother I am Sugar Dating to make ends meet. I am not an escort, but with one foot in the world I guess. I don't need anyone digging in my own activities, which is why I prefer to stay anonymous too … At this moment no one else is considering the book, but I only started submitting on Monday. If you have any other questions I will be happy to answer them.

Kind regards, M."

I get an answer back right away:

"You've done a good job on this book. I like the variety of it. Did she write the first draft or have you written from scratch based on interviews over Skype? Do you need a collaboration agreement between you?

Thanks for being so open about your own involvement, it must give useful insights? I can see the money from the book could be useful to you and repeat that everything is treated in greatest confidence with only me seeing material at this stage.

Is there a book in your experiences, if you were anonymous? Is there anything about your life I can see? I actually think you should start on your own book now.

Best wishes, The Agent"

Okay, so now I'm most definitely dancing. But when I text Amanda, she is a bit less enthusiastic. Now that I have found an agent who is interested and comes with agreements which have to be signed with real names – because these are legal contracts – she is freaking out. The last thing she wants is for her husband to find out.

So something I had never expected happens. It's me who signs a contract with The Agent. Therefore he is no longer The Agent, but now My Agent. How cool is that? Yes, this is most definitely going in a very good direction. Next, since Amanda is still not signing the contract, I agree with my agent to start writing my story. And I promise to finish it in three months.

Of course I have no idea what I'm signing up for. It's going to be crazy. I'm going to have to write three chapters a week during school time, take care of the kids *and* still make money through my Sugar Dating. But hey, when you get a chance to live your dreams, you do anything...

So I start writing like crazy. Then on Monday the 11th it's time for Sugar Dating again. After the kids are dropped at school – with the usual morning struggles – I start preparing for my new date. Oscar. He has contacted me a month ago and we have set our date for today.

Now we could have met before the sex. We both live close to London. But after we had agreed upon the allowance, he suggested we meet immediately in a hotel. *Well, why not.* I've travelled across the world to strangers. So why not meet him immediately in a London hotel? I know it comes close to another world. The escort world. But hey, I do have a choice. If I don't like the guy I just leave.

On date-day, Oscar has already sent a couple of messages since the morning. The guy is looking forward to it. But I'm not yet. I always feel a bit tense right before a date. Especially when it's a new one.

With the kids gone, I have two hours to prepare. But time flies and I close the front door behind me just in time, wearing a nice dress, high heels and a classy raincoat. Underneath I wear my best underwear, black, including holdups.

I take the bus and train to meet him. In a way it's funny, sitting in between all the 'normal' people going to their jobs or studies, knowing what I am about to do. What I like is that nobody will suspect. I look classy. Hard to get.

Now I know where the hotel is. I accidentally – or coincidentally – passed it last weekend with the kids, on our way to the Science Museum. And it made me smile inside. *It's sweet to have spicy secrets.* Oscar is already texting me: "Checking in. Want me to wait for you or shall I just give you my room number?" I think for one split second. Then I reply: "Give me your room number 😊"

Another first one. I've never met someone directly in their room. Let alone someone I have never met. Farshad always comes to pick me up in London, both India's pick me up at reception. *But new things are exciting…*

Walking into the hotel, I do feel like I'm on an episode of 'Diary of a Call Girl' as I walk in my classy rain coat right through reception to the elevators. From the corner of my eye I see a security guy, but I ignore him. I make sure I walk as confident as if I've always been staying in their hotel.

In the elevator I notice I held my breath and let go. *I'm in.* Using the big elevator mirror, I quickly brush my hair and put on some more lip gloss. Then the doors open and I walk up to his room. I take in some air, knock and he opens his door.

At first I'm a little disappointed. Now I *knew* the guy was bald. And he is. It's just that he had seemed a bit better looking on the picture. His profile says he is 47, but the guy looks older. Way older. But when he smiles I immediately decide I like him. He has this naughty smile that lightens up the room.

At first it's a bit uncomfortable. I take off my coat and we talk some stupid small talk. But then he starts kissing me. Now Mr. Tantra was the first moustache I kissed and Oscar is the first goatee. *Ew…*

I never thought I would be kissing men with moustaches and goatees, they don't particularly appeal to me. But I have to say, kissing them is okay. While we kiss I can feel his hard-on pushing against me. It feels good. I can already feel he is well-shaped. I softly rub over his dick and he moans.

Now there is something about sex...I just love it. I love the heat. The passion. The smell that lingers on my skin afterwards. So getting hot is never an issue. When I first met Farshad, Amanda advised me to use lubricant. It's what she always used before meeting her escort dates, to make them think she was horny.

Now I do have a bottle, but so far I have never had to use it. Only sometimes, when Farshad and I fuck for a really long time and the condom gets dry. But I always get wet. Always. The moment someone touches me I react.

I don't have my clothes on for very long. He takes off my dress and happily adores my lingerie. But not for long either. *They never do.* I always spend so much time on my lingerie and it always goes out so fast.

Oscar undresses himself. He is wearing very decent underwear. No boxer shorts. But it doesn't stay on for long either. His dick is as promising as I had thought. It's not thick like Farshad's – thick is even better – but it's nice and big. It's comparable to Rudolph's. Oscar is in good shape I have to say. He has a nice body.

He is kissing me again and I slowly lead him towards the bed, throw him on it and climb on top him, still kissing. I know he has a nice view of the Happy Boobs this way. And my ass is sticking in the air as I slowly lick his chest. I lick his side down-down-down and then slowly start to tease.

His thighs are sensitive I notice, so I let the tip of my tongue slowly move from his knees up up towards his balls. I softly lick his balls, take both in my mouth and suck on them. He groans. Then I lick around his dick. I keep teasing for some time, until I take his dick in my mouth.

Oscar is leaning on his elbows. He is a watcher, I notice, so I make sure he can watch. And I make sure I keep eye contact as I take his long dick deeper and deeper into my mouth. Going deep throat, licking and sucking in between. After a while he lets himself fall down and is moaning below me. *Jeez how I love it when a man enjoys a good blowjob…*

When he gets real close to coming he stops me. He flips me over, opens my legs and starts licking. He's good I have to day. Oscar knows exactly where to lick – up front, on and around the clitoris. Now I like masturbation, but my Sugar Dates have taught me that oral sex is way better. The tip of a tongue is so soft, so wet. No finger or dildo can compete.

When I'm hot I can never stay still. I hold the bedframe behind me, bite the pillow, hollow my back and get very, very close to an orgasm. I can come this way, but it's hard. Especially with someone I don't know yet.

Oscar comes back up and starts sucking my nipples. He puts my legs over his shoulder. I can feel his dick pushing against my pussy. *Ay, here is another guy trying to enter without a condom.* I make sure I hold him with my knees, so he can touch me with his dick but not enter, until he gets a condom.

We start missionary style. He puts my legs over his shoulders and then enters me forcefully. He keeps pushing hard. The guy has passion. I love it. But after some time I flip him over and sit on top of him. Riding him. Putting one hand on his chest, the other one playing with his balls behind me.

His naughty eyes go all over my body. Over the Happy Boobs, which he grabs. He comes half up and sucks my nipples. Then I squat on my feet and move fast. Oscar now starts to lose it. His naughty eyes are closed, his face tense, I know he is about to come. I make sure I keep up the speed until he comes with a big roar.

As Oscar is getting back to his senses, I first lie on him, then slide off and into his arm. After a few minutes he hugs me and starts chatting. We talk for maybe an hour about all kinds of things. Traveling. Different countries. Different cultures.

When Oscar gets up to check the time, we have ten minutes left. *I almost need to pick up the kids from school.* He comes back into the bed, flips me over and starts kissing again. Now Oscar has no more condoms, but luckily I do. I still have my 'family package'. Well, my second one since I started this Sugar Life... I put on a condom and Oscar turns me around.

Ay, I'm going to love this. I already know. You know how I love doggie and it's been way too long since I had a good one. Yeah I know. Japan was very doggy. But that was a rather unusual one. I love the regular one. I love to be taken hard from behind. First of all, because it makes for a real deep penetration. And also because it allows me to play with myself. And as you know the only way I can come from penetration is with extra stimulation.

So as he holds my ass and I feel his dick move in and out of me deeply, his balls bouncing off my ass, I start to stimulate myself. It doesn't take long before I totally, utterly, thoroughly come. *Wow...*

But there is no time to linger. I have to go. As I dress, Oscar takes a shower. After he is dressed he says: "I still have a gift for you" and he gives me the envelope with my allowance. I thank him and kiss him.

We kiss at the exit and then we each go our own way. One thing I notice when I'm on my way back to the station. It's like men can sense that I've just had sex. For some reason I get way more attention after a good fuck.

And I'm sure I'll see Oscar again. But contrary to the others, I'm not having any kind of relationship with this guy. He is just a good fuck. And for one split second a thought crosses my mind. *Isn't this getting too close to being an escort?*

But on the commuter train back I remind myself that I can't afford to get squeamish about morals. I just had a great fuck. I truly enjoyed myself. I haven't hurt anyone. So what is wrong with that?

Also I can save some money this month. And I picture my girls' faces. Lisa, getting so big and wise. Sophie, every day more mischievous. And their beaming faces when I can buy them the food they love. *Getting close to escorts or not, it is all so totally worth it...*

CHAPTER TWENTY-SIX: SETTING UP BUSINESS

From September onwards my life is a whirlwind. I don't even have time to meet Sarah and my chats with Amanda, Barbara, Paul and Mr. Viking become less. Someone who does reappear is Ben the journalist, after I check out his LinkedIn profile when I'm writing about him. And though I have little time for chatting, it's nice to be in contact with him again. I tell him all. About the book. What I have been doing. He's the last one who judges. For the rest, I take care of the girls and when they are at school I have dates and I am writing like crazy.

See, I have to write three chapters a week to finish my own memoir by December. Finishing three chapters during school time is quite a challenge. And apart from that I have to make money to survive.

Now since The Widower I've decided to do it all differently. One thing is for sure, I can't depend on these men. So I need to have several, who rotate. And if I want to survive from Sugar Dating, I should maybe become more like Amanda. I should start to see it as setting up a business.

I'm meeting Oscar – alias Mr. Fuck – almost weekly, when he is not travelling. They are nice fucks during school time. Just two hours of no hassle fucks. But I need more school-time fucks. Luckily I soon get a new message in my mailbox:

"You sound nice and interesting and you look beautiful in your pictures. I am the type that doesn't like fuss and tries to live life to the fullest. Would like to get to know you. What do you say? X John"

I check out the profile of this new guy. It says he is 46 years old and divorced. His picture shows no face, just a big blue shirt with quite a belly beneath it. It's always fun to see the kind of pictures men put on the site, *why don't they even try to show their most attractive features?*

His profile text reads:

"Active adventurer always ready for interesting friends and settings. Lots of international work and travel, but also lots of sports and entertainment. Very health conscious and liking the good things of life. Looking for friends with benefits, for mutual benefits of course. Someone real, honest and natural."

Well, I'm all in for the mutual benefits, so I answer back: "Hi John, Thank you for your message. You also sound nice and interesting and you are wearing a lovely shirt ;-) Are you living in the UK or just visiting? I would definitely like to get to know you! X Monique"

John Replies: "Hi Monique, Hahaha, yes no sexy pictures of six packs here... even if I had one ;) I am concerned with discretion and therefore do not show too much. What is a beautiful woman like you doing on this site and what would you like to find? X"

So I reply with my usual. That I'm a single mom with kids, how it's hard to make ends meet and that I would like to meet someone interesting for fun times, but also someone who can help me. But since Japan I'm adding something new. I can be his geisha, in a separate world from his normal one.

John replies: "Okay I see. Well, that's exactly what I'm looking for ... Friends with benefits, parallel to normal life, discrete, exciting, warm ... But for me it should definitely not be: fake, mechanical and things like that. I had too much of those already. I have no kids myself by the way, and no girlfriend. I'm divorced. X"

By now I'm an arrangement pro. I had too many time wasters. So I make sure we agree upon the amount of our arrangement before I arrange the babysitter and set up a meeting. See, quite some men on SA are not as generous as you would expect. But to meet them I still need to arrange babysitters and pay for them. So I now only meet men once we have agreed upon the money-part of the arrangement.

Once John and I have agreed upon the arrangement we set up a meeting for a Tuesday the next week. And like a real gentleman, John offers to come and pick me up. Now I don't want him in front of my house, so I give him the address of the shopping centre close by.

Not long after, I get a message from another guy called AmericanGigolo. He is three years younger than I am, married and is rather handsome so I am thrilled and ask him whether he is visiting the UK or living here. It turns out he is living in London. Now we have the usual talk. First we agree upon the arrangement. AmericanGigolo already comes up with the amount I have in mind, so that's all settled.

When I go to bed that evening, after I have tucked up the girls and looked at them lying snuggled under their duvets, I feel rather happy. I have two meetings coming up! This is going well ...

I'm a little late for my Tuesday meeting with John, since I had to cook dinner for the girls and the babysitter, which left me with little time to prepare. And then last minute I decide that maybe it isn't a very smart idea to get into a strangers car, so I delve into my own car looking for its safety hammer. *I might be able to break the window with that if needed.*

When I don't find it, I settle for the ice scraper instead. I have no idea what I can do with it, but it's better than nothing. *There must be something I can do with it…* So when I arrive, John is already waiting for me in his car.

When he sees me, he gets out and gives me a polite peck on my cheeks saying: "You are just as gorgeous as on your pictures!" and he walks around his car to open the door for me. I smile.

"I'm sorry I'm a little late," I tell him. "You were still within the ten minutes," he answers. "I beg your pardon?" "I always give girls ten minutes. If they are any later, I leave." "Always? Weren't you new to SA?" "Yes I am. But before I used other services. Escorts. Tinder…" *Yes. Well. Aren't they all? But at least the guy is honest…*

I check him out while he is driving. He looks like a regular middle-aged businessman. He has short salt and pepper curls, blue eyes and looks a bit older than 46, but most men on SA seem to lie about their age. Which is funny right? I'm a woman and completely honest about my age. *I should be the one lying…*

John gives me a sideways look and asks me: "Do you like pancakes?" *Pancakes? He's going to take me out for pancakes? This doesn't sound much like Sugar…* But I nod. "Sure." I laugh and then add: "Maybe I should have brought my girls too!"

Inwardly I sigh. *I'm already looking forward to my meeting tomorrow. At least that will be in a nice club.* Pancakes…. This is something I should text to Amanda so we can laugh about it. And I do realize how spoiled I've become…

But to my surprise he parks his car close to the Heron Tower. And he even leads me in. Now this is where Sushisamba is. One year ago I was here with Rudolph… And for a moment I miss him. *My Mr. Handsome. How is he doing?*

John catches my look and smiles. "We are just going to have a drink," he says as the panoramic glass elevator whisks us from the ground to the 39th floor and makes my ears pop.

We settle down in the bar area. He is a detailed guy I notice. When I put off my coat, his eyes go all over my dress as he says: "Now that's a beautiful dress you're wearing!" And he touches me for a moment to feel the material. He seems to be taking in the view with every detail.

We both order cocktails. I choose a Padron pepper margarita – once chosen for me by Mr. Handsome – John has a margarita. Then he gets up and whispers for a while with the bar tender before he gets us two more cocktails.

When they are finished, he walks into the main dining room with its dramatic ceilings and gob-smacking views of London. I follow him, feeling puzzled. *I thought we were going for pancakes?* But he says: "Don't worry, we're not going here. I'm just checking it out."

Apparently he has made a reservation though. And I strongly suspect that he did so when he was whispering with the bar tender, though he insists that's not true. I actually think he wanted to check me out first. If he liked me well enough, he would take me for an expensive dinner. Otherwise pancakes it was. But of course I will never know for sure.

We are shown to a semi-booth facing outwards. By now I'm not shocked about the menu anymore. But I still let him choose from the unique blend of Japanese, Brazilian and Peruvian cuisine.

We start with crispy yellowtail taquitos with avocado and roasted corn miso and green bean tempura with black truffle aioli. John appreciates everything. The cups, the plates. And we talk about Japan, which he also visited a couple of times. Of course I don't tell him for which reason I went to Japan. I tell him I was there for business. And, well, in a way I was, wasn't I?

Next we have the wagyu gyoza with kabocha puree and sesame snow, then the El Topo with salmon, jalapeno, shiso leaf, crispy onion, spicy mayo, fresh melted mozzarella and a nigiri selection with akami, sake and hamachi.

John grins when our lovely waitress bends over him to refill his glass. "You know, Japanese women like me," he says. And I smile politely. *Sure they do, John. They are nice to everyone.* But I do make a mental note of it. *John likes to feel special.*

Next comes lamb chop with coconut and red miso and heritage carrots with quinoa. And as a desert chocolate banana cake with maple butter, plantain chip and vanilla rum ice cream. All washed down with several bottles of sake.

"Have you seen the colour of my eyes?" John asks. I look him into his eyes. They are just blue eyes to me, but apparently he wants to hear something special about them. "They are very special," I tell him.

He beams for a second and then he shrugs as if indifferent. "Yes, I have heard that before … They are a very special shade of green, aren't they?" *Green?* I look a bit better at his eyes. They really are blue to me. But well, whatever the guy wants to hear. So I nod and say: "Yes indeed …"

After dinner John offers me a ride home. Now I'm quite drunk by now, and I think of Rudolph. So when we're driving on the highway, I decide: *what the hell. Let's give John something to remember.* He has taken me to the same place as Rudolph, let's give him a similar treatment.

First I caress his dick for some time. It's rock hard. Then I open his zipper and take it in my hand. John gulps with surprise. And his dick is quite surprising. It's nice and thick. When I tell him, he shrugs. "Yes, I have been told so before …"

I ignore him, lick my hand and start jerking him off. And he reacts strongly. Good. This is a man who openly enjoys it. I like that. Getting even more in the mood, I bend down and take his dick softly in my mouth. First licking it, sucking, then moving slow, faster, faster. The guy gasps as he drives on.

Now I don't have sex in the car with John. I don't make him come. This was our first dinner and so far I haven't seen any money yet. So I keep him hard and wanting me, as I kiss him goodbye and leave the car that evening…

The next morning he texts me and we set up a meeting for the next Tuesday. Now John is nice enough. He sends messages from time to time, keeping it personal and he doesn't send too many, making it bothersome. But I'm not thinking too much of him anymore. Because it's Wednesday. It's time for my date with the AmericanGigolo.

By now I have a whole collection of babysitters. I don't want to use one too much, I like to rotate. Though it's hard to find sitters that both girls like. So that evening when the girls are asleep and the new sitter has settled with chips on the sofa, I head off towards my commuter train to London. I'm wearing the same dress as yesterday, but who will know. John liked it well enough.

Outside it's cold and dark. The leaves are whirling around in the wind. And for one moment I feel lonely. For a moment there is nothing I would like to do more, than be home and snuggle up with my girls. But I need to make money…

When I'm on the train, I'm texting with Ben the journalist. He's all excited now that he is back in my life again and keeps texting me about my date. "Are you excited? What are you wearing? What kind of underwear?"

When I finally find the bar, I'm a little late. But there is no AmericanGigolo to be seen. So I sit at the bar and get a glass of water while I text Ben. "He's not here yet." Ben reacts fast. "Oh, oh, are you being stood up?" "I'm not. He's probably just late."

I try to contact the AmericanGigolo on KIK. But my messages simply aren't delivered. And I don't even have his phone number. So I think of what John said: "Normally I wait ten minutes. After that I am gone."

"I would love to join you," Ben writes, "But I have this school thing of my son..." Now I think quickly. I have a babysitter whom I need to pay anyway and I don't want to go home now. That would feel like a complete failure. *So why not have some fun?*

So I text Paul. He reacts back immediately. "Sure I'd love to meet you. Take the train back, I will come to pick you up." So I walk back to the station and take the train back home.

Paul is waiting for me at the station in his sportive car. And the moment I see him I smile. He's just so tall and handsome, as he walks around the car to open the door for me. He is wearing a handsome brown leather jacket that fits him nicely.

The moment I enter the car, he gets my cold hands and holds them for a while to warm them. "Nice to see you Monique," he says, as his light brown eyes flame up. "It's been a while..." But I do notice the bags underneath his eyes.

He starts the engine and drives us to a pub close by. Now I'm starving so Paul orders me fish and chips and doesn't touch them himself. And it's just so nice to be there with him.

We chit-chat for some time. Then I ask him what I have always wondered. "Paul," I ask "How come you don't mind what I am doing?" Paul shrugs. "Twenty years ago I would have. But now I know if I judge you, I lose you. And I don't want to lose you. You are special to me." He smiles and softly caresses my cheek before he continues.

"You know, sometimes I think you are doing it for the adrenaline," he says. "Now that you have tasted this way of life, I'm sometimes afraid that you will never be able to have a normal life anymore. You are used to the kick. To the thrill of this life." He looks at his hands for a moment before he continues: "Other times I think Amanda is too much of an influence..."

Then he takes my hand and we are silent for some time. And I notice the tired look has returned. "So how are *you* doing?" I ask him. He sighs. "Not that well … We're divorcing …" And I see tears welling up, so I squeeze his hand. "I'm so sorry Paul." Paul shrugs.

"It's okay. Our relationship was finished a long time ago. I was just staying for the kids. But now she wants me to see them only every other weekend. We're still fighting on that one. I want shared custody."

It's so good to hear a father talk like this. I'm used to The Ex, who so gladly stepped out of the girls' lives. It's just so good to hear from a father who wants to be there for his kids. One who really cares. *If only I had found the girls a father like this …*

He watches his hands for some time before he says: "I'm going to miss them." And he is fighting back his tears again. "Any other girls you're seeing?" I ask him to brighten up things. He shrugs. Then he looks up into my eyes and says "You are the one baby."

Now that should feel great right? It's lovely. I really do like Paul. Whenever I see him I get this warm feeling. I look forward to seeing him. But truth is that it freaks me out. This guy is divorcing and telling me I'm the one, even though he knows about the crazy stuff I'm doing. And I'm convinced that I just don't want a normal relationship anymore. So after those words I make sure I keep my distance.

When the sitter's time is up, Paul drives me back home. He gives me money to pay for the sitter and he kisses me before I get out. And there is something I notice. It's different with Paul. It's different from Sugar Daddies. Paul really cares for me. He is in love with me. And that gives such a totally different feeling. I get this warm, tingly feeling inside.

For one split second I wonder whether in the end Sugar Dating may be empty. And whether in a way the emptiness is hollowing me out. But I quickly push that feeling away.

I go in, pay the sitter, slip into something comfortable and tuck in the girls, looking at their sleeping faces. Sophie is tossing around in her little bed, fighting another nightmare. So with a blanket wrapped around her, I scoop her and Big Bear up and carry her to my bed where I cuddle up against her.

Just before I drift off, I remember how The Ex hated it when I would take the kids in bed. *See, there is no need for a guy in my life. No need for someone to mess up our balance. Our life is perfect the way it is.*

CHAPTER TWENTY-SEVEN: SELLING DREAMS

Next Tuesday John comes to pick me up at ten. He's taking me to his home. And he is the first Sugar Daddy whom I'm meeting home. In a way that makes me nervous. But the other option is my place, and I most definitely don't want to meet him here.

John is already waiting for me in front of the grocery store. He smiles when he sees me, gets out, opens the door for me and we drive off. Now last time I was quite excited with the guy, but then I had drunk. Now I'm sober. Real sober.

John smiles at me and says: "You know, you are the first one I'm taking home ..." I smile back and say: "You're the first one I'm going home with." And we both laugh. But soon John is serious again.

"Monique there is something I need to tell you," he says. And because of his serious tone I winch. *Now what is this going to be? He has another couple waiting for us? He has a torture room in his house?*

But John says: "I'm not divorced. I'm a widower. I just wanted you to know. Normally I tell girls that I'm divorced because it just makes it easier. Less emotional and all."

I touch his hand and say: "I'm so sorry, John." John nods. "It was the cancer ..." and he swallows hard before he continues. "It was horrible. It took ages before she had peace. She had so much pain …"

John clears his throat. "That's why I'm doing this now. I'm not going to fall in love again. I don't want to attach to someone I can lose." I don't know what to say to that, so I kiss his hand and he smiles.

When we arrive at his house, he seems a little stressed. "Please get in fast," he says, as he quickly looks me over. "You look decent enough, so I guess it will be okay. You could be my lawyer or something like that."

He quickly glances around. "It's the neighbours you see," he says while we enter his house and two cats curl around his legs. "Shall we take off our shoes?" As I'm zipping out of my decent-enough suede booties, he continues.

"They are always gossiping, you see. Sometimes I work till late at night and I just *know* what they must be thinking. 'Now what is John doing this late at night?' I hate it when people talk about me …"

I nod, while I walk into his living room. *People talk. I get that. Sometimes I think like that as well.* At times I wonder what people in my street think about me. Whether they suspect anything. And I hate it when some married mothers at school avoid me, since they consider single mothers as a threat. *Maybe I am, but not for them. I wouldn't give their husbands one second look.*

But then I always remember what Mr. Viking said. People mostly think about themselves. They don't even think that much about others. And caring about what other people might or might not think is simply a waste of good drinking time.

One of John's cats carefully comes to me and nuzzles my feet. "These are my cats," John says. "The one with you is Bella and this is Luna". And he bends down to scratch Luna under her chin. "You're special," he says. "They like you. Normally they run away from strangers."

While John prepares us tea, I walk around his living room. It's not as I had expected. It's rather empty, more like a hotel room. Or a room in an elderly home. It has tiles on the floor, no personal pictures, and absolutely nothing that reminds of a deceased wife. The only framed pictures are of his cats.

When tea is ready, John invites me to sit down on his sofa, clearing away two cat blankets. So we sit down next to each other, sipping from our tea and talking about his cats. Sometimes he touches me, telling me that he likes the softness of my dress.

After some time my tea is finished. Since John is not really making any move, I decide I will. So I start kissing him. And he reacts strongly, so I climb on his lap and we kiss passionately for some time.

Then he strips me down, right there on the sofa. Taking off my skirt, my bra, my stockings and my slip before he strips down himself. He has quite a belly I notice, and his body is covered with freckles. It's not the most attractive body, but I'm now used to focusing on the positive. I do like his dick. It's nice, thick and has a little curve going up. If I have Happy Boobs, John has a Happy Dick. It's as if his dick is cheering up.

But the sofa is not that comfortable, so I take his hand and he leads me up to his bedroom. His bedroom is also like a hotel room. It's a neat middle-class bedroom with only the most basic furniture.

But his bed is big. And that's all that counts for now. The guy has a nice cock, he has passion and he is going to pay. *What else can I want for now?* He likes different positions too, just like Farshad and Rudolph. He takes me missionary, doggy, with me on top and from the side.

And he acts like he is really in love. He tells me how beautiful I am. He caresses me, kisses me, and tells me my skin is so soft. Now with him being so loving, I would expect to be feeling like I did with Farshad and Rudolph.

But it's different. I really liked them, but I'm not really attracted to this guy. This is business. I'm even making sure I'm not spending too much time with him, making sure I'm getting enough for each hour spent.

Mr. Fuck is just business as well. And I'm not really attracted to Mr. Fuck either. But Mr. Fuck is easier. He is just a fuck. He has passion, fucks and afterwards it's done. We dress and go our own ways. There is not even the slightest hint of love.

John – the guy who doesn't want to love again – seems to be longing for love. When he asks me what I like about his body, that's a hard one since I'm not attracted to him. So I tell him he has a wonderful dick.

But the real problem is that he just doesn't come. I try everything. Really. Everything. For three hours I'm riding on top of him, under him, sucking him, doggy, but he just doesn't come.

Three hours later, when he is licking me again – he does a lot of that – I really don't feel like fucking anymore. So I kindly pull him up, kiss him and tell him that I'm actually a bit hungry and I soon have to pick up the girls from school.

John reacts fast. "You're hungry? I don't have much food in the house right now…" And he is already pulling on his trousers. "Do you like a fried egg?" I smile while I get into my dress. "Darling, I *love* fried eggs."

John happily goes down to fry some eggs, while I have a quick glance in his bathroom mirror. Then I go down and caress his cats. When he is finished, John puts our plates on the little saloon table in front of the sofa and we sit next to each other eating our eggs.

In a way this is so weird. We're complete strangers behaving in this homely way. And John seems to love this fake-homely thing. He is beaming, while we sit next to each other eating our eggs.

"It's so nice to have you here," he says between bites. But then a cloud passes over his face as he says: "You know, sometimes I just don't know the meaning of it all." I look at him. "What do you mean?"

John sighs. "It just feels like my life has no purpose." I caress his hand and say: "But it has, of course it has!" and John beams. But truth is that I don't really know what to say. With no kids, no spouse and not a too exciting job I would probably feel the same …

He drives me all the way back, just in time. And hands me the money when I go out. "You know, I don't make that much money," he says. "I save money for this." And he smiles.

Now I already kind of figured that out, I guess. Neither his house, nor his car or his clothes give the impression that he makes an awful lot of money. He looks like the average middle class man. And in a way I feel bad, taking his money. On the other hand, isn't this what he is paying for? For some dream he wants to live in?

"Thank you," I say as I take the money. "You really *are* helping me out." John smiles and says: "It was so lovely. I would love to meet you again. How about next Tuesday." "Sure!" I answer, and I kiss him one last time before I get out.

From then on we develop a regular meeting schedule. I meet him on Tuesdays. First we have tea, then sex in his bedroom and a fried egg afterwards. From the second time onwards he does come, though it still takes ages, and he manages to make me come without me even helping, which is quite an achievement.

But my attitude has changed. Before I had Sugar Daddies. Men whom I really liked, or with whom I liked the traveling. John is okay. I like him as a person. He is kind. But I don't have any deeper feelings for him.

If I wouldn't have to, I'd rather not have sex with him. I'm doing this for one thing only. Money. And I guess that is not making it Sugar anymore. John is my client. Going to him is my work. I even tell people I have a work meeting on Tuesdays, though of course I don't tell anyone what kind of work it is…

Do I feel bad about it? Not really. I'm happy with the money. With both Mr. Fuck and Mr. Happy Dick, my financial situation is finally improving. And it's not like I have a whole bunch of Mr. Fucks and Mr. Happy Dicks. But do I feel good about it? *Not really…*

Then on a Sunday morning I am up early. No surprise there of course. I'm always up early. I can hear Lisa and Sophie playing together. I yawn, scratch Fuzzy behind his ears and get my phone. There is a pop-up from SA. Someone favorited my profile.

When I check him out, there is not much information about him. Just that he is 53 years old and married with three kids. But the guy must also be up, because the moment I check him out, I get a new message in my mailbox:

"You're up early on a Sunday morning, but maybe that's because your children are still small? Your profile is a relief compared to what is usually to be found here. It is also rather intriguing, not to say intimidating!

We undoubtedly have enough discussion topics, although I do not know whether I fully meet the requirements in your profile. Cultured, certainly. Interesting, sophisticated, fun: all right, maybe a bit. But enjoying life to the fullest? That is the question…

Of course I would like to know more about such an interesting lady…Like what exactly does your work involve, what do you write, how old are your children, do you care for them on your own?

Another question is of course what someone with your talent, your possibilities, your track-record (and your looks!) is looking for on this site that she could not possibly find in the real world, where your admirers should be as numerous as the number of planes that take off over Heathrow every day?

Please excuse me if I ask too many questions, and fire questions back to me in reverse! I will answer everything, although I do not have such an exciting story... I used to work in the business world, I now work at a university, I teach literature and I have a great love for pre-revolutionary Russian literature – and also for some Spanish authors. Like Calderon, La Vida es sueño!

I am also a writer, but in scientific and popular science, not novels – the latter is a secret ambition, to pursue later... but when? The art of living is probably not to wait too long to make your secret dreams work... but then there are laws and practical objections...

A dreamy but warm greeting, M."

I smile when I read it. Not many men on SA are able to touch me with what they write. Rudolph did. And this new guy most definitely does. So I yawn one more time, sit up in my bed and answer. Soon he writes:

"Could I get an email address so that next time I can send a message to your email address? I feel a bit awkward inside the walls of this site, not only because I feel quite out of place among all those sugar babes (who send you one-line messages like 'Hey! I like your profile! Wanna meet soon?' Or messages from three lines with five spelling mistakes, and whose beautiful pictures cannot compensate for that).

But also because the annoying rectangle in which I have to type my messages is very awkward and I have the impression that sometimes pieces of text are also mutilated. As a writer you will agree that what we need is not a small rectangle, but a large white sheet on which (sometimes, sometimes) something can arise.

So what do you say? Shall we stay here or have our first small jump over the walls of this site? Looking forward to hear from you! M."

So I give him my email address. We mail back and forth and with every email he makes me smile. M. is a professor and not the typical SA man. Not at all. What he seems to be looking for, is a dream. He is not looking for sex. He is looking for a woman to write letters with, to go to museums and dinners with. A Soul Mate.

Our first meeting is in Brighton, at a beautiful pavilion right on the beach. Now it's still early, I just dropped the girls off at school and at this early hour there are only two men in the pavilion. One is facing the entrance and looks at me the moment I enter, but I have seen The Professor's picture. I know this guy isn't him.

So The Professor must be the other one, sitting with his back to the entrance, dreaming over the ocean. I walk up to him and he gets up and politely shakes my hand. Now The Professor really looks like one. He has dark hair, messy eyebrows and a dreamy look in his eyes. His clothes are very decent. A tweed jacket with matching trousers.

And he looks rather excited. Meeting Sugar Babies aka Soul Mates is something he obviously doesn't do daily. He has probably just pulled himself out of a book to shyly enter the wild outside world.

His cheeks and even the tip of his nose get a little red as he starts talking. He talks a lot, with wide hand gestures. But not in a bad way. The Professor wants to know everything about me. Everything. And I feel like all I do is talk.

Now The Professor talks as well. He talks about literature. About the romantic view of love. How he believes that love is something which doesn't necessarily needs to be consummated in any way. And I smile. I like him. He has something enchanting over him. His enthusiasm is one you don't find often with adults. It's the enthusiasm of a kid.

I have totally lost time, so when I check my watch I have to run. But just before I leave, he hands me a book. It's a small book with children stories about friendship. I thank him and run out. When I look back one last time, he isn't looking at me. He is again dreaming over the ocean...

I'm just in time at school and afterwards it's busy with friends, homework and dinner, so I don't open the book until it's evening, after bedtime stories, when the girls are tucked into their beds and I've settled with Fuzzy on the sofa to write on my memoirs. It's that moment that the book catches my attention again...

When I open the book it has an envelope inside. Now I didn't expect any money, this was our first meeting, but six £50 bills are neatly tucked inside. I smile. Receiving money has never felt bad, but with The Professor it just feels so pure.

Also included is a postcard with a quote from Roald Dahl: "'A dream,' he said, 'as it goes whiffling through the night air, is making a tiny little buzzing-humming noise. But this little buzzy-hum is so silvery soft, it is impossible for a human bean to be hearing it." And The Professor has written underneath: "With thanks for our first exploration of the silvery soft humming world of dreams!"

And I realize something. The Professor is right. This is all about the dream. Sugar Dating – and probably also the top-end escort world – is like the geisha world that Natasha talked about.

What we are really selling is a dream. An illusion. As long as our date lasts, men can escape their normal world with all its stress and responsibilities. For some frail moments, they can forget all about their kids, wives and jobs.

As long as the date lasts, they spend time with us in an illusion. An illusion of homely love, courtly love, of feeling desired and wanted. Of being seen. Because, as The Professor has stated so nicely in one of his letters: "in the end isn't that universal – the hope to be seen and recognised …"

CHAPTER TWENTY-EIGHT: MISSING THE TRAIN TO THE CITY OF ROMANCE

My life is still a whirlwind. I write, meet my Daddies and the weeks are full of school, playdates and sports. It's now a cold rainy November evening. The girls are colouring at the big kitchen table, while I am preparing the children's tea and juggling with the messages I'm getting in.

First Paul, The Viking and Mr. Happy Dick ask me how I'm doing. Then, as I am stirring the baked beans, Sarah is telling me about some new trouble she is having with her Stepmother and Barbara is telling me her husband has a rebound and is starting to turn into himself again.

And as I grill sausages and turn over the oven chips, I suddenly get a message from Mr. Tantra, telling me he is remembering our night together. He tells me how busy he has been these last few days and that he just wants to relax in some good company.

Apparently it's chatting day today. So maybe it shouldn't have been such a surprise when I get a message from Farshad, asking me how I'm doing and telling me he misses me 'too much'.

Now, as I said, it's November. It's exactly one year since I last met him. And it has been half a year since I last heard from him. I used to get a little annoyed with that, but now I'm used to it.

This is Sugar Dating. We spend months without the expectation to see each other, still it feels like we share a special bond. So I reply back that I miss him too and hope to meet him soon. He reacts back fast:

"I have 2 chances to meet you

1: I can meet you from tomorrow afternoon till Sunday!
2: meet you 17th afternoon till 19th morning.

Please let me know how we can meet each other and where we go. Roma? Venice? Milan? Paris? Big kiss, Farshad"

As I stir the beans once more, I write to him that I'd love to meet him. Tomorrow is a bit hard, but his second option could work. *And for a moment I wish that things wouldn't be so last minute with him.* See, I need to arrange things for the girls, I need lies to be constructed...

Then, after that message, he is silent again. So I have no idea whether I will meet him. I hate that with him. I really do. I'm really quite fond of him, but I hate never knowing what will happen. It makes it so tough to arrange it all. And for a moment I even miss dependable Mr. Yoga. So the 16th comes, and it's only in the evening that I hear from him and hold a ticket in my hands for the next day. *Jeez...*

Now I'm flying at two in the afternoon and there's a lot of last-minute arranging to do. So I ask The Ex to pick up the girls from school at three, instead of me bringing them to him at six. He is rather annoyed with it being so last minute and tells me he has to work. So I arrange for a mother to have the girls with her until The Ex will pick them up at six and I arrange the cat-sitter.

But flying at two leaves me tons of time to prepare, which is nice. I shower, try on different dresses, pack my suitcase and leave a note for the cat sitter before I close the door behind me and take the commuter train to Heathrow.

I am flying with EasyJet, just like I did last year with Robert. Which means I am allowed one carry-on bag, but no extra purse, so I have to push my purse into my hand luggage and carry my book, passport, phone and water bottle in my hands, realizing that Easy Jet is just *not* my favourite company.

Yes I know, I've changed. And I shouldn't complain. Fact is that it has actually been quite a while since I last travelled. Japan was my last Sugar Trip and that was in the end of August. *Damn, that's more than two months ago …*.

And I simply love traveling. See, this is something that I have discovered with this Sugar Life. I love the different cities, the posh hotels, the exclusive restaurants. I guess I just like adventure and the good things of life. Now I'm pondering over all this on the flight, but it isn't too long and Milan Malpensa airport is small which is great – I'm out in a second.

Farshad is waiting for me at the exit and it's so lovely to see him again. I will always have a weak spot for him. He was the first who paid to spend the night with me and he is the only one who helps me without an arrangement. He is the one who takes me shopping for presents. Whatever happens, he will always have a special place in my heart.

But when I see him again, I realize that Farshad has changed this last year. He looks tired and aged. His hair is greying, he has bags underneath his eyes and I miss the sparkle in them. He used to be such a vibrant, happy man. *What has happened with him?*

When he sees me, he puts his arms around my waist and still kisses me like a long lost lover. Then he takes my arm and leads me to the train station to look for a train to Venice. Milan would be perfectly fine for me, but for some reason he has put his mind on going to Venice together.

When he asks at the counter, most trains are sold out. But there is still one at 8:45 PM which will reach Venice at eleven. The guy behind the counter smiles at us. "That still leaves time for a nice dinner here, no?" And we can only agree.

So we take a train towards Central and I snuggle up against Farshad while he starts searching hotels on his phone. He finds one and makes a booking, but it soon gets rejected because his credit card is over date. Farshad shrugs and starts looking for a hotel that accepts cash.

Then when we have to change trains at Duomo, Farshad says: "Come. You have to see the Duomo!" I hesitate. I would love to see it, I have never been to Milan, but we just don't have an awful lot of time. So I say: "We still need to have dinner and have a train to catch…" But Farshad is decisive. "We eat here. At Duomo."

And the moment we get out of the subway, the Duomo is right in front of us. It's a stunning, pink-hued white marble Gothic cathedral. Farshad smiles and says: "First time I came to Europe thirty years ago I came here. To Milan. Duomo was the first thing I visited." And he looks up with a smile. "Can you imagine? They made it all by hand. Thousands of people."

But we don't have too much time to admire it, we still need to have our dinner and we have a train to catch. So Farshad leads me to the beautiful Galleria Vittorio Emanuele, a 19th century arcade to the right of the Duomo. It's stunning, with a glass dome and a mosaic. There is a Christmas tree under construction and there are stores of Prada, Gucci and Borasalino.

"This is too much beautiful," Farshad sighs while he leads me into a classy restaurant called Biffi. It's an all-glass construction right inside the beautiful old Galleria and we get a lovely table by the window. When we get the menu Farshad chooses a lovely fish-dish with olives and I choose delicious Gnocchi with Gorgonzola. Farshad has a red wine, while I have a white one.

"So what do you do now?" Farshad asks me, while we dip our homemade bread into olive oil. "I have been writing," I tell him. "Your old books?" I shake my head. "No, do you remember my friend, Amanda?" Farshad nods. "I have been writing her memoirs." *Which is in a way true, right? I did write those before I started writing mine.*

"Did she have such an interesting life?" Farshad asks me, as he cuts his fish and takes a bite. I smile and nod as I say: "She was a top-end escort." Farshad almost chokes. "She was a *what*?" And it takes him a while to recover.

As he dries his lips with his linen napkin, he says: "Good. That is too much interesting. That will be a hit. I am sure." He takes one more bite, then he asks: "Am I also in this book?" I smile sweetly at him and lie glibly: "Of course not darling. It's a book about Amanda's life, right? Not mine." *And for a second I muse about how horribly good I've become at lying.* He keeps nodding and says: "You found a good subject honey. It's too much interesting."

After dinner we have to hurry, we have a train to Venice to catch. So we rush through the Galleria, past the Duomo, into the subway. But the subway train is late, so we are late at the grand Art Deco Central Station and we just miss our train to Venice.

As we watch the train ride away, Farshad sighs. "I'm so sorry," he says. I kiss him. "Why darling? It's okay. Milan is beautiful. Let's enjoy Milan together. Come I saw a ticket-office on the way, let's try to get your money back for the return trip."

Farshad looks at me. "Are you sure honey? Is Milan good enough for you?" "Of course it is!" And I gesture to the beautiful building around me. "Look, Milan is beautiful!" Farshad looks around. "It is, isn't it?" "It is honey, it's stunning. And you are with me. That's the most important." Farshad smiles and kisses me.

But the Italian guy at the railway desk thinks otherwise. He looks with sparkling eyes from over his glasses at both of us. "Why you cancel?" he asks. "You go to Venice together. Venice is romantic, no?" Farshad smiles and says: "Too much romantic." "Don't lose this chance!" the Italian says. So he changes our train tickets to the next day.

When we get out of the station, Farshad gets his phone and starts searching for a hotel in the neighbourhood. He finds a Crowne Plaza, books online and off we go. It's not a long walk and the area is beautiful with old stately buildings.

At the hotel a friendly Italian checks us in. "So sorry," he says. "You just got one of our last rooms. We only have two rooms left. A small one with a queen size bed," he looks at us and gestures with his hands. "Too small for you," he says. "You need the space."

I smile. *This is so Italy.* Even our receptionist is concerned about our love life. I guess in Sugar Life, Italy is *the* place to go. I guess only in Italy they don't even think about arrangements, but just about people enjoying love, no matter with whom you show up and no matter what the differences are.

The receptionist is still worried about our room. "The other is big one," he says. "But with two beds," and he sighs a sad little sigh. "Ok," Farshad says. "I will come and check with you." So up they go together, checking out which bed will be most suited for our lovemaking.

I walk towards a desk which has flyers of things to do in Milan. There are tours and things like that, but there is one thing that catches my eye. It's an exhibition about Leonardo da Vinci. And knowing Farshad, that will be exactly what he likes.

When they come back down, they both smile contently. "We take the big one," Farshad says and the receptionist nods in agreement. "Look," I tell Farshad and show him the flyer. "They have an exhibition you'd like here in Milan. It's about Leonardo da Vinci." Farshad starts to beam. "Leonardo. I love Leonardo. Maybe we stay in Milan!"

When we are in the room, Farshad is busy for some time. "I already checked with receptionist," he says. "It can all move." So he removes the nightstand and pushes the beds against each other. Then he gives me a sideways look, asks: "No sex, right?" and he bursts out laughing.

But once the beds are done, Farshad has no patience. He strips off my clothes and starts kissing me. It has been ages since we last made love, but it still feels so familiar. His soft chest hair, his huge dick. Damn it's lovely.

He first takes me in missionary. And it takes some time before he can enter me all the way. As always, his dick is simply too big to enter in one thrust. But once he can enter me thoroughly, he turns me around, puts a pillow under my belly and takes me from behind. He comes quite fast like that. It must have been a while since he last had sex. And he looks even more tired afterwards, so we go to sleep at ten.

Normally I sleep lousy in hotels, but not this time. I lie in his arms and sleep amazingly well throughout the whole night. When I wake up, Farshad is smiling at me and says: "Honey you cuddled the whole night with me. I'm loving it!"

I smile and follow the scar underneath his lip with my finger, then lazily turn with my back to him while he cuddles me. I still love being cuddled by him. And he is already hard. I can feel his huge dick against my bum. Well, you understand that Farshad doesn't let me lie like that for long.

Soon I can feel him entering me. I push my ass towards him as he holds my hip and thrusts his dick deep inside of me. It's a nice lazy lovemaking, still lying on our sides. But soon I'm not lazy anymore. I get hot and climb of top of him.

"Honey," Farshad whispers. "You are so beautiful when you are hot. You get all red and you look like such a young girl. I love it." But soon he isn't talking anymore. He gasps as I ride him faster and faster. Then I turn around on top of him. I ride him with my ass towards him – so I know he has a nice view of his dick entering me – and I hold his feet with my hands. He comes quite fast like that.

After sex we dress for breakfast. Farshad is still wearing the same clothes as the last time I met him, I notice. And I can only wonder. *Does he take the same clothes with him every time he travels? Or is his business just not going so well?*

The breakfast buffet is nice. It's not as luxurious as I'm used to – god am I getting spoiled – but it's nice. I have toast with eggs and peach juice, while Farshad gets us a nice selection of fruits.

Then after breakfast we go to the station to cancel our tickets. Because with a Leonardo da Vinci exhibition in Milan, Farshad has decided we will stay. But cancelling takes ages. The Italian ticketing system is slow, inconvenient and antique. When he has finally gotten some of his money back – 70 euros from the 200 he paid – Farshad is relaxed and says: "Let's go to Da Vinci!"

'The World of Leonardo' is a temporary museum at the other end of Galleria Vittorio Emanuele II. A tiny elevator takes us up to the exhibition, where large installations of da Vinci's inventions are everywhere, hanging from the ceiling and displayed throughout the airy rooms.

There are exhibits of his contribution to town planning and his invention in flight, music, architecture, weaponry and even reproductions of the Mona Lisa and The Last Supper. I had no idea that da Vinci invented so much!

Farshad is bewitched at the multimedia stations. The interactive touch screens allow him to interact with more than two hundred digital reconstructions and show da Vinci's inventions, starting with his drawings.

They show how – at least on paper – he created such inventions as the bicycle, the helicopter, cannons, smoke machines, portable bridges, armoured vehicles and an airplane based on the physiology and flying capability of a bat.

Farshad marvels at the working models of machines designed by Leonardo, like a submarine, a mechanical lion, -eagle and -dragonfly and a rapid-fire crossbow, as well as reconstructions of his musical instruments.

I'm also impressed, though not as bewitched as Farshad is. As an engineer, he simply loves inventors like Leonardo and Gaudí. So we stay for a very long time. It's already three when we finally leave.

We take the elevator back down and have lunch at a restaurant close by. It's not as flashy as usual, just a regular place down the road, but that makes it rather nice and intimate. I have a lovely big tuna salad with olives, red onion, Italian olive oil and balsamic. Farshad orders two dishes – a pizza with salami and a folded pizza with fried vegetables – which he both manages to finish.

When we are finished with our lunch, dusk is already falling. We get out of the restaurant and walk through the Galleria towards the Duomo, where Farshad has a cigarette looking at the beautiful cathedral.

"You know," he says as he blows out some smoke, "When I first arrived here I had an Italian mentor. He was so nice to me. He showed me everything. He treated me like his own son." Farshad is quiet for a while, blowing out smoke, before he adds: "He has died. But I will always remember how he treated me. He opened the gate to the western world for me …"

He seems to be lost in thoughts for some time. But then he kisses me and says: "How about some shopping?" Well, sure! I guess Farshad has indeed made me a bit more Aphrodite, because I'm all in for shopping.

He first leads me into a sweetshop and says: "Find something for your girls!" I love that about him. I love how he always remembers my girls. We choose two bags with Christmas chocolates and an advent calendar with candies. Next he takes me into Zara and tells me: "Find something nice!"

Now Zara is not the place he would have taken me before and I'm starting to think that his business might really not be as successful as it used to be. But Zara is fine too. Truth is that I'm happy with anything, getting presents is always fun.

Still there is nothing at Zara's that takes my fancy. Zara is just not what it used to be. Or maybe the fashion isn't right now. It's big and shapeless. And fashion or not, that's simply not my style. I like elegant and feminine.

Then Farshad asks me: "Honey, can you help me? I never have time. And I don't really know ... I am a man ... Can you help me buy some clothes?" I smile and kiss him. "Of course darling. I'd love to!" So we go up to the Men's section of Zara, where Farshad tries on several coats. It's endearing in a way, he is like a small boy. He keeps putting things on and asking me whether I think it looks good on him.

In the end we find him a lovely black business coat that looks nice and classy on him. When we get out, I spot a Benneton opposite the road. "Darling, do you need some sweaters?" I ask him. "Benneton has really nice soft sweaters." Farshad nods. "I do honey. I do."

Now Zara may not be my style anymore, but apparently Benneton still is, I realize the moment I get in. It has soft materials and all the clothes here have a nice feminine cut. "Honey, you try a coat on," Farshad says. So I try on several and Farshad marvels at all of them. "Honey, you are like a model. You have a too much delicious body. Anything you put on suits you."

Now that is something you could hear every day, right? So I kiss him and choose the first coat I tried. It's a beautiful tight black coat made of soft wool. And then I tell him: "But we came here for your sweaters," and I drag him up to the first floor.

"I'm sure you can use some nice soft sweaters," I say. *Especially since he is still wearing the same ones from one year ago…* Now here he is also like a little boy, trying on his sweaters. He is insecure, asking me whether the colour suits him. And not happy because he used to be a Large and now he is an XL.

He first still tries to push himself into a Large, with bad results. It makes him look like a sausage. Not that I say that of course, I just tell him an XL would be better. "But I need L," Farshad insists. "I'm going to lose weight again." I smile at him and say: "Darling, you are a real man. Look at your broad shoulders. A real man needs XL." And with that he beams and accepts an XL.

After our shopping, we sit next to each other for some time watching the Duomo while Farshad smokes a cigarette. We are both rather quiet and lost in our thoughts. Farshad seems to be remembering the first time he came to Milan. I am thinking about my book. Because I know I am going to write about this the moment I'm back home. *I have three chapters to go…*

Then Farshad points at a terrace op top of the Galleria overlooking the Duomo. "Shall we go there for a drink?" he asks. I smile and say: "That would be lovely, darling." So up we go, to the terrace for an aperitivo – which is one of the city's oldest traditions. It means having a drink including a huge buffet from which you can eat your fill from 6 to 7 pm. We sit for some time with our drink, overlooking the Duomo. But Farshad is looking tired again. And soon he says: "Honey let's go back."

We walk back to the hotel. It's quite a walk, but it's beautiful. We walk past stately houses, palaces, cosy restaurants. "Why did you want to go to Venice?" I ask him. Farshad laughs. "I had no idea about Milan," he says. "I went here a hundred times. But I had no idea that it is so beautiful." He is quiet and grabs my hand before he continues. "Also when I am alone, I just don't really feel like exploring …"

He looks at me for a second. Then he asks me: "Why didn't you get angry, honey?" "Angry? About what?" "About missing the train…" I laugh. "Why would I get angry about that? It wasn't your fault!" He shrugs. "My ex-wife would have," he says. I ponder on that for a moment. "You know, so would my ex," I then tell him. "He also would have been angry at me." And we both laugh at that.

He takes my hand. "You are such an easy-going woman," he says. "I wish we had a chance to be together." I smile. *Me too.* In a way, Farshad is someone I could consider something serious with. And I suddenly realize that I guess I always hoped we could, in some way.

But right at that moment, walking through the beautiful Milan streets, I also see the reality of our situation. Farshad will always be living like this. Would I move to Iran? Hell no. And he has his life there. He would never leave. So this is all there is. All there ever will be. *And will that be enough for me?* For some reason realizing this makes me sad.

It's only eight when we are back in the hotel, but Farshad looks exhausted. "Darling, are you okay?" I ask him. He shrugs. "I just do too much working. I am always busy. I want to work less." "So what would you like to do when you work less?" I ask him. He starts beaming. "Make things," he says. "Like art. Make things for myself. And explore the world." He sighs. "But it's no use. All my money is in my company. So I need to go on …" And he looks even more tired now.

I promised you to be honest, right? In a way, I hoped he would mention something about me. About us. That he would want to spend more time with me. *Isn't that stupid. This is all we have. All there will ever be. Some stolen moments together. And why does that make me sad?*

"Honey, do you mind if I take nap in your lap?" he asks me. I smile. "Of course not darling." So he takes off his glasses and lies down on my lap. Soon he falls asleep. I read my book, drink some wine from the mini bar and softly caress him.

At ten I wake him. "Honey, you are so tired. Maybe you should just go to sleep." Farshad nods, ponders off and is busy in the bathroom for some time. When he comes back, he starts kissing me and climbs on top of me. We make love in missionary until he comes and he falls asleep at eleven.

The next morning we make love one last time and he comes quite quickly. Somehow his tiredness seems to affect our love-making too. Also I haven't had an orgasm this whole trip. And for the first time I realize something. Now that I have had so many men trying to please me, I realize that Farshad doesn't really do anything to please me. He has a great dick. He loves different positions. But he doesn't try to make me come in anyway.

I don't really mind though. I enjoy being with him. I enjoy his dick. And I will be with Mr. Happy Dick next Tuesday. He will make me come, I know. But it's an interesting observation. And it's interesting that I never even noticed.

After we dress, he gets his money out of the safe and starts counting his hundred dollar bills. Then – to my surprise – he hands me 2000 euros. *What? Two thousand euro's??* It's the biggest amount I have ever gotten, and we're not even in a real arrangement.

So I look at him with shock and say "Are you sure?" He smiles. "Just a little something, because I haven't been able to look after you for so long. You just write that book. I know it will be a hit. "I give him a long kiss. "Thank you honey," I say. "Thank you so much. This will definitely help me out until I have finished my book…" *But somehow, this feels like a goodbye…*

After a quick breakfast we take a cab to the airport. Now Farshad is leaving from Terminal 1 and I am leaving from 2. Mr. Yoga would have said goodbye in 1 and let me go to 2 by myself, but not Farshad. He is like a lover, as long as I am with him.

After we say our goodbyes he will forget me and I know it will take ages before I next hear from him. *If* I ever hear from him again. Because somehow this time felt different. And I realize that moment that if something would happen to him, I would never know.

So Farshad sees me off at terminal 2 and I have to hurry, so I kiss him and rush through to customs. I can still see him waiting for me for quite some time and I wave, but he doesn't see me.

And when I see him like that, I do feel a little sad. *What has happened to him?* He's looking so old and tired. I wish I could have helped him more, or done something for him, though I don't know what. I wish I could hug him right there and then and take all his tiredness away.

But then he catches my eye and his whole face starts to beam. And for one second he is the sparkling Farshad I remember …

CHAPTER TWENTY-NINE: FATA MORGANA

One morning after I've brought the girls to school, I just don't feel like writing. I've been writing so much these last months. And I'm pondering over something... See, Mr. Tantra has contacted me to let me know that he is coming to the UK next week and asked me whether I'm interested to visit a Swingers Club with him. So I wonder. *AM I interested?* I make myself a hot cup of coffee and contemplate about my life these last twenty-one months.

See, I've been living on the periphery of the escort world for almost two years now. And more and more frequently the voice inside of me asks me how long I am going to do this – even though I squash it the moment it comes up.

I have changed these twenty-one months. I now view each message I get not as a potential fun date, but as potential business. But even though I have a degree of financial security now, I still feel insecure about my future. And I am lying to so many people... Fact is that the lies are breaking me up.

So in a way I am longing to stop. I clearly can't make money like this forever. I do realize that I simply have to think of some other way to support my little family. I have to come up with an alternative income stream. The answer is just around the corner.

Because I'm writing. Thanks to the help of my Sugar Daddies, I have been able to start doing the things I really feel passionate about. And following my passion gives real satisfaction. Ben the journalist has even proposed that, once my memoirs are finished, we will start writing erotic memoirs together. *Now that will be fun!* And my agent is all for this idea.

Also I have saved enough money these last months to be able survive for some time. So maybe it's time to get out. Maybe it's time to see whether I can stand on my own feet.

I take a big sip of my coffee, scratch Fuzzy behind his ear and then open my laptop. Seeking Arrangement is easy to log into. And once again, I deactivate my account. But this time, I tell myself, it's forever.

By now, my memoirs are almost finished. I'm editing the last chapters and I have two more chapters to write. Writing about Amanda was fun, but writing about myself has been even more fulfilling. It makes me realize that I've had two great years through Sugar Dating. I almost can't believe myself all the stuff that I've done. The things that almost no one knows about.

Skydiving seems like a dream. So do all the trips I've made. Japan, Singapore, Hong Kong, Dubai, Paris, Barcelona, Vienna, Milan... Milan was only weeks ago, so that one still feels real. All the rest now feel like dreams. Like nice sparkly bubbles in my otherwise so normal life.

Also, I've discovered my sexual drive. I have experienced a whole new range of sexual fantasies. But there still is one fantasy I haven't experienced yet. My very first contact – with the American with his three girlfriends – has sparked my fantasy for one thing. So far I have never kissed a girl.

So maybe I should have this one last experience with Mr. Tantra. A Swingers Club would be a wonderful place to have a first girl-experience. At least I'll be able to choose the girl. And

I like Shiva. Since our Tantra-experience, it's like there is this special bond between us.

When I look at the pictures of the club online I have to admit that I'm surprised how cool it looks. It looks classy. Like a high-end night club. And I am intrigued... So I tell Shiva that yes, I would love to join him. It will be one hell of a last experience.

The evening he arrives, I arrange for the girls to stay with friends and take a train to Heathrow. Shiva is already waiting for me. Okay, so maybe he is short with a moustache and a protruding belly, but somehow after experiencing Tantra with him, it feels like we have a special connection. And I melt at the intense gaze he gives me. "Hi sweetheart," he says, "how wonderful to see you. Are you ready for your Fata Morgana?" And he smiles.

We take a cab to the club, where we are greeted by a warm, friendly girl who explains all the rules to us. Basically, the club is very female friendly. No means no, if anyone bothers me I should talk to the guards and things like that. Next Shiva pays the "membership fee" and in we go.

Inside a nice, friendly couple welcome us warmly and give us a tour. It feels like we are checking out a model home here and I am almost embarrassed to admit that I am surprised at how 'normal' the patrons are.

They suggest we start downstairs, so we follow them down a long and narrow stairway. And I am wondering what I am going to see... *Will there be whips and scenes? Or group sex in full force?* Well, not quite yet. It's 11 PM, which is still early and not much activity is going on. Yet.

We begin with a trip to all the different rooms. You name it and it's here. There are theme rooms, a sex dungeon complete with a chain and a leather sex swing, voyeur rooms, group rooms full of beds and platforms and there are round beds that people can rotate from the outside window by pushing a button for an optimal view.

Red lights above each door indicate what's free, and you have to schedule with the hostess to arrange a room. But all is still empty. "Don't worry," our hostess tells us. "Things will heat up later."

Next they show us a heated outdoor pool, a hot tub, steam room and sauna. And on the second floor there is a locker room where everyone changes into lingerie at a specific time.

Once the tour is over, we are left at the bar. Shiva orders me a glass of Chablis and has a Whiskey himself. He is so relaxed and casual about this. He behaves as if we are in just a regular bar, while I feel adrenaline racing through my body. But it's nice to be here with him. In a way his attitude reassures me.

Slowly the place is filling up. Couples of all ages and races gather up. They are drinking, chatting and many greet each other warmly. Now this bar could have been a regular bar anywhere, except that several women smile right at me.

I had expected to feel sleazy here – especially with Mr. Tantra who is so obviously not my boyfriend – but the opposite is true. I feel sexy, beautiful and respected. No one is manhandling me or making any unwelcome gestures or movements towards me.

Soon it's time to change into our lingerie and it doesn't take long until the party is in full swing. In the beginning I feel rather self-conscious walking around in my underwear, but soon that feeling is gone. Because the club is packed with people in sexy underwear and everyone is in a great mood. This place is surreal. And so sexual.

Now one couple seems to be especially interested in us. Or maybe I should say that the girl seems to be interested in *me*. And she is simply gorgeous. She is Asian, with beautiful long black hair and full lips. The guy with her is just a regular guy. Not especially attractive, but also not unattractive. But it's not the guy whom I'm interested in. I'm mesmerized by the girl. And to my shock she walks straight up to me.

I take a deep breath. *Now fantasies are nice, but am I really going through with this? Am I going to live out my fantasy?* But I don't have much time to think. She says "Hi, I'm Alice," takes my hand and pulls me onto the dancing floor, while Shiva gives me an encouraging smile.

So, suddenly we are dancing. Then we are dirty dancing. And before I know it Alice presses her lips on mine. And for a split second the world seems to be in slow motion. The main thing that strikes me is the softness. She is just so soft. And kissing her is nothing like I had expected it to be. It doesn't feel bad. Or lesbian. Or any other label that things tend to get.

It feels pure, warm, soft and just so delicious. Soon her tongue is inside my mouth and we are kissing, long and deep. I love the way she tastes, I love to feel the curves of her body. Everything about her is soft and sweet. We don't even look at our men, who simply stand on the sidelines for now, watching and waiting.

Finally Alice takes my hand again and leads me downstairs, while our men follow. Downstairs, the atmosphere is very different. Here the air is musky with the smell of sex. We come across a large square bed surrounded by thin curtains. And I can see dark shadows of people who peer through, watching the action.

When I go closer, I see countless naked bodies intertwined. And in a way I feel like a pervert, standing in the dark watching strangers having sex. But surprisingly, it's also exciting…

Now this is the first time ever that I see other people having sex. And it's like there is porn everywhere. But I'm not sure this big group-thing is it for me. I prefer something a bit more personal.

It's all arms, legs, tits and asses. There are quiet moans and slow movements. In a way I feel awkward, standing there in my garters. For a moment I just feel awfully silly and I'm sure my face is as red as a tomato. So thank goodness that it's so dark in here. The only light is a faint, red glow that illuminates the play area.

Alice pulls me out of my awkwardness. She pulls me along and our men follow. Now we pass several other intimate alcoves, all occupied by people in various states of sex. Everyone seems to be enjoying themselves here. We walk past the giant spa, which is filled with naked bodies. I take a peek inside the playroom and see a couple trying out a bondage board.

But the room Alice chooses is for just the four of us. It has a plushy red mattress that spreads from wall-to-wall and one-way windows that look in from the corridor. Perfect for a voyeur, I can't help thinking. And in a way, knowing that strangers will be able to see us is highly arousing.

Alice starts kissing me as soon as we are on the mattress. And though I'm focused on her lips and the tip of her tongue, I also feel her hand which is softly caressing my leg and then going up, slowly, very slowly until she is touching me in my slip for a while before taking it off.

I pull my corset over my head, while she takes off her own bra and I softly kiss her nipples, while my hands cup her breasts. I have never felt another woman's breasts before. But it feels good. They are nice and soft. Then she pulls up my chin and we are kissing again. Softly. Slowly.

I hesitate when Alice softly pushes me down. *I'm not sure I'm into this…* But I see Shiva looking at us with a reassuring smile and before I know it Alice is licking me. She is sucking my clit, licking slowly and really taking her time.

I gasp. Now in my whole life, I never expected to do this with a girl. Nor could I have imagined that I would be enjoying it this much. This is totally new for me. It's just so different. But at no point does it feel uncomfortable or wrong. So I just let my desires take over. I do as I please.

After some time, Alice comes up again and we continue our kissing. We kiss for some time, while the men just watch. They are coming closer now, touching our bodies without being intrusive.

I flip Alice around and start licking her. Now I've never done this before, but Alice instructs me. "Do it slow. Real slow." So I oblige. I draw my tongue from her cunt to her clit in long, slow laps, slipping my finger inside of her and smile when she moans.

The men are now getting closer. Don bends over Alice and starts licking her together with me, while she takes his cock in her mouth. At the same time Shiva slowly moves behind me and starts licking me from behind.

So Alice and Don are in 69 – she is giving him a blowjob, while he is licking her. And at the same time I'm bending down in front of her, also licking her, while Shiva is licking me from behind, holding me tight, his hands caressing my body.

After some time I turn towards Shiva and push him on his back. I softly take his dick in my mouth, giving him a nice deep blowjob. I can see Alice next to me, Don is now taking her from behind. Sometimes Alice reaches out for me and we kiss each other.

When Shiva finally penetrates me, he takes me on my back, with my leg over his shoulder giving a nice and deep penetration. Alice is moaning next to me while she is still taken doggy by Don. We still reach over and kiss from time to time.

Until Shiva flips me over and Alice and I are both taken doggy, next to each other. I start pushing my hips back into Shiva, feeling him get further inside me until it almost hurts. Though we are here with four persons, I still feel so close to him.

Being in doggy, I start helping myself and quickly have a real intense orgasm, while Shiva holds my body close to him. He comes quite soon afterwards. When I look next to us, Alice and Don are already panting. They must have finished before us.

For a while we lie together, panting. I'm lying close to Shiva, while he is holding me. But then it's time to leave the room. We get dressed, make some small talk and go back up to the bar, where Alice and Don mingle with friends.

While Shiva and I are sitting at the bar, smiling and sexually satisfied, I think about how different this place is from what I had imagined. It's definitely naughty. And it isn't for everyone. But it's far from the sleazy place I'd imagined it to be.

It's clear everyone here is having fun. They are embracing their sexuality in ways many people can't and won't. The atmosphere is playful and friendly, and personal limitations are respected. It's a place where fantasies can become a reality, and anything goes.

We take a few more drinks and then we go back to Shiva's hotel. In his room we make love once more. It's a lazy, easy lovemaking. We've already been sexually satisfied. But after Shiva falls asleep, I lie awake for some time pondering over the night.

So I have been to a sex club. I had my first girl experience. And it was interesting, no doubt. I truly enjoyed it. But I'm not sure group sex is my thing. At least not on a regular basis. I prefer sex in an intimate one-on-one contact. In a way, the Tantra with Shiva was way more intense than this was. This was just pure lust. Tantra touched something deeper.

But this experience *did* open my eyes to a world where no one is afraid of who they are and what they want – and I liked it. A lot. The purely sexual connection established between complete strangers was really interesting.

In a way, that's no different from Sugar Dating of course. I've been having sex with complete strangers for almost two years now. And it has been fun. No doubt about that. I've had a lot of fun. And some of my Sugar Daddies I have grown quite fond of. But there's an intimacy that I'm missing.

I miss being loved. I miss loving someone. I miss someone caring about me for who I am, not just for my body. Someone who is interested enough to really care. And someone whom I'm really interested in.

Now I'm not sure I will find that. But the Sugar Life is starting to feel hollow. It's time to move on. And just before I fall asleep – for one moment – Paul's face comes up, but I quickly push him away just before I drift off to a deep dreamless sleep ...

CHAPTER THIRTY: MAGIC CHRISTMAS

Another Christmas is fast approaching, so the days are a whirl again of end-of-term plays, carol concerts and the special school Christmas dinner. Now as I said before, I had decided that my girl experience would be my last one. My account on SA is deleted and now it's time to say goodbyes.

Mr. Tantra already knows I'm quitting. We had our goodbye swingers club experience and he let me know that I should text him if I ever feel like having another Tantra experience.

The Professor is an easy goodbye. He quickly moves on to catch other dreams -I don't think I could have lived up to his dream anyway. See, that's the thing with dreams, they will always be different from reality. But in a way I do miss his long rambling emails. They always made me smile.

I send a goodbye email to Farshad, but I hear nothing back. No surprise there of course. Maybe I will, one day. And I'm sure he wishes me well. It still feels like we have some special connection. But maybe that's also just an illusion.

Then I have one last mind-blowing fuck with Mr. Fuck before saying our goodbyes. And I have no doubt that a replacement will be easily found.

But Mr. Happy Dick makes our last time a special one. He has champagne and Christmas pudding ready – at 9 in the morning, but who cares – and we wish each other a great life. Then we have our last fuck. And it's funny, with some people the sex only gets better the more you do it. But this time is definitely the last.

So now my days as a Sugar Babe are behind me. And with the Daddies gone, it's time to focus on my girls. The Ex and I have divided the Christmas holidays again. The first week the girls are with me, and this time I have *chosen* to have them for Christmas Eve. Our Christmas Eve dinner will be our new family tradition. Now the second week they will be with their father, including the New Year. But I force myself not to think about that. Let's just focus on the positive …

Thanks to my arrangements, I don't have to worry about money this Christmas either. So we do all the things we did last year. The first day of the holidays, we head off to London to see the decorations. We go to the butcher where the girls choose a big juicy turkey. We buy a real Christmas tree. And back home we put on our Christmas CD while the girls spend the whole day decorating our tree, ending with a fairy on top.

But there is one big difference. Because this time I have decided to invite my family. Mr. Viking totally agrees with that of course. See, he's the only SD who's staying. We never had sex, we never had money transactions, we have become friends. And I don't feel like losing a good friend. But he's not chatting too much. He's preparing his own Danish miracle of Christmas.

So the girls and I visit my parents in their damp villa, where I interrupt my father just in time as he starts saying: "Watch out for the sss …." *I am not going to let him finish that in sperm stains …* The moment I invite them, they are beaming. And it makes me smile. *I never realized they cared.*

Therefore that early afternoon before Christmas Eve my father is sitting in an easy chair in front of the open fire. He has taken on the mission of keeping the fire alive. And he is taking his mission quite seriously, with his wild curls all in a mess.

My mother is helping the girls with the food, as we prepare our Christmas pudding and the Mince Pies. Soon the whole kitchen is covered with dough, raisins and almonds and the house is smelling like a Christmas dream. And when the girls hug her, my mother is shining. I've never seen her like this. In a way, she reminds me of a little girl herself. And I love seeing her like that.

Soon the house is filled with family and Fuzzy purrs away in all the cosiness. Laughs are being laughed, tears are being shed. And I love the jokes, the thrill, the buzz. Two years have passed and I'm no longer in awe with how my cousins are with their kids. The girls and I have the same naturalness now. Things go easy. Smooth. With laughs and love. Just like with the rest of my family.

I look at my girls with a smile. Both of them are running wild around the house with their cousins. And I notice that Lisa is no longer staying close to me, observing me. She is not trying so hard to be big. She knows I'm happy now. So she is playing around and laughing out loud. Lately she is just so happy and playful. And I realize that since Greece I haven't seen her carry all that burden on her thin little shoulders anymore. Looking at my girls makes my heart swell.

And it's like my mother can read my thoughts. She comes next to me and says: "You've done damn well, Monique. Your girls are happy little beings. You are making it work on your own. You can be proud of yourself." And she gives me a heart-warming smile. Now I know this is all. I won't get hugs or other ways of affection from her. But *this* is her giving me affection. Her letting me know she loves me. And I have never felt this close to her. It warms my heart.

When it's dinner time everyone gathers around our big kitchen table. The girls, my parents, great-uncle's wife, cousins, anyone whom I could fit around I have invited. They all have taken their share of food and drinks with them and the table is a loud and happy place.

Now I haven't been too creative, we're having the same as last year. But except for the three of us, no one else has tasted it before. So as a starter we have smoked salmon and the main course is what makes everyone cheer. It's the turkey, with roasted potatoes, vegetables, roasted parsnips and a stuffing with gravy and bread sauce. And after that everyone attacks the Christmas pudding.

I simply relish this Christmas dinner, watching all the happy faces of my family around the dinner table. My father, his grey curls all wild, making strange jokes and getting happily drunk. My mother with her short cropped black hair and her red lipstick, smoking thin cigarettes from her long cigarette holder and beaming like a little girl. Maybe she doesn't organise things like this, maybe she is shy, but she does seem to enjoy the same cosiness which I do.

And suddenly I realize something. See, all this time I have been looking for the family-feeling that I had with my Grandmother. I was hoping to find it with a man, in my own little family. But fact is, it's right here. Under my nose. *I* am with the girls the family I always wanted. I *have* the family I always dreamt of. *I* am the one who can give my girls that same feeling. And that just feels so grand.

After dinner we take out our family board games and everyone is playing games until we wave the family goodbye and it's time to go to bed. Sophie still believes in Father Christmas this year, though I don't know how long she will, so I enjoy it thoroughly as the girls hang up their stockings, leave mince pies and milk for Santa and carrots for his reindeer.

Then the girls jump in my bed and I read them the last chapter of Richard Scarry's 'The animal's Merry Christmas.' Yes, we still read that book. And we will keep reading it with Christmas, until they are too old to enjoy it. And I'm sure one day I will read the same book to my grandchildren.

After their story I tuck both of them in, cuddling and kissing them. And when I sit down on the sofa, scratching Fuzzy under his chin, I get a message. It's Paul. Asking me whether I want to celebrate New Year's Eve with him. Now normally I would have turned him down with some excuse. But this time I hesitate. And as I hear the rain hitting on the window pane, I ponder over my life these last two years.

My first year of Sugar Dating was marvellous. But if I'm totally honest the second year wasn't so swell. When money became my main focus – after I lost my job and The Ex stopped paying alimony – the Sugar Dating lost its Sugar. Let's face it. This last year I've been more an escort than a Sugar Babe.

Now I know this will be considered morally questionable by most of society, but fact is that it made me survive. And in my opinion it was all worth it. I don't regret how I have lived. Fact is, if I had to, I'd do it again. I will do anything to safeguard my girls. To keep a roof over their heads. And I mean literally anything. Also I have the living proof that I did the right thing – my girls are happy, stable and confident human beings now.

Do I ever feel guilty about how I survived these two years after my divorce? Not at all. I don't consider myself as having done anything wrong. I certainly haven't hurt anyone. In fact, most of the time accepting hard cash in exchange for intimacy has felt far from dishonourable. Most of the time I didn't feel degraded. I was the one with the power. In a way I have gotten a new sense of independence through meeting strangers. And I have definitely discovered my sexual drive.

And that's funny. As you may remember, I started this whole thing thinking that 'I wasn't on SA for new sexual experiences, as tempting as they may be'. Well, I ended up getting a whole range of them. I have experienced the joy of oral sex, Tantra, anal and had my first girl. I have dated men I would never have dated before. I have learned that I love doggy, soft SM, a thick dick and chest hair. That I'm not necessarily monogamous. That I like dominant men in bed.

But it hasn't been all about the sex. And though I preferred my first year, this last one has also been interesting. I've visited Dubai, Japan, Vienna and Milan. I did sky diving. I met two men from India that I was quite fond of. And I've had two first experiences that I'll always remember.

And then there are all the things I have learned. I learned about the Danish miracle of hygge – and I put it into practice. To focus on the positive the Pakistani way and to accept and move on if something is out of my control the Japanese way. To stop believing in my own limiting beliefs. To enjoy being alone. To accept myself and my body.

I have learned not to care so much what people think of me. That the best things in life are on the other side of my maximum fear. That I love traveling. I've kind of learned how to deal with people like Wilma. Kind of. Though I know it will always be a challenge. At least I've learnt not to let her get under my skin. *Most of the time.* And I've learned to stop believing that a man will get me out of trouble. In the end, it's me who has gotten myself out of my trouble.

My Sugar Daddies did help me of course. Even if it wasn't just one, or 'The One' that I was all the time looking for. Truth is that with the help of all of them I could survive. Also they helped me to take the girls on vacation. To make Christmas magical. And thanks to them I am now writing. These last two years have made it all possible.

Now in these two years I've met two men – Farshad and Rudolph – that I could have had 'real' relationships with.

Whatever those are. For I still don't believe in 'regular' relationships. I don't want to live together with a man. I still believe in LAT – Living Apart Together. But one thing I have learned. Never say never. You never know what turns your life can take.

In a way, realizing that I could have had relationships, has made me open up again. Open up to the possibility of romance. See, till now my motto was 'if I don't lose my heart, I can't get hurt'. But truth is that if I don't lose my heart, I can also not be loved. And in the end, relationships without love become hollow after some time.

So right there and then I decide to answer Paul. And I tell him that yes, I would love to celebrate the New Year's Eve with him. I have no idea where that will lead to. He's single now. So I'm celebrating the beginning of a new year with a single guy who thinks that 'I'm the one' and who makes me melt inside. But one thing I do know now. Whatever happens, I can deal with it.

Next I take out my diary and read my last year's resolutions. It makes me smile. It's amazing how many of them really happened. I can't even imagine how much my life has changed these past two years. They have been two hell of a years. So why wait? I take a pen and write down my resolutions for 2018:

- Get my memoirs published
- Make them a success
- Make my own money – outside the Sugar World
- Spend more time with people that matter
- Find love?

Next I make myself a cup of hot milk and look around my own hygge home. At the girls' paintings stuck on the walls. At Fuzzy, purring on our cosy sofa. At our big kitchen table where we draw, make cookies or play games. A fire is still smothering in the open fireplace. And tomorrow the house will be filled with children voices, whispers, games and laughs again.

Next I go check on my girls. I tuck up Lisa and look down at her, lying snuggled under her duvet. My neat, serious Lisa, who has learned to laugh again. Sophie has been tossing around in her little bed and has kicked her blanket off. I tuck her – and Big Bear – back in and kiss her on her wild ginger hair, while she softy moans and reaches her arms up for a cuddle. Wild Sophie, who has conquered her nightmares and is not wetting herself anymore.

Then I snuggle under my own duvet. I'm just feeling so damn happy. It feels like I'm glowing inside. Soon it's going to be 2018, a brand new year full of possibilities. And I'm sure it's going to be swell. One thing I know for sure. It's going to be My Year. And that's my last thought, just before I drift off in a deep peaceful sleep ...

Lightning Source UK Ltd.
Milton Keynes UK
UKHW01f1932170618
324368UK00001B/33/P